ADVANCES IN ECONOMETRICS

Volume 6 · 1987

COMPUTATION AND SIMULATION

GP89 01732

ADVANCES IN ECONOMETRICS

A Research Annual

COMPUTATION AND SIMULATION

Editors: THOMAS B. FOMBY
Department of Economics
Southern Methodist University

GEORGE F. RHODES, JR.
Department of Economics
Colorado State University

VOLUME 6 · 1987

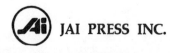 JAI PRESS INC.

Greenwich, Connecticut   *London, England*

Copyright © 1987 JAI PRESS INC.
55 Old Post Road, No. 2
Greenwich, Connecticut 06836

JAI PRESS LTD.
3 Henrietta Street
London WC2E 8LU
England

ISBN: 0-89232-795-2

Manufactured in the United States of America

CONTENTS

LIST OF CONTRIBUTORS

Ronald Bewley

University of New South Wales
New South Wales, Australia

Herman K. van Dijk

Erasmus University
Rotterdam, The Netherlands

Thomas B. Fomby

Department of Economics
Southern Methodist University

K. J. Hayes

Department of Economics
Southern Methodist University

David F. Hendry

Nuffield College
Oxford, England

R. Carter Hill

Department of Economics
Louisiana State University

Joseph G. Hirschberg

Department of Economics
Southern Methodist University

Adrian J. Neale

Nuffield College
Oxford, England

Simon Power

Department of Economics
University of Regina
London, Canada

Georege F. Rhodes, Jr.

Department of Economics
Colorado State University

D. J. Slottje   Department of Economics
                              Southern Methodist University

Henri Theil   Department of Economics
                              University of Florida

Aman Ullah   Department of Economics
                              University of Western Ontario
                              Canada

INTRODUCTION

The editors are happy to present the 1987 volume of *Advances in Econometrics*. The subject area covered is "Computation and Simulation." The advent of the high speed computer has, in recent years, offered much scope for the use of computer intensive techniques in such diverse fields as Bayesian inference, Monte Carlo integration, simulation of estimator properties, nonparametric density estimation, and computer algebra. The fact that computer intensive techniques are receiving increased attention is witnessed by the recent comprehensive surveys by R. E. Quandt (1983) and D. F. Hendry (1984). The purpose here is to bring recent developments in such techniques to the reader's attention.

We briefly review the contents of this volume. Bewley and Theil consider the problem of testing for heteroscedasticity in equation systems and, in particular, the Rotterdam system. Given the inherent difficulties in deducing the small sample properties of test statistics in equation systems, Bernard's Monte Carlo approach and Bootstrap extensions are considered and found to be very informative. Bewley and Theil's results confirm that computer intensive techniques can very effectively augment our understanding of empirical problems even when analytical statistical results are unavailable. In fact, even now, micro computer simulation programs are available to provide the empirical investigator with simulation capability on a problem-by-problem basis. See the paper by D. F. Hendry and A. J. Neale reviewed below and contained in this volume.

Fomby's paper discusses and brings to some closure the controversies surrounding the Monte Carlo literature that examines the ridge regression method as an alternative to least squares in the presence of multicollinear designs. In particular, several authors have claimed that the conventional Monte Carlo designs are biased in favor of ridge methods because the implicit priors of these designs coincide with the priors inherent in ridge regression itself. Counterclaims have been put forward based on certain invariance results. Fomby puts these claims and counterclaims into perspective with a set of experiments of his own. He concludes that minimaxity is an important considertion when deciding which side of the ridge Monte Carlo controversy holds, at present, the upper hand.

Hayes, Hirschberg and Slottje inform us that a quiet revolution has been taking place right under many of our noses. Natural scientists have become increasingly reliant on the computer to manipulate symbols as well as numbers. Algebraic manipulation by the computer has allowed heretofore intractable problems in physics and mathematics to be reduced to expressions that are quickly solved. Curiously, as they note, social scientists, and in particular, those who might benefit the most, economists, have not appeared to have taken advantage of the available computer algebra technology. The authors proceed to provide a brief overview of several popular algorithms and then present actual examples in economics where the algorithms are found to greatly simplify the problems under study.

Hendry and Neale are interested in simulation methodology (e.g., control variates and response surface methods) and, in particular, efficient Monte Carolo experimentation for teaching and research. The authors introduce the newly available PC program for on-site Monte Carlo simulation, PC-Naive. PC-Naive is a menu driven program that provides an interactive environment, allows ease of design of an experiment at the presimulation stage, and, as well, flexibility and speed in selecting results for postsimulation analysis. Special features of the program include graphical presentation especially suited to Monte Carlo summarization and the availability of a recursive simulation mode which reduces the comparative disadvantage of current personal computer technology (i.e., speed for pre-80386/7 microchips). The recursive Monte Carlo methods that Hendry and Neale develop simultaneously compute outcomes at all sizes up to the largest of interest. There is little increase in cost over direct methods, but duplication of experiments at different sample sizes is eliminated, reducing the number of experiments needed for a given level of specificity. The recursive Monte Carlo methods can be viewed as a technique for variance reduction by minimizing uncertainty between the outcomes at successive sample sizes. Hendry and Neale also demonstrate the usefulness of PC-Naive as an instruction tool.

Hill's paper examines two aspects of designing Monte Carlo experiments when the purpose of the Monte Carlo is to study properties of estimators for linear and nonliner models. The first aspect considered is multicollinearity. That is, what are alternative ways of representing multicollinear design matrices and what are the implications of each choice for both linear and nonlinear models? The second aspect considered is extrapolation and the accuracy of various predictors. In particular, how should extrapolation be characterized for the purpose of examining the relative accuracies of competing predictors? Measures of extrapolation are defined that include not only distance between in-sample and out-of-sample data ellipsoids, but also rotation and elongation, which allow for changes in collinearity patterns.

Power and Ullah explore the integration of nonparametric density estimation and Monte Carlo methods in a study of two-single-equation estimators in the context of a rational expectations simultneous equations model. Their study illustrates how nonparametric density summarizations of Monte Carlo results can significantly enhance the information provided by and therefore the value of Monte Carlo experiments. What is emphasized by their work is that a nonparametric density estimate will almost always reveal additional information to that available in summary statistics of whatever kind. In the study at hand Power and Ullah find that the substitution estimator of Sargeant and Wallis appears to dominate the errors-in-variables estimator of McCallum in the context of rational expectations simultaneous equations models.

Rhodes' paper is concerned with the interpretation and documentation of simulation studies appearing in an increasing number of contexts: the classroom, the research institute, the consulting firm, public and quasi-public agencies, and the board room. The first question addressed is "What is a simulation study?" Rhodes then proceeds to divide simulation studies into categories according to alternative features and purposes of the experimental design. Other important questions addressed are: "Is the study design capable of producing valuable information"? "Did the execution of the study actually produce the information sought"? and "What are the valid interpretations of the results"? Rhodes goes on to discuss the potential limitations of simulation studies and measuring the completeness of the documentation. Finally decision model simulations are examined as a special case. A careful examination of the intended audience and purpose should be instrumental in shaping presentation methods used.

Finally van Dijk discusses some Monte Carlo integration methods that can be used for the efficient computation of posterior moments and densities of parameters of econometric and, more generally, statistical models. The methods utilize the principle of importance sampling and are intended for the evaluation of multidimensional integrals where the integrand is unimodal and multivariate skew. That is, the integrand has different tail behavior in different directions. Illustrative results are presnted on the dynamic behavior and probability of explosion of a small-scale macroeconomic model. This application involves nine-dimensional numerical integration.

The editors hope the readers of this volume benefit from the research of the contributing authors and thereby enhance their own research by adopting readily available computer intensive techniques.

Thomas B. Fomby
George F. Rhodes, Jr.
Series Editors

REFERENCES

Hendry, David F. (1984) "Monte Carlo Experimentation in Econometrics," chapter 16 in Z. Griliches and M. D. Intriligator, eds., *Handbook of Econometrics*, volume II (Amsterdam: North-Holland).

Quandt, Richard E. (1983) "Computational Problems and Methods," chapter 12 in Z. Griliches and M. D. Intriligator, eds., *Handbook of Econometrics*, volume I (Amsterdam: North-Holland).

MONTE CARLO TESTING FOR HETEROSCEDASTICITY IN EQUATION SYSTEMS

Ronald Bewley and Henri Theil

ABSTRACT

In this paper we consider the problem of testing for heteroscedasticity in equation systems and, in particular, the Rotterdam demand system. Owing to the inherent difficulties in deducing the small sample properties of test statistics in equation systems, Barnard's Monte Carlo approach is adopted. Two Monte Carlo tests, and bootstrap extensions of them, are considered. The tests are used on observed Dutch data using the Rotterdam demand system and in a series of simulation experiments.

Advances in Econometrics, Volume 6, pages 1–15
ISBN: 0-89232-795-2

I. INTRODUCTION

Autocorrelation and heteroscedasticity in the disturbances of a single-equation regression model produce the same undesirable effects. In both cases the parameter estimates are inefficient and the associated variances are biased. Thus, hypothesis tests based on such estimates are inappropriate.

Although the effects of these two breakdowns of the classical assumptions are similar, there is a widespread acceptance of the need to test for autocorrelation that certainly does not apply to the heteroscedastic case. There are two obvious reasons for this disparity.

First, in the case of heteroscedasticity, there is no well-defined alternative hypothesis to the homoscedastic assumption and this is to be contrasted against the almost universal acceptance of the need to test for first-order autocorrelation with the Durbin–Watson statistic. Although some tests for heteroscedasticity, such as that proposed by Goldfeld and Quandt (1965), only require the data to be ranked according to increasing variance in the disturbances, the increasingly popular Breusch and Pagan (1979) test requires an explicit alternative model to be defined. Secondly, there is a finite sample test for autocorrelation, but as Breusch and Pagan (1979, p. 1293) note for their statistic, "even in this special case [of two distinct values for the disturbance variance] the distribution of the statistic does not appear tractable analytically"; this is due to the fact that the statistic involves the ratio of quadratic forms of ordinary least squares (OLS) residuals that are not independent. The situation is exacerbated by the degree of approximation in finite sample work: "the adequacy of the asymptotic theory to indicate correct significance levels is rather suspect" (Breusch and Pagan 1979, p. 1291).

In the present paper we are concerned with the problem of testing for heteroscedasticity in the multivariate regression model of which demand systems form an important special case.[1] It is well known that, even in the homoscedastic case, inference based on small samples can be extremely misleading. Except in a few special but nonetheless important cases, all inference has only asymptotic justification and small sample approximations can be extremely poor (see Laitinen, 1978; Meisner, 1979; Bera et al.,

1981; Bewley, 1983, 1986). The essential problem in testing hypotheses in equation systems is that the estimate of the disturbance covariance matrix needs to be inverted and the estimate of the inverse is extremely poor unless very large samples are available. This problem is highlighted by the calculation of the degrees of freedom in the system. When there are no cross-equation restrictions in the multivariate regression model, each equation has the same regressors and so OLS, generalized least squares (GLS), and maximum likelihood (ML) are identical. Whereas the degrees of freedom for an individual equation are $T - k$, using obvious notation, the degrees of freedom for the system are $T - k - n + 2$, where $n - 1$ is the number of estimated equations (see Bewley, 1983).[2] Thus, for the estimate of the disturbance covariance matrix to be nonsingular, a considerably greater number of observations is required to perform joint tests, rather than tests on single parameters, unless the equation system is particularly small. Clearly the inference problem will not be improved by the presence of heteroscedastic disturbances, and so the testing of this assumption is of particular importance in equation systems.

Theil and Shonkwiler (1986) have stated that it is worthwhile to consider Barnard's (1963) Monte Carlo test procedure whenever there are problems with the distribution of a test statistic. The essence of the Barnard approach is to compute *any* data-based statistic and to compare it to the empirical distribution for that statistic generated in a Monte Carlo experiment. The approach can be made even less dependent on theoretical distributions by replacing, say, normally distributed pseudorandom numbers in Monte Carlo testing by a bootstrap distribution. The principle of Monte Carlo testing has been successfully applied to testing for homogeneity and symmetry restrictions in demand systems by Shonkwiler and Theil (1986), Taylor et al. (1986), and Theil et al. (1985); Theil and Shonkwiler (1986) considered the problem of testing for autocorrelation in equation systems. It is our aim to use the principle of Monte Carlo testing to investigate the degree of heteroscedasticity in the disturbances in certain Dutch data using a Rotterdam demand system.

The Rotterdam demand system and the Dutch data are described in Section II. The test statistics are introduced in Section III and are used to analyze the Dutch data in Section IV. The results of

a simulation experiment are reported in Section V, and this paper
concludes in Section VI with a brief summary and suggestions for
testing for heteroscedasticity in equation systems.

II. THE ROTTERDAM DEMAND SYSTEM
AND THE DUTCH DATA

In consumer theory, an individual is assumed to maximize the
utility gained from consuming a bundle of goods at given prices
subject to the budget constraint. The demand equations that result
from the optimization procedure are dependent on the choice of
utility function, and one popular way to circumvent the need to
arbitrarily specify a utility function is to use a first-order approximation to the underlying demand equations. This method, known
as the Rotterdam demand system from the affiliation of its proponents Barten (1964) and Theil (1965), can be used in several
different forms; here we consider the homogeneity-constrained
absolute price version:

$$\bar{w}_{it}Dq_{it} = \theta_i DQ_t + \sum_{j=1}^{n-1} \pi_{ij}(Dp_{jt} - Dp_{nt}) + u_{it}, \qquad i = 1, \ldots, n, \quad (1)$$

where the p_{it} $(i = 1, \ldots, n)$ are the prices for the n goods at time
t; q_{it} are the corresponding quantities and DQ_t is the Divisia
volume index $\sum \bar{w}_{it}Dq_{it}$; w_{it} $(i = 1, \ldots, n)$ are the average budget
shares; $\bar{w}_{it} = (w_{it} + w_{i,t-1})/2$; D is the log-change operator $D(x_t) =$
$\log_e(x_t/x_{t-1})$; u_{it} is the disturbance term in the ith equation; θ_i is
the marginal budget share; and π_{ij} is the Slutsky parameter.

The choice of this particular functional form (1) is particularly
appropriate for our study because not only is it used in many
applied studies but also it has become the standard for simulation
experiments that examine the small sample properties of test
statistics in demand analysis (for example, see Laitinen, 1978;
Meisner, 1979; Bera et al., 1981; Bewley, 1983, 1986—inter alia).

The observations used for the application and those which form
the basis of the simulation experiment in Section V are the Dutch
data published in Theil (1975). In this data set there are 14 goods
(that is, $n = 14$) and 31 annual observations ($T = 31$) comprising
a period of 17 interwar years and one of 14 post–World War II
years.[3]

In estimation and inference, it is assumed that the unknown parameters π_{ij} and θ_i are fixed over time, but clearly the underlying demand equations being approximated possibly have Slutsky parameters and marginal budget shares that evolve over time. Byron (1984) and Barnett (1984) had an interesting interchange over the interpretation of flexibility in this context and the result appears to be that while the Rotterdam system appears to have negligible approximation errors it can have nonnegligible truncation errors when evolving parameters are considered to be fixed. Given that the Dutch data set includes behavior from quite different historical periods, it is reasonable to question the validity of this model, or indeed any other demand system, to cope with the transition from pre- to post-World War II behavior and attitudes. One way in which problems might manifest themselves is via the disturbance covariance matrix. It is our working hypothesis that we should test for there being a different disturbance covariance matrix in each regime, but within each regime we assume serially independent, homoscedastic disturbances.

III. TESTS FOR HETEROSCEDASTICITY

Given the problems that have been noted with regard to testing for heteroscedasticity in single equations and the general testing problems in systems of equations, Barnard's Monte Carlo testing procedure has an important role to play in choosing a system test for heteroscedasticity. The strength of Barnard's procedure lies in the fact that *any* test statistic can be chosen and one is assured that the size of the test can be approximated to *any* desired degree of accuracy. Since size is no problem, all efforts in designing a test statistic can be directed toward the power of the test and ease of computation.

The heteroscedastic model under consideration for the Dutch data is one in which the variance of the disturbances in each equation can take two distinct values—one value for the interwar period, and another for the postwar period. The appropriate single-equation Lagrange Multiplier (LM) test has been detailed by Breusch and Pagan (1979, p. 1293). Apart from the constant terms, this test involves the ratio of the residual sum of squares for the first period to the residual sum of squares for the total data set.

Since these two residual sums of squares are not independent, the analytical distribution is intractable. On the other hand, the Gold-feld and Quandt (1965) test has a known exact distribution because it only involves the ratio of residual sums of squares from two nonoverlapping sample periods and separate regression estimates.[4]

In a recent paper, Griffiths and Surekha (1986) compared the power of the Breusch-Pagan test, the Goldfeld-Quandt test, and two further tests that have only asymptotic justification. Their results indicate that the Goldfeld-Quandt test has greater power than the Breusch-Pagan test in their experimental design. Although it does not necessarily follow, we have opted to use nonoverlapping periods in the design of our statistic on the grounds that it might be more sensitive to departures from homoscedasticity than the Breusch-Pagan test. Specifically, we consider

$$\tau_i = \left[\frac{1}{17} \sum_{t=1}^{17} (e_{it})^2 \right] \Big/ \left[\frac{1}{14} \sum_{t=18}^{31} (e_{it})^2 \right], \qquad i = 1, \ldots, n, \qquad (2)$$

for each equation in the system, where e_{it} is the residual in equation i at time t from OLS applied to (1). The system analog is defined to be the arithmetic mean of the statistics (2):

$$\tau = \frac{1}{n} \sum_{i=1}^{n} \tau_i. \qquad (3)$$

Although the distributions of (2) and (3) are unknown, it can be noted that all of the τ_i and τ statistics should be close to 1 if the null hypothesis is true.

The test statistics (2) and (3) involve mean squares of residuals, but Monte Carlo testing can just as easily be based on other functions of residuals. An alternative set of statistics, which is less influenced by outliers, is that based on mean absolute values:

$$\tau_i' = \left[\frac{1}{17} \sum_{t=1}^{17} |e_{it}| \right] \Big/ \left[\frac{1}{14} \sum_{t=18}^{31} |e_{it}| \right], \qquad i = 1, \ldots, n; \qquad (4)$$

$$\tau' = \frac{1}{n} \sum_{i=1}^{n} \tau_i'. \qquad (5)$$

Obviously analytical expressions for the distributions of all of the statistics in (4) and (5) are intractable.

It is important to note the differences in the information con-tained in the single-equation statistics, (2) and (4), compared to the system versions, (3) and (5). In a demand system, the sum of the residuals across equations is identically zero from the budget constraint:

$$\sum_{i=1}^{n} e_{it} = 0. \tag{6}$$

This in turn implies that the disturbance covariance matrix Ω_t, where $\Omega_{ijt} = E(e_{it}e_{jt})$ is singular and of the form

$$\sum_{i=1}^{n} \Omega_{ijt} = \sum_{j=1}^{n} \Omega_{ijt} = 0. \tag{7}$$

From (7) it is not possible to have heteroscedasticity in only one equation without placing severe restrictions on the shifts in the correlation structure. It is important, therefore, to test for heteroscedasticity in the system as a whole or in some submatrix of Ω_t. It also follows that if the null hypothesis of homoscedasticity is true and the same level of significance were to be used for all of the single-equation tests, the probability of rejecting homoscedasticity in any one equation increases with the number of equations in the system. Indeed, if all of the residual series are uncorrelated there is a probability of $(1 - .95^{14}) = .512$ of rejecting homoscedasticity in at least one equation with the Dutch data, even if the null is true, when each test is carried out at the 5% level.[5]

Clearly, there is some relationship between the notions of testing for heteroscedasticity in a system and for demand homogeneity. In both cases one can test at the individual level, but it is rare to find support for testing homogeneity at anything but the system level.

IV. AN APPLICATION TO DUTCH DATA

The Rotterdam system (1) was estimated for the 31 annual observations of Dutch data by OLS. The numerical values of the statistics (2) and (3) are shown in column 2 of Table 1. To verify whether the value of $\tau = 0.78$ is significant at the 5% level, we apply Barnard's test procedure by simulating (1) under the null hypothesis. This is performed by using the observed DQ_t's and Dp_{jt}'s and the data-based LS (least squares) estimates of the θ_i's

Table 1.   Heteroscedasticity Testing for Observed Dutch Data

Equation (1)	τ_i, τ (2)	Rank		τ_i', τ' (5)	Rank	
		N (3)	B (4)		N (6)	B (7)
1. Bread	1.35	53	52	1.11	64	68
2. Groceries	1.19	68	59	1.05	97	72
3. Dairy products	0.47	324	310	0.68	324	312
4. Vegetables	0.49	318	315	0.78	255	250
5. Meat	0.27	387	380	0.55	381	374
6. Fish	3.10	4	4	1.68	9	5
7. Beverages	0.32	370	378	0.48	393	392
8. Tobacco	0.37	356	371	0.58	361	366
9. Pastry	0.71	208	214	0.94	145	131
10. Clothing	0.35	368	362	0.60	357	352
11. Footwear	0.47	311	337	0.71	283	306
12. Other durables	0.43	319	343	0.69	308	324
13. Utilities	0.52	282	307	0.61	350	360
14. Other goods	0.94	143	117	0.93	154	141
System	0.78	242	238	0.81	308	309

and π_{ij}'s. Independent pseudonormal error vectors are generated with zero means and a covariance matrix equal to the matrix of mean squares and products of the data-based LS residuals (the e_{it}'s).[6] We can then compute the implied simulated values of the dependent variables of (1) and, from them, the associated values of the statistics (2) and (3). This is repeated 399 times, so that each τ_i and τ takes 400 values: the data-based value shown in column 2, and 399 replications. Column 3 of Table 1 shows the rank of the data-based value among the 400 values. If the rank exceeds 390 or is less than 11 in magnitude, homoscedasticity should be rejected at the 5% level in a two-sided test. The actual rank of the system is 242, indicating that no such rejection is warranted.

The other entries in column 3 provide the analogous ranks of the data-based statistics (2). Although the result just mentioned implies that there is no reason to reject homoscedasticity for the system as a whole, the entries in rows 6 and 5 (column 3) suggest that there may be heteroscedasticity in the equations for fish and meat.[7] However, without a more specific alternative hypothesis to *all* of the equations having a shift in the variance, one rejection out of 14 tests at the 5% level should not cause too much concern for an overall 5% test.

The Monte Carlo test as presented is based on an assumption of normality, but it is certainly not the case that such an assumption is universally acceptable. For example, in the present application it was noted that some of the residuals are rather large and their size contributed to the possible rejection of the homoscedasticity assumption in certain equations. The justification for normality in the disturbances is usually based on the central limit theorem being applied to the sum of numerous nonnormal influences. If one or more of these influences is dominant, then a mixture of normal distributions might be more appropriate and outliers, such as those found in the meat, fish, and beverages equations, are produced. Whether or not such an assumption is warranted, it is still useful to consider modifying the Monte Carlo testing procedure by using Efron's (1979) bootstrap procedure. This amounts to assigning probability $1/T = 1/31$ to each of the T data-based LS residual vectors $(e_{it}, e_{2t}, \ldots)$ and by then drawing from this distribution (with replacement) T times. The advantage of bootstrapping is, of course, that no distributional assumptions are necessary and any biases due to a misplaced assumption of normality would evaporate. The results of bootstrapping the statistics (2) and (3) are presented in column 4 of Table 1. It appears from these results that the normal and bootstrap versions of the statistics produce similar results, indicating either that there are no major departures from normality in this data set or that the statistics are reasonably robust.

Another way in which sensitivity to outliers can be minimized is to consider the absolute value versions of statistics (4) and (5). These are presented in column 5 of Table 1, and the normal and bootstrapped rankings are given in columns 6 and 7, respectively. Although the general picture is much the same when τ' is employed, there are some slight variations for individual equations' statistics. In particular, heteroscedasticity has become significant at the 5% level in the beverages equation and is less of a problem in the meat equation. On balance, an insignificant system measure τ', coupled with only slight evidence of departures from homoscedasticity in two equations, does not constitute a rejection of a constant disturbance covariance matrix.

V. A SIMULATION STUDY

If the replications described in the previous section are considered to be an inner loop within an outer loop of simulations, a framework exists for examining power and departures from normality in the disturbance-generating process. The experiment in the outer loop is based on the 14 equation homogeneity-constrained absolute price version of the Rotterdam model, using Laitinen's (1978) design.[8] In order to consider power, the disturbance covariance matrix at time t, Ω_i, is specified as

$$\Omega_t = \begin{cases} \Omega & t = 1, \dots, 17 \\ d\Omega & t = 18, \dots, 31, \end{cases} \tag{8}$$

where d is a scalar and Ω is taken from Laitinen (1978). When $d = 1$, the null hypothesis is valid and size can be examined. Values of $d = \sqrt{2}$ and 2 are chosen for the alternative hypotheses, and the same generated disturbances are used for each value to aid comparison.

Because of the form of the postulated heteroscedasticity (8), one-sided lower-tailed tests are used: 100 simulations are used on the outer loop, and 99 in the inner. Thus homoscedasticity should be rejected at the 5% level if the rank of the statistics is numerically greater than 95. The number of times a rejection of each system statistic is made, out of the 100 outer loop replications, is presented in columns 2 and 3 of Table 2.

Table 2.   Heteroscedasticity Testing for Simulated Data

Null Hypothesis (1)	Zero Kurtosis		Kurtosis: 10.52	
	N (2)	B (3)	N (4)	B (5)
	Statisstic τ			
True ($d = 1$)	5	3	9	6
Untrue ($d = \sqrt{2}$)	17	19	25	19
Quite untrue ($d = 2$)	65	66	43	36
	Statistic τ'			
True ($d = 1$)	5	6	7	3
Untrue ($d = \sqrt{2}$)	18	17	17	16
Quite untrue ($d = 2$)	67	71	44	35

Under the null hypothesis ($d = 1$), the system measures are, of course, close to the expected value of 5. As the value of d increases, power increases rapidly. Since the disturbances on the outer loop are indeed normally distributed, there is no great difference between the normal and bootstrapped versions, nor between the τ and τ' versions of the statistics.

From this part of the experiment, the results are promising for the type of heteroscedasticity being considered. If, on the other hand, there are offsetting changes with Ω of the type hypothesized for the data-based experiment, it is likely that the system tests would be far less powerful. Clearly, testing for heteroscedasticity in a system is far more complicated than similar tests in single-equation studies, mainly due to the lack of well-defined alternative hypotheses.

It can be argued that the assumption of normality is too strict for the type of data commonly used in demand analysis; one possible cause of nonnormality was introduced in the empirical study. Following the work of Theil and Rosalsky (1985), we will now consider the effects of outliners, or "fat tails", on the τ and τ' statistics.

It is assumed that the disturbances are generated from a mixture of normal distributions and the time-dependent disturbance-covariance matrix:

$$\Omega_t = (1 - p)\Omega + p(\delta\Omega),$$

where δ is a scalar controlling the kurtosis; $(1 - p)$ is the probability that a vector of disturbances has covariance Ω, and p that it has covariance $\delta\Omega$.

For this series of experiments, $\delta = 16$ was chosen to give a disturbance-generating distribution with kurtosis 10.52 and $p = 2/31$. The implication of these values for δ and p is that, on average, 29 of the disturbance vectors have the same covariance structure as before, but two disturbance vectors are scaled up by a factor of 4 to give larger variances and covariances but with the same correlation structure. The distribution was made operational by drawing 31 independent uniform variates for each outer loop replication r_t ($t = 1, \ldots, 31$) and multiplying the $N(0, \Omega)$ variate by $\sqrt{\delta} = 4$ if $r_t < p$. On the inner loop, normality was assumed or bootstrapping was used as in the previous experiment. The number of rejections (again using the same sets of random disturbances) are given in columns 4 and 5 of Table 2.

The concept of fat tails is closely linked with the form of heteroscedasticity being postulated. The difference is that, instead of multiplying all of the disturbance vectors in one regime by a common factor, as in the heteroscedastic model, a small random number of disturbance vectors from either regime is multiplied by a common factor. Clearly, if it so happens that the outliers all appear in one regime, then a major effect will be felt by the test statistics: if they are in the first regime, the apparent heteroscedasticity will be masked; if they are in the second regime, the effect will be highlighted. It is immediately apparent that with no heteroscedasticity ($d = 1$) the effect of nonnormality has biased τ toward rejection when normal errors are drawn, but this effect is less pronounced when using τ'. Furthermore, the bootstrap method appears to be far more robust, with the τ and τ' rejections being quite similar.

When heteroscedasticity is introduced with $d = \sqrt{2}$ all four sets of rejections are almost indistinguishable, but when $d = 2$ it is quite clear that there are more rejections with the normal case.

A comparison of the normal and fat-tailed experiments reveals that departures from normality can cause a severe loss of power in the system measures. The single equation results, which are not presented, are in broad agreement with the system results.

VI. CONCLUSIONS

The Monte Carlo procedure described above can be used in conjunction with *any* statistic to give a correctly sized test. Therefore, it is important to define a statistic that will give good power against reasonable alternative hypotheses. The simulation experiment reported in Section V suggests that the τ' test might be useful in the demand context and this statistic is reasonably insensitive to misspecification. If the results of this experiment are taken to imply that the τ' and τ'_i tests are reasonably robust and powerful, then it can be concluded that the Rotterdam model and the Dutch data are consistent with an assumption of homoscedasticity, but some attention should be paid to two of the middle observations—specifically, those either side of the break.

ACKNOWLEDGMENTS

This research was conducted while Bewley was visiting the University of Florida, and the project was supported in part by the McKethan-Matherly Eminent Scholar Chair, University of Florida.

NOTES

1. In demand analysis, the budget constraint implies that the disturbance covariance matrix is singular. The standard procedure from Powell (1969) is to delete an equation before estimation. Once an equation has been deleted, a linear-in-parameters model, such as the Rotterdam system described in Section II, becomes a standard multivariate regression model.

2. In Bewley (1983), the "excess number of degrees of freedom over the minimum required to produce a nonsingular estimate of the disturbance covariance matrix" is defined to be $T - k - n + 1$. Thus, it follows that the number of system degrees of freedom is that number plus 1.

3. The 14 goods are implicitly defined in Table 1 (see Section IV).

4. The Goldfeld-Quandt test normally would involve deleting the central, say, 5 observations and taking the ratio of the residual sums of squares from regressions involving the first and last 13 observations with these Dutch data. Under these circumstances, there are insufficient observations to define a distribution for the test since there are 14 regressors in each submodel.

5. All of the residual series in a demand system cannot be uncorrelated because of (7) but, under rational random behavior (see Theil, 1980, Chaps. 7 and 8), pairwise correlations are usually small.

6. Kinderman and Ramages's (1976) algorithm was used to generate the error vectors. This algorithm is the one selected for the programming language GAUSS.

7. The fact that the goods with associated heteroscedasticity problems are closely related deserves special consideration. Meat rationing was lifted only shortly before the start of the second subperiod and could well have contributed to the large OLS residual in the first observation of that subperiod. In fact, this residual is the largest in absolute value in that equation. It is also interesting to note that the largest absolute residual in the beverages equation occurs in the same observation. The largest absolute residual in the fish equation occurs in the last observation in the first subperiod.

8. The data for the regressors are taken from Theil (1975, pp. 264-265) and for the parameters θ_i from Theil (1975, p. 277). The Slutsky parameters π_{ij} are defined to be $\pi_{ij} = -0.6(\delta_{ij}\theta_i - \theta_i\theta_j)$ and the (i, j)th element of Ω is taken to be $-\pi_{ij}/10,000$, where δ_{ij} is the Kronecker delta.

REFERENCES

Barnard, G. A. (1963) "Comment." *Journal of the Royal Statistical Society, Series B* 25, 294.

Barnett, W. A. (1984) "On the Flexibility of the Rotterdam Model: A First Empirical Look." *European Economic Review* 24, 285-289.

Barten, A. P. (1964) "Consumer Demand Functions Under Almost Additive Preferences." *Econometrica* 32, 1-38.

Bera, A. K., R. P. Byron, and C. M. Jarque (1981) "Further Evidence on Asymptotic Tests for Homogeneity and Symmetry in Large Demand Systems." *Economics Letters* 8, 101-105.

Bewley, R. A. (1983) "Tests of Restrictions in Large Demand Systems." *European Economic Review* 20, 257-269.

Bewley, R. A. (1986) *Allocation Models: Specification, Estimation and Applications.* Cambridge, MA: Ballinger.

Breusch, T. S. and A. R. Pagan (1979). "A Simple Test for Heteroscedasticity and Random Coefficient Variation." *Econometrica* 47, 1287-1294.

Byron, R. P. (1984) "On the Flexibility of the Rotterdam Model." *European Economic Review* 24, 273-283.

Efron, B. (1979) "Bootstrap Methods: Another Look at the Jackknife." *Annals of Statistics* 7, 1-26.

Goldfeld, S. M. and R. E. Quandt (1965) "Some Tests for Homoscedasticity." *Journal of the American Statistical Association* 60, 539-547.

Griffiths, W. E. and K. Surekha (1986) "A Monte Carlo Evaluation of the Power of Some Tests for Heteroscedasticity." *Journal of Econometrics* 31, 219-231.

Kinderman, A. J. and J. G. Ramage (1976) "Computer Generation of Normal Random Variables." *Journal of the American Statistical Association* 71, 893-896.

Laitinen, K. (1978) "Why is Demand Homogeneity So Often Rejected?" *Economics Letters* 1, 187-191.

Meisner, J. F. (1979) "The Sad Fate of the Asymptotic Slutsky Symmetry Test for Large Systems." *Economics Letters* 2, 231-233.

Powell, A. A. (1969) "Aitken Estimators as a Tool in Allocating Predetermined Aggregates." *Journal of the American Statistical Association* 64, 913-922.

Shonkwiler, J. S. and H. Theil (1986) "Some Evidence on the Power of Monte Carlo Tests in Systems of Equations." *Economics Letters* 20, 53-54.

Taylor, T. G., J. S. Shonkwiler, and H. Theil (1986) "Monte Carlo and Bootstrap Testing of Demand Homogeneity." *Economics Letters* 20, 55-57.

Theil, H. (1965) "The Information Approach to Demand Analysis." *Econometrica*, 33, 67-87.

Theil, H. (1975) *Theory and Measurement of Consumer Demand*, Vol. 1. Amsterdam and New York: North-Holland Publishing.

Theil H. (1980) *The System-Wide Approach to Microeconomics.* Chicago: University of Chicago Press.

Theil, H., T. G. Taylor, and J. S. Shonkwiler (1986) "Monte Carlo Testing in Systems of Equations." In *Advances in Econometrics*, Vol. 5, D. J. Slottje and G. F. Rhodes (eds.), pp. 227-239. Greenwich, Ct.: JAI Press, Inc.

Theil, H. and M. C. Rosalsky (1985) "Homogeneity and Symmetry Testing When the Error Distribution Has Fat Tails." *Economics Letters* 18, 7–8.

Theil, H. and J. S. Shonkwiler (1986) "Monte Carlo Tests of Autocorrelation." *Economics Letters* 20, 157–160.

THE RIDGE REGRESSION
MONTE CARLO CONTROVERSY:
WHERE DO WE STAND?

Thomas B. Fomby

I. MONTE CARLO FAVORITISM?

Few discussions of Monte Carlo methodology have been livelier
than those surrounding small sample investigations of ridge
regression estimators. See, for example, Dempster et al. (1977)
with comments and rejoinder, Smith and Campbell (1980) with
comments and rejoinder, and the sequence of papers by Pagel
(1981), Farebrother (1983), and Silvapulle (1985). These papers
contain claims and counterclaims of biased Monte Carlo
methodologies which favor the proposed method, ridge regression.
Though 10 years have passed since the discussion began, there
seems to be little consensus on the desirability of adopting ridge

Advances in Econometrics, Volume 6, pages 17–49
Copyright © 1987 by JAI Press Inc.
All rights of reproduction in any form reserved.
ISBN: 0-89232-795-2

regression and the degree to which the chosen Monte Carlo designs might have unduly favored the proposed methods.

Naturally Monte Carlo investigators try to avoid experimental designs which favor one estimation (test) method over another a priori. This cannot always be done, however, since one of the purposes of Monte Carlo investigations is to examine small sample properties of which little is known analytically. Thus, in the spirit of scientific inquiry, commentaries as those previously mentioned are helpful in clarifying the "neutrality" of given Monte Carlo experiments. This paper is an attempt to bring the controversies surrounding ridge regression Monte Carlo methodology to some closure.

II. NOTATION AND OUTLINE

To set the notation for this paper, suppose the following regression model is appropriate:

$$y = \beta_0 \mathbf{1} + X\beta + e, \tag{1}$$

where X is an $(n \times p)$ matrix of regressor variables of rank p; $\beta = (\beta_1, \ldots, \beta_p)'$ is an unknown vector of regression coefficients; and e is normally distributed with mean $\mathbf{0}$ and covariance matrix $\sigma^2 I_n$. The design matrix X is standardized so that $X'X$ is a correlation matrix. The vector $\mathbf{1}$ denotes an $(n \times 1)$ vector of ones, and β_0 is the unknown intercept parameter.

Because of analytical convenience, many ridge regression discussions begin by rewriting the model (1) in canonical form

$$y = \beta_0 \mathbf{1} + W\alpha + e, \tag{2}$$

where $W'W = \Lambda$ and Λ is a diagonal matrix containing the eigenvalues of $X'X$. Also $\Lambda = \text{diag}(\lambda_1, \lambda_2, \ldots, \lambda_p)$, where $\lambda_1 \geq \lambda_2 \geq \ldots \geq \lambda_p$ are the ordered eigenvalues of $X'X$. There exists an orthonormal matrix Q such that $Q'X'XQ = \Lambda$. The canonical design matrix is then defined by $W = XQ$, and the canonical parameter vector is defined by $\alpha = Q'\beta$.

Considering model (2), the least squares (LS) estimator of α is

$$\hat{\alpha} = (W'W)^{-1}W'y = \Lambda^{-1}W'y. \tag{3}$$

Likewise, the LS estimator of α is linked to the LS estimator of

β by the equation $\hat{\alpha} = Q'\hat{\beta}$, where $\hat{\beta} = (X'X)^{-1}X'\mathbf{y}$. For any particular estimator $\tilde{\alpha}$, the corresponding estimator of β is obtained by $\tilde{\beta} = Q\tilde{\alpha}$. As a competitior to the LS estimator $\hat{\alpha}$ (and thus to $\hat{\beta}$), Hoerl and Kennard (1970a) proposed the ridge regression estimator:

$$\tilde{\alpha}(k) = (W'W + kI)^{-1}W'\mathbf{y} = (\Lambda + kI)^{-1}W'\mathbf{y}, \tag{4}$$

where $k > 0$ is the ridge shrinkage parameter. In a series of propositions they established an existence result of the following form: There exists a $k_0 > 0$ such that $\text{MSE}(\tilde{\beta}(k)) < \text{MSE}(\tilde{\beta})$ for $0 < k < k_0$, where $\tilde{\beta}(k) = Q\tilde{\alpha}(k)$ and $\text{MSE}(\tilde{\beta}(k))$ denotes the mean square error function $E(\tilde{\beta}(k) - \beta)'(\tilde{\beta}(k) - \beta)$.

A major limitation of this result, as pointed out by Conniffee and Stone (1973) among others, is that k_0 depends on unknown parameters, β and σ^2, and thus one needs to estimate k to make the ridge estimator $\tilde{\beta}(k)$ operational. Of course, once the ridge parameter is allowed to become data dependent, say $k = \hat{k}$, the MSE function of $\tilde{\beta}(\hat{k})$ becomes very complicated and simulation studies have frequently been used to evaluate the performance of stochastic ridge counterparts.

The purpose of this paper is to examine assertions that certain simulation studies have adopted designs which are biased in favor of ridge regression and what the consensus is concerning the appropriateness of adopting ridge regression techniques when data are multicollinear and LS is an imprecise estimation method. Next, Section III reviews a major criticism of some ridge regression simulation designs. Three different Monte Carlo designs and results therefrom are presented in Section IV. Section V concludes and summarizes the controversy as it now stands.

III. A MAJOR CRITICISM OF RIDGE REGRESSION SIMULATION METHODOLOGY

A popular design for ridge Monte Carlo experiments might be termed the "unit p sphere" (UPS) design. This design was used in the simulation studies of Hoerl, Kennard, and Baldwin (HKB) (1975), Lawless and Wang (LW) (1976), and Dempster et al. (1977), all of which strongly supported the use of ridge estimators as an alternative to LS in the presence of multicollinear data.

The UPS design for randomly selecting the $\boldsymbol{\alpha}$ vector of model (2) is as follows: Choose an arbitrary (though fixed) vector, say ℓ, of unit length, $\ell'\ell = 1$. A random orthonormal matrix G is generated. Consequently, $\boldsymbol{\alpha} = G'\ell$ has a uniform distribution on the UPS. As Thisted (1977) noted, repeated selection of $\boldsymbol{\alpha}$ vectors in this way implies

$$E\alpha_i = 0, \qquad i = 1, 2, \ldots, p;$$

$$\text{var}(\alpha_i) = 1/p; \tag{5}$$

$$E(\alpha_i\alpha_j) = 0, \qquad i \neq j.$$

That is, the implicit prior associated with this method of generating $\boldsymbol{\alpha}$'s for simulation purposes is such that $\boldsymbol{\alpha}$ has mean zero, equal component variances, and zero component covariances.

Coincidentally, Dempster et al. (1977) and Smith and Campbell (1980) have shown that the ridge estimator $\tilde{\boldsymbol{\alpha}}(k)$ can be motivated from a Bayesian point of view if one has prior information of the form $E(\boldsymbol{\alpha}) = \mathbf{0}$, $\text{var}(\boldsymbol{\alpha}) = (\sigma^2/k)I_p$. As Smith and Campbell (1980, p. 78) note, this is equivalent to stating that the ridge estimator is a posterior mean corresponding to orthogonal priors with common variances centered at the origin. Since the method of generating the design coefficient vectors, $\boldsymbol{\alpha}$, implies the same distribution as the implicit prior assumed by ridge regression, several authors have claimed that the UPS design is biased in favor of ridge estimators (see, in particular, Thisted, 1977, pp. 102–103; Pagel, 1981, pp. 2364–2366. Pagel (1981, p. 2366) concluded: "Most importantly, the effectiveness of ridge shrinkage for non-null prior coefficients must be further studied."

As a rebuttal to the criticisms of prejudice implied by the UPS design, Silvapulle (1985) proved an interesting ridge regression invariance result. This result states that the unconditional MSE of the stochastic ridge estimator, $\tilde{\boldsymbol{\alpha}}(\hat{k})$, is the same whether $\boldsymbol{\alpha}$ is chosen uniformly from the UPS or uniformly from the positive orthant of the UPS. The nature of the rebuttal will be made apparent after the formal presentation of the result.

INVARIANCE RESULT (SILVAPULLE): Consider the class of stochastic ridge estimators of the form

$$\tilde{\boldsymbol{\alpha}}(\hat{k}) = \{\tilde{\alpha}_i(\hat{k})\} = \frac{\lambda_i\hat{\alpha}_i}{\lambda_i + \hat{k}}, \qquad i = 1, 2, \ldots, p, \tag{6}$$

where $\hat{k} = k(\hat{\alpha}_1^2, \hat{\alpha}_2^2, \ldots, \hat{\alpha}_p^2, \hat{\sigma}^2, \Lambda)$ is a function of the data. Let

$$\text{MSE}\{\tilde{\alpha}(\hat{k}) | \alpha\} = E\{(\tilde{\alpha}(\hat{k}) - \alpha)'(\tilde{\alpha}(\hat{k}) - \alpha) | \alpha\}$$

denote the conditional MSE and

$$E_F\{\text{MSE}(\tilde{\alpha}(\hat{k}) | \alpha)\}$$

denote the unconditional MSE where α is assumed to be distributed according to a distribution function F. Let G denote the distribution function of the random vector $(|\alpha_1|, |\alpha_2|, \ldots, |\alpha_p|)$, where α is distributed according to F. Then it follows that

$$E_F\{\text{MSE}(\tilde{\alpha}(\hat{k}) | \alpha)\} = E_G\{\text{MSE}(\tilde{\alpha}(\hat{k}) | \alpha)\}. \quad \blacksquare \quad (7)$$

Now for a specific application of this theorem to the present controversy. Let α be distributed uniformly over the UPS and furthermore let this distribution be denoted by F. Then $|\alpha|$ is uniformly distributed over the positive orthant of the UPS. Denote this distribution by G. The above theorem then guarantees that the unconditional MSE of a stochastic ridge estimator $\tilde{\alpha}(\hat{k})$ is invariant to the choice of UPS design vs. a positive-orthant UPS design, hereafter denoted POUPS.

If the Thisted (1977) claim of biasness in simulation were to be substantiated, one would have suspected that

$$E_F\{\text{MSE}(\tilde{\alpha}(\hat{k}) | \alpha)\} < E_G\{\text{MSE}(\tilde{\alpha}(\hat{k}) | \alpha)\}. \quad (8)$$

The POUPS design has the same characteristics as the UPS design except the mean of $|\alpha|$ is

$$E|\alpha| = (1/\sqrt{p}, 1/\sqrt{p}, \ldots, 1/\sqrt{p})'. \quad (9)$$

In this instance the implicit prior of the POUPS design would not coincide with the Bayesian ridge prior in the first moment but would with regard to zero covariance and common variance. The Silvapulle (1985) invariance result implies that the zero mean of the UPS design is not crucial in determining the performance of the class of ridge estimators $\tilde{\alpha}(\hat{k})$, contrary to the claim by Pagel (1981). This substantiates the unpublished finding of Farebrother and Thompson (1983), reported by Farebrother (1983), that ridge estimators perform well in experimental designs with fixed nonzero α apart from the performance in the UPS design.

The disagreement does not stop here. Van Nostrand (1980) notes the contradictory simulation results found by Draper and Van

Nostrand (1978). Van Nostrand (1980, p. 93) states: "This lack of consistency does not bolster one's faith in ridge regression." In fact several simulation studies have tested the effectiveness of ridge regression methods for different *fixed* orientations of the coefficient vector relative to the eigenvectors of the data moment matrix $X'X$ (see Newhouse and Oman, 1971; McDonald and Galarneau, 1975; Gunst and Mason, 1977; Wichern and Churchill, 1978; Gibbons, 1978). In these studies ridge estimation performed poorly when the fixed β vector was aligned with the eigenvector associated with the smallest eigenvalue of $X'X$, whereas β orientations near the eigenvector associated with the largest eigenvalue of $X'X$ gave rise to good ridge performance.

In the next section the contrasting styles (and results) of the UPS and POUPS designs vs. the "fixed coefficient" (FC) design are presented in such a way as to make them comparable. In addition to illustrating the sensitivity of some Monte Carlo results to the choice of experimental design, some interesting invariance results are uncovered as well.

IV. A CONTRAST OF EXPERIMENTAL DESIGNS

A. The Unit p Sphere (UPS) Design

In the HKB and LW simulation studies, several regression models were considered which yielded a variety of choices of the dimension of the regression vector α (that is, p), degrees of freedom $(n - p - 1)$, and eigenvalue spectrum Λ. Only one model is required here for contrasting the various experimental designs and highlighting interesting invariance results. In particular, the standardized regression design matrix X considered here is called the "10-factor basic model" by Lawless and Wang (1976, p. 314). This data set is the standardized form of the classic Gorman–Torman multicollinear data set reproduced in many sources including Hoerl et al. (1986, Table 2, p. 371). The specifications of this design matrix are $p = 10$, $n = 36$ (the sample size), with the correlation matrix $X'X$ having eigenvalues 3.6864, 1.5496, 1.2966, 1.0515, .94467, .65709, .36047, .23176, .14792, and .074018.

The present author duplicated, as far as different random numbers will allow, the 10-factor basic model by choosing 5000 different α's from the surface of the UPS for each of 10 values of $a^2 = 1/\sigma^2$.

This was accomplished by generating uniform $(-1, 1)$ random numbers so as to construct a $p \times p$ (10×10) correlation matrix and therefrom deriving a random orthonormal matrix G. Thereafter, random α's were generated from $\alpha = G'\ell$, where $\ell = (1/\sqrt{10}, 1/\sqrt{10}, \ldots, 1/\sqrt{10})'$. For each model, the $\hat{\alpha}_i$ terms (the LS estimates of the α_i) were independently generated so that $\hat{\alpha}_i \sim N(\alpha_i, \sigma^2/\lambda_i)$, for $i = 1, 2, \ldots, p$, and $\hat{\sigma}^2$ (the LS estimate of σ^2) was generated so that $(n - p - 1)\hat{\sigma}^2/\sigma^2 \sim \chi^2_{n-p-1}$. As in the LW simulation, the values of a^2 chosen were 1, 4, 9, 25, 64, 200, 900, 1600, 2500, 10,000. The simulation program was written using SAS PROC MATRIX language and routines UNIFORM (for computing uniform random numbers), RANNOR (for computing normal random errors) and EIGVEC (for generating the columns of the random orthonormal matrix G). The program was executed on Southern Methodist University's IBM 3081 computer using version 5 SAS.

B.   Estimators and Risk Functions Considered

The estimators of α considered in the LW simulation were primarily of the ridge family, the principal components estimator being the exception. Of the ridge estimators considered there, the HKB and LW estimators are considered here.

The HKB and LW estimators are of the form

$$\tilde{\alpha}_i(k_i) = \left(\frac{\lambda_i}{\lambda_i + k_i}\right)\hat{\alpha}_i, \qquad i = 1, 2, \ldots, p, \tag{10}$$

where k_i depends on the data. Let $\hat{\sigma}^2 = \text{RSS}/(n - p - 1)$, where RSS denotes the LS residual sum of squares. HKB suggest the use of the ridge parameter

$$k_a = p\hat{\sigma}^2 \Big/ \sum_{i=1}^{p} \hat{\alpha}_i^2, \tag{11}$$

while LW suggest the use of the ridge parameter

$$k_b = p\hat{\sigma}^2 \Big/ \sum_{i=1}^{p} \lambda_i \alpha_i^2. \tag{12}$$

The same risk functions of LW are considered here, namely,

$$M_1 = E(\tilde{\beta} - \beta)'(\tilde{\beta} - \beta) = E(\tilde{\alpha} - \alpha)'(\tilde{\alpha} - \alpha)$$

$$= \sum_{i=1}^{p} E(\tilde{\alpha}_i - \alpha_i)^2 \tag{13}$$

and

$$M_2 = E(\tilde{\beta} - \beta)'X'X(\tilde{\beta} - \beta) = E(\tilde{\alpha} - \alpha)'\Lambda(\tilde{\alpha} - \alpha)$$

$$= \sum_{i=1}^{p} \lambda_i E(\tilde{\alpha}_i - \alpha_i)^2. \tag{14}$$

To serve as a contrast to the heuristically developed HKB and LW ridge estimators, Stein-like estimators (see Stein, 1955; James and Stein, 1961) are considered here as well. Such estimators are minimax, and risk gains are guaranteed over LS. The two positive-part Stein-rule estimators examined are those discussed in Judge and Bock (1978, pp. 179–180 and 240–244). The first is

$$\alpha_1^+ = [1 - as/(\tilde{\alpha} - \alpha_0)'\Lambda(\hat{\alpha} - \alpha_0)]^+(\hat{\alpha} - \alpha_0) + \alpha_0, \tag{15}$$

where $a = [\text{tr}(\Lambda^{-1})\lambda_p - 2]/(n - (p + 1) + 2)$; $s = \hat{\sigma}^2/(n - p - 1)$; and $[\cdot]^+$ is the positive-part operator. That is, $[\cdot]^+$ takes the value $\cdot$ when $\cdot > 0$, and zero otherwise. The vector α_0 is nonstochastic and represents the user's choice of shrinkage point. Equivalently, α_0 can be thought of as a prior vector for α. This estimator is minimax relative to the risk M_1. As might be expected, the risk improvement offered by α_1^+ increases as α_0 approaches the true value of α.

The second positive-part Stein-rule estimator is of the same form as α_1^+ except the shrinkage constant takes the form $a = (p - 2)/(n - (p + 1) + 2)$. This estimator is denoted by α_2^+ and is minimax with respect to the risk M_2. Again the improvement offered by α_2^+ depends on the proximity of α_0 to the true value of α.

As an alternative to the sampling theoretic estimators presented above, Zellner's Bayesian g-prior estimator (see Zellner, 1980; Judge et al., 1985, pp. 110–111) is considered as well. The g-prior estimator is of the form

$$\alpha_g = \frac{g\alpha_0 + \hat{\alpha}}{1 + g}. \tag{16}$$

This estimator is the posterior mean of a joint posterior density arising from a normal likelihood function and prior distributions of σ and α of $p(\sigma) \propto \sigma^{-1}$ and $p(\alpha) \sim N(\alpha_0, (g\Lambda)^{-1})$, respectively. The parameter g can be thought of as the precision of the prior information relative to the sample information. Letting $g = 1$, that is, assuming the prior and sample information should carry equal weights, Zellner's g-prior estimator becomes

$$\alpha_g = \frac{\alpha_0 + \hat{\alpha}}{2} \tag{17}$$

and is the simple average of the LS estimator and the prior mean. Though not minimax, this estimator does minimize average risk (see Zellner 1971, p. 424). As several Bayesian estimators have performed well in many contexts (see, for example, Fomby and Guilkey, 1978), it was thought appropriate to include this estimator here for comparison purposes.

C. Results of UPS Design

Given a value of $a^2 = 1/\sigma^2$, 5000 replications of the UPS design were generated, and for each iteration the norms

$$S_1 = \sum_{i=1}^{p} (\tilde{\alpha}_i - \alpha_i)^2 \tag{18}$$

and

$$S_2 = \sum_{i=1}^{p} \lambda_i(\tilde{\alpha}_i - \alpha_i)^2 \tag{19}$$

were computed for each estimator. Over all 5000 replications the summary measures $\text{AVE}(S_1)$ and $\text{AVE}(S_2)$, that is, the average of the S_1 and S_2 values obtained over the 5000 replications, were calculated as well as the percentage of replications for which the given estimator produced a smaller value of S_1 then the LS estimator, and similarly for S_2. For the purpose of providing accuracy measures, the standard errors of the empirical MSEs $\text{AVE}(S_1)$ and $\text{AVE}(S_2)$ are reported in parentheses. The performances of the various estimators, given the setting of the UPS design, are detailed in Tables 1, 2, and 3a,b. The column headings denote the various estimators considered. HKB and LW represent, respectively, the Hoerl, Kennard, and Baldwin (1975) and Lawless and Wang (1976) ridge estimators of Eqs. (10)–(12). The labels STI∅ and STIM denote the Stein rules of Eq. (15), where in the former case $\alpha_0 = \varnothing$ (the null vector) and in the latter $\alpha_0 = \ell = (1/\sqrt{10}, \ldots, 1/\sqrt{10})'$, the mean of the POUPS design. The notation of I in the middle of these labels is to emphasize the fact that the risk weight matrix used for constructing the Stein rules was chosen

(Text continues on page 30)

Table 1. Average S_1 values for estimators (based on 5000 runs): UPS Design

(Standard errors in parentheses)

a^2	HKB	LW	STIØ	STIM	STXXØ	STXXM	ZELGØ	ZELGM	LS
1	7.7809 (.115141)	3.13293 (.0381394)	30.33 (.313806)	30.5023 (.314142)	7.24372 (.151968)	8.57937 (.158273)	8.38274 (.0822634)	8.63587 (.0830894)	32.5455 (.325481)
4	2.19831 (.0285461)	1.18724 (.0102798)	7.68955 (.0786404)	7.78263 (.0789654)	2.68799 (.0411267)	3.568 (.045852)	2.28228 (.0212579)	2.5378 (.0222321)	8.13637 (.0813703)
9	1.14228 (.0127056)	0.775963 (.0054118)	3.46607 (.0351106)	3.51146 (.0353475)	1.66582 (.0202493)	2.1634 (.0236302)	1.15283 (.00994461)	1.40915 (.0110121)	3.61616 (.0361646)
25	0.556384 (.00493624)	0.480584 (.0031555)	1.27162 (.012766)	1.28342 (.0128548)	0.875219 (.00891916)	1.02591 (.0103299)	0.574729 (.00410303)	0.831688 (.00532609)	1.30182 (.0130193)
64	0.299284 (.00245675)	0.293117 (.00218787)	0.502873 (.00503262)	0.505295 (.00505451)	0.424015 (.00418046)	0.458131 (.00455458)	0.376677 (.00201715)	0.633995 (.00342239)	0.508523 (.00508565)
200	0.129855 (.00114814)	0.135436 (.0012147)	0.162087 (.00162097)	0.16237 (.00162379)	0.152811 (.00151419)	0.157022 (.00156391)	0.290425 (.000976552)	0.548003 (.00261447)	0.162727 (.00162741)
900	0.0343655 (.000332529)	0.0359407 (.000359864)	0.0361288 (.000361302)	0.036143 (.000361451)	0.035646 (.000355553)	0.0358609 (.000358169)	0.258919 (.000428751)	0.516676 (.00232056)	0.0361616 (.000361646)
1,600	0.0197844 (.000194)	0.020473 (.000205)	0.0203305 (.000203)	0.0203349 (.000203)	0.0201768 (.000201)	0.0202436 (.000202)	0.254995 (.000318)	0.512791 (.002282)	0.0203409 (.000203)
2,500	0.0127946 (.000126)	0.0131284 (.000131)	0.0130139 (.000130)	0.0130157 (.000130)	0.0129508 (.000129)	0.0129775 (.000129)	0.253182 (.000253)	0.511002 (.00226)	0.0130182 (.000130)
10,000	0.0032413 (.0000323)	0.00326797 (.0000326)	0.00325428 (.0000325)	0.00325438 (.0000325)	0.00325034 (.0000324)	0.00325178 (.0000325)	0.250777 (.000126)	0.508645 (.00224)	0.00325455 (.0000325)

Table 2. Average S_2 Values for Estimators (Based on 5000 Runs): UPS Design

(Standard errors in parentheses)

a^2	HKB	LW	STIØ	STIM	STXXØ	STXXM	ZELGØ	ZELGM	LS
1	4.63449 (.0443195)	2.81238 (.0318289)	9.40712 (.0640204)	9.46572 (.0637706)	2.58278 (.038316)	3.26139 (.0379904)	2.77082 (.0177599)	3.02234 (.0194591)	10.0833 (.0644448)
4	1.26272 (.0109151)	0.91443 (.00809457)	2.38791 (.0158657)	2.41787 (.0158237)	1.07388 (.00944144)	1.42556 (.0106842)	0.880215 (.00566611)	1.13658 (.00754632)	2.52081 (.0161112)
9	0.623244 (.00485002)	0.517833 (.0038739)	1.07689 (.00702895)	1.0907 (.00704229)	0.662886 (.0046614)	0.815654 (.00555872)	0.530103 (.00341699)	0.788083 (.00537113)	1.12036 (.00716053)
25	0.270159 (.00185115)	0.256211 (.00169904)	0.394912 (.00253968)	0.39824 (.00255158)	0.318629 (.00207787)	0.351473 (.00228091)	0.350846 (.00225443)	0.610118 (.00425936)	0.40333 (.00257779)
64	0.125146 (.000812062)	0.12548 (.000806345)	0.156015 (.000998551)	0.156665 (.00100182)	0.14229 (.000913741)	0.148433 (.000950411)	0.289402 (.0018493)	0.5494 (.00387134)	0.157551 (.00100695)
200	0.0459894 (.000293744)	0.0470379 (.000301601)	0.0502451 (.000321177)	0.0503176 (.000321605)	0.0487177 (.00310955)	0.0493789 (.000315302)	0.262618 (.00166933)	0.523143 (.00369498)	0.0504163 (.000322224)
900	0.010972 (.0000699)	0.011168 (.0000716)	0.0111949 (.0000715)	0.0111983 (.0000715)	0.0111182 (.0000709)	0.011145 (.0000711)	0.252815 (.00160)	0.513702 (.00362)	0.0112036 (.0000716)
1,600	0.00622937 (.0000397)	0.00631011 (.0000404)	0.0062993 (.0000402)	0.0063029 (.0000402)	0.00627518 (.0000400)	0.00628218 (.0000401)	0.25159 (.00159)	0.512558 (.00361)	0.00630204 (.0000402)
2,500	0.00400368 (.0000255)	0.00404179 (.0000258)	0.00403218 (.0000257)	0.00403256 (.0000257)	0.0040224 (.0000256)	0.00402465 (.0000257)	0.251023 (.00158)	0.512039 (.00360)	0.0040333 (.0000257)
10,000	0.00100645 (.00000643)	0.00100945 (.00000645)	0.00100826 (.00000644)	0.00100827 (.00000644)	0.00100768 (.00000643)	0.00100762 (.00000643)	0.250267 (.00158)	0.51138 (.00360)	0.00100833 (.00000644)

27

Table 3a. Percentage of Time Better Than LS Using S_1 as Norm (5000 Runs):
UPS Design

a^2	HKB	LW	STI∅	STIM	STXX∅	STXXM	ZELG∅	ZELGM
1	.9998	.9998	1.0	1.0	.9998	.9994	1.0	.9998
4	.9994	.9994	1.0	.9998	.9980	.9852	.9998	.9968
9	.9914	.9884	.9996	.9970	.9818	.9706	.9974	.9658
25	.9356	.9212	.9952	.9766	.9574	.9384	.9286	.7186
64	.8272	.8012	.9634	.9132	.9138	.8664	.5990	.3002
200	.6930	.6580	.8610	.7874	.8136	.7512	.1142	.0294
900	.5870	.5620	.6984	.6498	.6724	.6268	.0002	.0002
1,600	.5652	.5440	.6566	.6148	.6332	.5940	0.0	0.0
2,500	.5534	.5346	.6216	.5920	.6016	.5794	0.0	0.0
10,000	.5272	.5156	.5616	.5512	.5544	.5438	0.0	0.0

28

Table 3b. Percentage of Time Better than LS using S_2 as Norm (5000 runs): UPS Design

a^2	HKB	LW	STI∅	STIM	STXX∅	STXXM	ZELG∅	ZELGM
1	1.0	.9998	1.0	.9998	.9988	.9906	1.0	.9994
4	.9982	.9968	.9996	.9950	.9648	.9158	.9944	.9510
9	.9900	.9792	.9954	.9736	.9080	.8550	.9478	.7446
25	.9462	.9122	.9618	.9012	.8292	.771	.5986	.2678
64	.8410	.7948	.8728	.7966	.7416	.6888	.1502	.0400
200	.7080	.6692	.7504	.6834	.6462	.6128	.0032	.0008
900	.5990	.5720	.6170	.5926	.5680	.5562	0.0	0.0
1,600	.5738	.5516	.5882	.5706	.5496	.5444	0.0	0.0
2,500	.5570	.5390	.5710	.5580	.5388	.5366	0.0	0.0
10,000	.5274	.5216	.5304	.5314	.5174	.5200	0.0	0.0

to be I. The labels STXX$\varnothing$ and STXXM denote the predictive Stein rules of Eq. (15) with $a = (p - 2)/(n - (p + 1) + 2)$ and with $\alpha_0 = \varnothing$ and $\alpha_0 = \ell$, respectively; XX denotes the risk weight matrix chosen for constructing the Stein rules, that is, $X'X$. The labels ZELG$\varnothing$ and ZELGM denote the Zellner g-prior estimators [Eq. (17)], with prior vectors $\alpha_0 = \varnothing$ and $\alpha_0 = \ell$, respectively.

In Table 1 the empirical unweighted MSEs, AVE(S_1), and weighted MSEs, AVE(S_2), of the various estimators support the following conclusions:

a.   The reported MSEs for the HKB, LW, and LS estimators coincide, apart from sampling error, with those reported by Lawless and Wang (1976, Table II, p. 318). That is, the empirical MSEs reported by LW are almost always within two standard errors of the empirical MSEs reported here. This is as it should be since the UPS design executed here is the same as LW's except for the use of different random numbers.

b.   The HKB ridge estimator performs uniformly better than LS, substantially so for low a^2, with the advantage over LS diminishing as $a^2 \to 10,000$.

c.   The LW ridge estimator offers substantial improvement over LS for low-to-moderate values of a^2, but the improvement offered is not universal. For large a^2, the LW estimator is less efficient than the LS estimator but not substantially so.

d.   With respect to the AVE(S_1) measure, the minimaxity properties of the Stein rules STI$\varnothing$ and STIM are empirically supported. The gains offered by the STI$\varnothing$ estimator are greater than those offered by the STIM estimator because the null shrinkage point associated with STIM was generally closer to the actual α value chosen in each iteration than the $\ell = (1/\sqrt{10}, \ldots, 1/\sqrt{10})'$ shrinkage point chosen by the STIM estimator. The mean of the α vectors chosen over all 5000 iterations for each a^2 value (the same 5000 random numbers were used for each value of a^2) was $(-0.00506019, -0.00174056, -0.00905797, -0.0152578, -0.018198, -0.00844654, -0.000927088, 0.00252029, 0.00387665, 0.00222919)$. This is obviously much closer to the null vector than it is to ℓ. This goes to show that the better the choice of shrinkage point (prior vector) the greater the improvement offered by Stein rules. However, the stringency of the minimaxity requirement did lead to gains which were substantially less than the HKB ridge estimator. In compensation the Stein rules did not succumb to the inefficiency of the LW estimator for large values of a^2. Percentage gains offered by the STI∅ estimator relative to LS range from 6.8% for $a^2 = 1$ to 0.008% for $a^2 = 10,000$.

e. Somewhat surprisingly, the Stein rules STXX∅ and STXXM were empirically minimax with respect to AVE(S_1) as well, even though the choice of the risk weight matrix ($X'X$) is not appropriate in this context. Moreover, these estimators dominated their counterparts STI∅ and STIM, yielding gains more in line with those offered by the HKB ridge estimator. In this instance the greater shrinkage offered by the predictive Stein rules yielded greater risk gains, though this particular outcome need not apply generally.

f. With respect to AVE(S_1), the Bayesian estimators are not empirically minimax. Though the ZELG∅ estimator does quite well for small a^2, it becomes inefficient relative to LS as a^2 nears moderate-to-large values. The ZELGM estimator is, as expected, dominated by the ZELG∅ estimator because ZELG∅ uses a more appropriate prior mean. The same conclusions hold for these Bayesian estimators when one is considering AVE(S_2).

g. With respect to AVE(S_2), the minimaxity properties of the Stein rules STXX∅ and STXXM were empirically supported. As expected, the gains offered by the STXX∅ estimator were greater than those offered by the STXXM estimator. The choice of shrinkage point was more appropriate in the former case. In this instance, the HKB ridge estimator did not display the distinct advantage it has in the context of AVE(S_1) over the Stein rules. In fact, the STXX∅ estimator dominated the ridge estimators for $a^2 = 1$ and exhibited comparable risk for the remaining a^2 values. Percentage gains offered by the STXX∅ estimator relative to LS ranged from 74.4% for $a^2 = 1$ to 0.064% for $a^2 = 10,000$.

h. The Stein rules STI∅ and STIM were empirically minimax with respect to AVE(S_2), a result again not expected given the incorrect choice of weight matrix. The estimators did not, however, dominate their counterparts STXX∅ and STXXM.

Table 3 contains basically the same information as contained in Tables 1 and 2 except here the performance of the various estimators is measured as the percentage of the time that the given estimator has smaller norm (S_1 or S_2), see equations (18) and (19), than the LS estimator.

i.   When one uses this measure of performance, the appropriate
Stein rules perform acceptably relative to the ridge estimators. In
the case of $AVE(S_1)$, the STI∅ estimator uniformly dominates its
ridge competitors.

D.   Results of POUPS Design

The positive-orthant UPS (POUPS) design is suggested by the
Silvapulle invariance result presented in Section III. Thus, the
POUPS design is such that the α vector for each iteration of the
simulation is chosen to be the absolute value of the α vector chosen
uniformly from the UPS. The corresponding results of the POUPS
simulation as they parallel those of the UPS simulation are presented in Tables 4, 5, and 6a,b. The same random numbers (and
thus α and $\hat{\sigma}^2$ values) used to generate the UPS results were used
in producing these results. The major conclusions drawn here are
as follows:

j.   Apart from the minor discrepancies arising from the finite-
ness of the number of iterations, the invariance result of Silvapulle
(1985) is empirically supported here. That is, the performance of
the ridge estimators are not affected by the fact that with this
design the mean of the α vectors chosen over all 5000 iterations
for each a^2 was (0.255626, 0.259146, 0.256957, 0.261439, 0.258016,
0.255822, 0.258272, 0.258907, 0.257608, 0.258131), which is much
closer to $\ell = (1/\sqrt{10}, \ldots, 1/\sqrt{10})'$ than the null vector.
k.   As noted by Breusch (1980), other things held constant, the
risk of the LS estimator is invariant to the choice of α. Compare
the $AVE(S_1)$ and $AVE(S_2)$ values across the UPS and POUPS
designs.
l.   An inductive conclusion offered by the simulations of the
UPS and POUPS designs is that the risks of the STI∅ and STXX∅
estimators are invariant across these designs. By inspection, these
Stein rules are in the same class as those of the HKB and LW
ridge estimators, and thus the Silvapulle result likewise applies.
The risks of the STIM and STXXM estimators are not, however,
invariant. They perform better in the context of the POUPS design
because the prior vector ℓ is more appropriate there. As noted by
Judge et al. (1985, p. 86), the performance of Stein rules is not
invariant to the choice of shrinkage point.

(Text continues on page 37)

Table 4. Average S_1 Values for Estimators (Based on 5000 Runs): Positive Orthant Design

(Standard errors in parentheses)

a^2	HKB	LW	STIØ	STIM	STXXØ	STXXM	ZELGØ	ZELGM	LS
1	7.77611 (.115079)	3.13135 (.037532)	30.3296 (.313752)	30.2161 (.313756)	7.20251 (.152421)	6.39103 (.149942)	8.38727 (.0822905)	8.22457 (.0814879)	32.5455 (.325481)
4	2.19663 (.0285091)	1.18669 (.0100187)	7.68958 (.078619)	7.60381 (.0784855)	2.66933 (.0412007)	1.96324 (.038885)	2.28454 (.0212692)	2.12423 (.020585)	8.13637 (.0813703)
9	1.14099 (.0126789)	0.775198 (.00527986)	3.46607 (.0351046)	3.40866 (.0349339)	1.65648 (.0202119)	1.10907 (.0182114)	1.15434 (.00995054)	0.994826 (.00932694)	3.61616 (.0361646)
25	0.555065 (.00491784)	0.479309 (.00311696)	1.27156 (.0127652)	1.2481 (.0126429)	0.871624 (.00890737)	0.59744 (.00743167)	0.575635 (.00410489)	0.416757 (.00357959)	1.30182 (.0130193)
64	0.298289 (.00244856)	0.292003 (.00217589)	0.502846 (.00503259)	0.496029 (.00498263)	0.42339 (.00418372)	0.329731 (.00346631)	0.377244 (.00201714)	0.218724 (.00162612)	0.508523 (.00508565)
200	0.129548 (.00115318)	0.135012 (.00121487)	0.162085 (.00162105)	0.16106 (.0016116)	0.152786 (.00151652)	0.136925 (.00135976)	0.290746 (.00097584)	0.132486 (.000796686)	0.162727 (.00162741)
900	0.034322 (.000333)	0.0359104 (.000364)	0.0361288 (.000361)	0.0360685 (.00360)	0.0356461 (.000355)	0.0346612 (.000344)	0.259071 (.000428)	0.100989 (.000513)	0.0361616 (.000361)
1,600	0.0197622 (.000194)	0.0204621 (.000207)	0.0203305 (.000203)	0.0203109 (.000203)	0.0201769 (.000201)	0.0198549 (.000197)	0.255108 (.000318)	0.0970665 (.000481)	0.0203409 (.000203)
2,500	0.0127818 (.000126)	0.0131221 (.000132)	0.0130139 (.000130)	0.0130058 (.000130)	0.0129509 (.000129)	0.0128168 (.000127)	0.253273 (.000253)	0.0952552 (.000466)	0.0130182 (.00130)
10,000	0.00323934 (.000323)	0.00326647 (.0000327)	0.00325428 (.0000325)	0.00325376 (.0000325)	0.00325034 (.0000325)	0.00324169 (.0000323)	0.250823 (.000125)	0.092853 (.000447)	0.00325455 (.0000325)

Table 5. Average S_2 Values for Estimators (Based on 5000 Runs): Positive Orthant Design

(Standard errors in parentheses)

a^2	HKB	LW	STIØ	STIM	STXXØ	STXXM	ZELGØ	ZELGM	LS
1	4.63629 (.0443566)	2.81449 (.0317478)	9.40718 (.06401)	9.3667 (.0642496)	2.57776 (.0382699)	2.11934 (.039233)	2.77656 (.0178104)	2.60996 (.0166639)	10.0833 (.0644448)
4	1.26416 (.0109272)	0.91602 (.00805327)	2.38796 (.0158624)	2.35901 (.015972)	1.07380 (.00942354)	0.728713 (.00949386)	0.883134 (.0055513)	0.721283 (.00460978)	2.52081 (.0161112)
9	0.624285 (.00485569)	0.518819 (.00384136)	1.07686 (.00702797)	1.05837 (.0070601)	0.663427 (.00464669)	0.440727 (.00420093)	0.532049 (.00338581)	0.371813 (.00238547)	1.12036 (.00716053)
25	0.270559 (.00185051)	0.256469 (.001678)	0.394874 (.0025395)	0.387818 (.00253046)	0.317584 (.00205269)	0.239337 (.00170873)	0.352014 (.00222185)	0.193069 (.00125584)	0.40333 (.00257779)
64	0.125241 (.000809983)	0.125503 (.000798646)	0.156007 (.000998693)	0.15407 (.000991518)	0.142085 (.00909527)	0.122259 (.00812437)	0.290131 (.00182467)	0.131914 (.000875731)	0.157551 (.00100695)
200	0.0460083 (.000293645)	0.0470373 (.000301081)	0.0502458 (.000321266)	0.0499643 (.000319701)	0.0487308 (.000312268)	0.0458661 (.000294365)	0.263031 (.00165456)	0.105339 (.000714164)	0.0504163 (.000322224)
900	0.0109742 (.0000700)	0.0111703 (.0000718)	0.0111952 (.0000715)	0.0111785 (.0000714)	0.0111225 (.0000712)	0.0109473 (.0000698)	0.25301 (.00159)	0.0956804 (.000656)	0.0112036 (.0000716)
1,600	0.00623017 (.0000397)	0.00631137 (.0000405)	0.0062994 (.0000402)	0.00629389 (.0000402)	0.00627716 (.000401)	0.00621829 (.0000397)	0.251736 (.00158)	0.0944872 (.000649)	0.00630204 (.0000402)
2,500	0.00400403 (.0000255)	0.00404244 (.0000258)	0.00403224 (.0000257)	0.00402991 (.0000257)	0.00402346 (.0000257)	0.00399815 (.0000255)	0.25114 (.00158)	0.0939393 (.000646)	0.0040333 (.0000257)
10,000	0.00100648 (.00000642)	0.0010095 (.00000645)	0.00100826 (.00000644)	0.0010081 (.00000644)	0.00100782 (.00000644)	0.00100591 (.00000642)	0.250325 (.00158)	0.0932216 (.000642)	0.00100833 (.00000644)

34

Table 6a. Percentage of Time Better Than LS Using S_1 as Norm (5000 runs): Positive Orthant Design

a_2	HKB	LW	STIØ	STIM	STXXØ	STXXM	ZELGØ	ZELGM
1	.9998	.9998	1.0	1.0	.9998	1.0	1.0	1.0
4	.9992	.9992	1.0	1.0	.9972	.9998	.9998	.9998
9	.9900	.9884	.9998	1.0	.9082	.9976	.9970	.9998
25	.9386	.9252	.9936	.9998	.9580	.9850	.9260	.9942
64	.8290	.7980	.9624	.9932	.9146	.9640	.6106	.9946
200	.6884	.6530	.8596	.9478	.8068	.9034	.1074	.5622
900	.5848	.5530	.7004	.7974	.6686	.7622	.0004	.0520
1,600	.5608	.5402	.6514	.7382	.6270	.7070	0.0	.0112
2,500	.5506	.5320	.6212	.6948	.6012	.6694	0.0	.0018
10,000	.5244	.5142	.5616	.5996	.5524	.5846	0.0	0.0

Table 6b. Percentage of Time Better Than LS Using S_2 as Norm (5000 Runs)
Positive Orthant Design

a_2	HKB	LW	STI∅	STIM	STXX∅	STXXM	ZELG∅	ZELGM
1	1.0	.9998	1.0	1.0	.9988	1.0	1.0	1.0
4	.9972	.9956	.9996	1.0	.9644	.9978	.9960	.9998
9	.9898	.9820	.9956	1.0	.9084	.9748	.9488	.9970
25	.9394	.9104	.9626	.9938	.8288	.9054	.5962	.9392
64	.8412	.7960	.8786	.9610	.7430	.8404	.1496	.6250
100	.7088	.6636	.7376	.8590	.6482	.7360	.0020	.1294
900	.5976	.5698	.6152	.7022	.5708	.6274	0.0	.0018
1,600	.5696	.5470	.5906	.6576	.5544	.5984	0.0	0.0
2,500	.5538	.5364	.5712	.6298	.5426	.5810	0.0	0.0
10,000	.5274	.5158	.5336	.5698	.5182	.5452	0.0	0.0

36

m. The Bayesian estimator ZELG∅ is also subject to the Silvapulle invariance result, though the ZELGM estimator is not. The ZELGM estimator naturally performs better in the context of the POUPS design.

E. Results of the Fixed Coefficient (FC) Vector Design

As previously mentioned in Section III, not all investigators have chosen to use a random coefficient design when evaluating the performance of ridge estimators. In fact, several authors have found that the alignment of the coefficient vector relative to the eigenvector associated with the smallest eigenvalue of $X'X$ is crucial.

To contrast the fixed coefficient (FC) design to the random coefficient methods previously discussed, and FC experiment was run on the same standardized Gorman–Toman regressor data used in the previous designs. Also to accentuate the nonminimaxity of the HKB and LW ridge estimators, a very unfavorable orientation of the α vector was chosen. That is, the *fixed* α vector was chosen to be $\alpha = (0, 0, \ldots, 0, c)'$, where c denotes an appropriately chosen constant. The α vector is collinear with the eigenvector associated with the smallest eigenvalue of $X'X$. Furthermore, $\sigma^2 = 1$ was chosen.

In the case of the POUPS design, the corresponding coefficients of determination (R^2) implied by the various a^2 values are (in expectation) given by

a^2	1	4	9	25	64	200	900	1600	2500	10000
R^2	0.5	0.8	0.9	0.96	0.9846	0.995	0.9989	0.9994	0.9996	0.9999

The coefficient of determination is calculated in each case as

$$R^2 = \frac{\sum_{i=1}^{p} \lambda_i \alpha_i^2}{\sum_{i=1}^{p} \lambda_i \alpha_i^2 + \sigma^2}$$

$$= \frac{1}{1 + \sigma^2} = \frac{1}{1 + (1/a^2)} \tag{20}$$

if we let $\alpha = (1/\sqrt{10}, \ldots, 1/\sqrt{10})' = \ell$, the expected value of the coefficient vector in the POUPS design.

For $\sigma^2 = 1$, the values of c which yield the corresponding R^2 values for the FC design are as shown here:

c	3.6756	7.3513	11.0269	18.0068	29.3901	51.8511
R^2	0.5	0.8	0.9	0.96	0.9846	0.995

	110.7633	150.0118	183.7446	367.5442
	0.9989	0.9994	0.9996	0.9999

Obviously, as the length of c increases, the R^2 of the regression model of the FC design likewise increases. The prior vectors for the Stein rules STI∅ and STXX∅ are as before the null vector, whereas the prior vector for STIM and STXXM is taken to be the true parameter vector $(0, 0, \ldots, 0, c)'$.

The results of the FC design are summarized in Tables 7, 8, and 9a, b, standing in stark contrast to those from the previous random designs. In particular:

n. Except for $a^2 = 1$ ($c = 3.6756$), the HKB and LW ridge estimators are uniformly worse than LS with respect to AVE(S_1). The situation improves only slightly with respect to AVE(S_2).

o. With respect to AVE(S_1), the Stein rule one would prefer a priori is STIM. The prior vector is the true parameter vector, and the risk weight matrix chosen to construct the estimator is I. This estimator is minimax as is supported by the observed AVE(S_1) values. The percentage improvement offered is a constant 7.99% because of the invariance properties of STIM and LS in this setting. The STI∅ estimator is likewise minimax but provides much less risk improvement because the null vector is not equal to the true parameter vector. In fact as the true vector α moves farther away from the origin, the risk improvement offered by STI∅ deteriorates rapidly. Thus, the selection of the shrinkage point in Stein-rule estimation is very instrumental in determining the risk properties of the Stein rule.

p. With respect to AVE(S_1), the STXX∅ estimator proves to be inefficient (and nonminimax) for moderate values of c. This might be suspected because the shrinkage point is not optimal and the estimator is designed to perform well in the context of $X'X$ being the risk weight matrix rather than in the the present context, where the weight matrix for evaluation purposes is I.

(*Text continues on page 43*)

Table 7. Average S_1 Values for Estimators (Based on 5000 Runs): Fixed Vector Design

(Standard errors in parentheses)

a^2	c	HKB	LW	STIØ	STIM	STXXØ	STXXM	ZELGØ	ZELGM	LS
1	3.6756	15.8805 (.106557)	13.9293 (.0402384)	30.4786 (.313246)	30.1381 (.313741)	13.494 (.131418)	5.86674 (.147886)	11.5205 (.126325)	8.13637 (.0813703)	32.5455 (.325481)
4	7.3513	33.5941 (.212841)	46.3345 (.0988632)	31.1749 (.315142)	30.1381 (.313741)	29.57776 (.245151)	5.86674 (.147886)	21.6599 (.207743)	8.13637 (.0813703)	32.5455 (.325481)
9	11.0269	48.1778 (.405648)	94.9355 (.234396)	31.7584 (.319778)	30.1381 (.313741)	41.8067 (.447659)	5.86674 (.147886)	38.5542 (.297015)	8.13637 (.0813703)	32.5455 (.325481)
25	18.0068	56.2689 (.623943)	208.247 (.681152)	32.2799 (.326152)	30.1381 (.313741)	46.1229 (.59981)	5.86674 (.147886)	89.2298 (.472178)	8.13637 (.0813703)	32.5455 (.325481)
64	29.3901	49.3132 (.595598)	366.907 (1.67666)	32.4739 (.327312)	30.1381 (.313741)	40.8355 (.511538)	5.86674 (.147886)	224.133 (.762146)	8.13637 (.0813703)	32.5455 (.325481)
200	51.8511	39.6135 (.451692)	441.199 (2.89914)	32.5275 (.326417)	30.1381 (.313741)	35.7759 (.400927)	5.86674 (.147886)	680.363 (1.33776)	8.13637 (.0813703)	32.5455 (.325481)
900	110.7633	34.2465 (.358982)	244.802 (2.23584)	32.5415 (.325784)	30.1381 (.313741)	33.296 (.344848)	5.86674 (.147886)	3075.46 (2.85113)	8.13637 (.0813703)	32.5455 (.325481)
1,600	150.0118	33.4795 (.344819)	166.221 (1.65584)	32.5431 (.325677)	30.1381 (.313741)	32.9543 (.33671)	5.86674 (.147886)	5634.29 (3.85994)	8.13637 (.0813703)	32.5455 (.325481)
2,500	183.7446	33.168 (.338898)	127.229 (1.32986)	32.5438 (.325629)	30.1381 (.313741)	32.8166 (.33332)	5.86674 (.147886)	8448.98 (4.72708)	8.13637 (.0813703)	32.5455 (.325481)
10,000	367.5442	32.6979 (.329472)	58.5307 (.669071)	32.5449 (.325541)	30.1381 (.313741)	32.6103 (.327898)	5.86674 (.147886)	33781.0 (9.45237)	8.13637 (.0813703)	32.5455 (.325481)

39

Table 8. Average S_2 Values of Estimators (Based on 5000 Runs)
Fixed Vector Design

(Standard errors in parentheses)

a^2	c	HKB	LW	STIØ	STIM	STXXØ	STXXM	ZELGØ	ZELGM	LS
1	3.6756	5.56602 (.0448356)	3.43693 (.0317449)	9.40899 (.639909)	9.33969 (.0644088)	2.58925 (.0380215)	1.8201 (.0398927)	2.7713 (.0175878)	2.52081 (.0161112)	10.0833 (.0644448)
4	7.3513	7.81945 (.0459748)	6.18254 (.0308569)	9.56042 (.0633599)	9.33969 (.0644088)	4.37571 (.0354124)	1.8201 (.0398927)	3.5218 (.0213765)	2.52081 (.0161112)	10.0833 (.0644448)
9	11.0269	9.70479 (.0529942)	10.2614 (.0311495)	9.70866 (.0631447)	9.33969 (.0644088)	6.14337 (.0393664)	1.8201 (.0398927)	4.77228 (.0265034)	2.52081 (.0161112)	10.0833 (.0644448)
25	18.0068	11.1141 (.0681123)	19.6315 (.0500565)	9.88614 (.0634734)	9.33969 (.0644088)	8.09283 (.0520151)	1.8201 (.0398927)	8.52319 (.0379203)	2.52081 (.0161112)	10.0833 (.0644448)
64	29.3901	11.0276 (.0713821)	32.6108 (.120539)	9.99741 (.0639663)	9.33969 (.0644088)	9.21785 (.0593713)	1.8201 (.0398927)	18.5085 (.0582626)	2.52081 (.0161112)	10.0833 (.0644448)
200	51.8511	10.5076 (.0675826)	39.2943 (.21468)	10.0538 (.0642738)	9.33969 (.0644088)	9.78483 (.0627299)	1.8201 (.0398927)	52.2777 (.0398927)	2.52081 (.0161112)	10.0833 (.0644448)
900	110.7633	10.1872 (.0652126)	25.5163 (.173393)	10.0766 (.0644073)	9.33969 (.0644088)	10.0153 (.0640901)	1.8201 (.0398927)	229 558 (.211464)	2.52081 (.0161112)	10.0833 (.0644448)
1,600	150.0118	10.1404 (.0648822)	19.8215 (.134755)	10.0796 (.0644249)	9.33969 (.0644088)	10.0458 (.0642634)	1.8201 (.0398927)	418.957 (.285996)	2.52081 (.0161112)	10.0833 (.0644448)
2,500	183.7446	10.1213 (.0647468)	16.9861 (.113988)	10.0808 (.0644319)	9.33969 (.0644088)	10.0581 (.0643312)	1.8201 (.0398927)	627.296 (.350108)	2.52081 (.0161112)	10.0833 (.0644448)
10,000	367.5442	10.0925 (.0645345)	11.9798 (.0772429)	10.0826 (.0644421)	9.33969 (.0644088)	10.0767 (.0644267)	1.8201 (.0398927)	2502.32 (.699705)	2.529 81 (.0161112)	10.0833 (.0644448)

Table 9a. Percentage of Time Better Than LS Using S_1 as Norm (5000 Runs): Fixed Vector Desgin

a^2	c	HKB	LW	STIØ	STIM	STXXØ	STXXM	ZELGØ	ZELGM
1	3.6756	.852	.8374	.9954	1.0	.8822	1.0	.9804	1.0
4	7.3513	.3984	.2116	.8862	1.0	.5542	1.0	.6248	1.0
9	11.0269	.2904	.0438	.7166	1.0	.4202	1.0	.2996	1.0
25	18.0068	.2824	.0122	.6152	1.0	.3900	1.0	.0828	1.0
64	29.3901	.3216	.0056	.5664	1.0	.4064	1.0	.0050	1.0
200	51.8511	.3782	.0108	.5394	1.0	.4404	1.0	0.0	1.0
900	110.7633	.4386	.0434	.5198	1.0	.4678	1.0	0.0	1.0
1,600	150.0118	.4522	.0778	.5152	1.0	.4770	1.0	0.0	1.0
2,500	183.7446	.4624	.1124	.5122	1.0	.4818	1.0	0.0	1.0
10,000	367.5442	.4810	.2544	.5062	1.0	.4896	1.0	0.0	1.0

Table 9b. Percentage of Time Better Than LS Using S_2 as Norm (5000 Runs): Fixed Vector Design

a^2	c	HKB	LW	STIØ	STIM	STXXØ	STXXM	ZELGØ	ZELGM
1	3.6756	.9994	.9996	.9998	1.0	.9996	1.0	1.0	1.0
4	7.3513	.8902	.9242	.9998	1.0	.9618	1.0	.9978	1.0
9	11.0269	.5374	.4302	.9966	1.0	.9054	1.0	.9572	1.0
25	18.0068	.3706	.0316	.9612	1.0	.8356	1.0	.6024	1.0
64	29.3901	.3734	.0096	.8698	1.0	.7494	1.0	.0706	1.0
200	51.8511	.4078	.0128	.7464	1.0	.6526	1.0	0.0	1.0
900	110.7633	.4512	.0462	.6184	1.0	.5762	1.0	0.0	1.0
1,600	150.0118	.4618	.0818	.5894	1.0	.5574	1.0	0.0	1.0
2,500	183.7446	.4698	.1158	.5740	1.0	.5440	1.0	0.0	1.0
10,000	367.5442	.4854	.2574	.5378	1.0	.5240	1.0	0.0	1.0

q. Somewhat surprisingly, in the context of $\text{AVE}(S_1)$, the Stein rule STXXM performs best overall and is empirically minimax in this particular instance. Evidently, the shrinkage constant

$$a = (p - 2)/(n - (p + 1) + 2) = 0.296296$$

adopted by the STXXM estimator is more appropriate for this particular experiment than the midpoint chosen for the STIM estimator

$$a = [\text{tr}(\Lambda^{-1})\lambda_p - 2]/(n - (p + 1) + 2) = 0.015238.$$

The larger shrinkage constant provided the greater gain in this particular case. Recall that the STIM and STXXM estimators are of the same form except for the choice of a. However, the choice of $a = 0.296926$ is outside of the region

$$0 < a \leq 2[\text{tr}(\Lambda^{-1})\lambda_p - 2]/(n - (p + 1) + 2),$$

which ensures the minimaxity of the STIM estimator. Another parameter vector orientation could well lead STIM to lose its dominance of LS should such a large value of a be chosen in general.

r. With respect to $\text{AVE}(S_1)$, the Bayesian ZELGM estimator did quite well, as might be expected with the use of such good prior information. The ZELG$\emptyset$ Bayesian estimator performed poorly because of the poor choice of prior mean.

s. With respect to $\text{AVE}(S_2)$, essentially the same conclusions hold true as did in the context of $\text{AVE}(S_1)$. The ridge estimators are not minimax, whereas the Stein rules STXX$\emptyset$ and STXXM are. The choice of prior vector is important in the Stein-rule and Bayesian estimators. The percentage risk improvements offered, however, by the minimax Stein rules are much greater in the prediction context, $\text{AVE}(S_2)$, than the point estimation context, $\text{AVE}(S_1)$. For instance, the STXXM estimator offers an 81.9% improvement over LS, whereas in the context of $\text{AVE}(S_1)$ the STIM estimator offers only a 7.99% improvement over LS.

t. Some interesting invariance properties appear in the FC design. The risks of the STIM, STXXM, and ZELGM estimators are invariant to changes in the true parameter vector as long as the prior vector coincides with the true parameter vector. The LS estimator is invariant to the choice of parameter vector, as shown by Breusch (1980).

V. WHERE DO WE STAND?

This brings us full circle—back to the point where the "random coefficient" (RC) adherents and "fixed coefficient" (FC) adherents still hold opposing views as to the appropriateness of the proposed ridge estimators of HKB and LW and the degree to which recommendations have been shaded by "prejudicial" experimental designs. The Silvapulle (1985) invariance result does, at first blush, seem to support the case of the RC adherents since the nonzero mean of the POUPS design does openly violate the zero mean prior implied by the Bayesian interpretation of the ridge estimator. The Silvapulle result does not, however, annul the fact that there do exist very unfavorable fixed orientations of the β vector which can lead the ridge estimators to be substantially inefficient relative to LS.

The basic viewpoint of the RC adherents is probably accurately expressed by Hoerl et al. (1986, p. 371) in the statement:

> It is well known that the performance of most biased estimators is affected by the alignment of β with the eigenvalues of $X'X$. Several simulations have, therefore, used β aligned with the maximum and minimum eigenvalues. ... Although these vectors represent the theoretically best and worst possible situations, we feel that they are not representative of the real world. Since β is a fixed parameter and the eigenvalues of $X'X$ are either random or determined by choice of a design, we believe generating β independently of X is most realistic.

From this quotation I conclude that the authors are willing to assume that:

1. No prior information is available on β or σ^2. Thus, ridge existence theorems are only suggestive.
2. β is fixed in repeated samples. This leaves three cases of the nature of the regressor matrix X to be considered.

CASE 1: Matrix X is designed. In this instance no collinearity problem exists and the impetus for biased estimation is much reduced. LS is quite acceptable in designed experiments.

CASE 2: Matrix X is fixed but collinear. The following question then naturally arises: "Is β in the 'proximity' of q_p?" The vector

$\mathbf{q}_p$ denotes the pth column of Q and is the eigenvector associated with the smallest eigenvalue of $X'X$. If it is, the performance of stochastic ridge estimators may leave much to be desired. Most importantly, the term "proximity" is ad hoc and is not operational as such. How close does β have to be to $\mathbf{q}_p$ before the stochastic ridge estimators perform poorly? If the direction angle between β and $\mathbf{q}_p$ is less than $15°$, is the performance of the stochastic ridge estimator acceptable? If it is less than $10°$? If it is less than $5°$? Even if such a "direction angle" rule did exist, recall that HSH appear to feel that the absence of prior knowledge on β is typical.

CASE 3:   Matrix X is random and collinear. The corresponding question then becomes "Is β in the 'proximity' of $E\mathbf{q}_p$?" Again any answer to this question is at best ad hoc since no operational rule exists nor in many cases is there any complete prior information available on β.

Thus, I would conclude that stochastic ridge rules like those of HKB and LW are ad hoc and leave much uncertainty in the user's mind. [This is a slight overstatement since recent research by Casella (1980, 1985) does allow one to determine sufficient conditions for the minimaxity of the LW estimator. More about this below.] Even in the presence of prior information on β, the term "proximity" used above is still problematic. Better yet, if prior information on β is available, even if only in linear combination form $R\beta = \mathbf{r}$, why not adopt a minimax Stein-rule estimator which properly takes account of the available (good) prior information? The only limitation of this approach is that the row dimension of R must be greater than 2. The risk improvement offered by the Stein rule in this case is likely to be quite substantial, and some gain is always guaranteed.

The philosophy of the original ridge theorists is quite different from that of more recent ridge theorists. The original theorists (Hoerl and Kennard, 1970a,b, among others) subscribed to the usefulness of existence theorems which guaranteed a risk gain in the presence of the knowledge of unknown parameters. The existence theorems "suggested" that stochastic ridge estimators might, like their theoretical counterparts, offer substantial gains over LS "in most typical situations." But what is typical for one investigator may not be so for another, and one must be satisfied with the claim that "poor performance is unlikely since so many simulation experiments have reported favorable results."

Ridge theorists of more recent vintage have begun their theoretical work by first defining a class of ridge-like estimators and then imposing the requirement of minimaxity and examining the type of data-based ridge parameters $(\hat{k})$ that would satisfy sufficient conditions for minimaxity. For a cross section of the minimax ridge literature see Casella (1977, 1980, 1985), Strawderman (1978), and Judge et al. (1985, pp. 925–926). These ridge estimators have the ridge property of inducing parameter estimate stability and at the same time are minimax. Interestingly, Casella (1985, Theorem 2.1, p. 754) examines a class of ridge estimators of which the LW ridge estimator is a special case. Casella's theorem proves that the LW estimator $\tilde{\alpha}(k_b)$ is minimax with respect to the risk function M_1 if

$$\frac{p}{\lambda_p} \le \frac{2m}{m+2}\left[\lambda_p^2 \sum_{i=1}^{p}\left(\frac{1}{\lambda_i^2}\right) - 2\right], \tag{21}$$

where $m = (n - (p + 1))$. This condition is not satisfied by the present 10-factor basic model (the standardized Gorman–Toman data).

The minimax ridge estimators are not without potential shortcomings, however. The extent of risk gains over LS could degenerate rapidly with only moderate degrees of collinearity. [See Hill and Ziemer (1983, 1984) for analyses of the effect that multicollinearity has on the risk gains offered by various Stein rules.] That is, there is a "tension" between minimaxity and the stability of estimated parameters, especially in the presence of multicollinearity (Casella, 1985).

Given this critique and the recent literature on minimax estimation (prediction) in the presence of multicollinearity, the ridge-type estimator, be it HKB, LW, or minimax, probably has passed its prime. Certainly, Stein rules which account for the relevant loss function and at the same time incorporate good prior information are to be recommended. In the absence of good prior information, Stein rules which use principal component restrictions probably should be considered. Employment of these restrictions is reasonable since they are maximum-variance-reducing restrictions (see Fomby et al., 1978). The principal components estimator appears to be a less arbitrary shrinkage point than the origin (Hill and

Ziemer, 1984; Hill and Judge, 1987). Tentative findings in Hill and Ziemer (1984) indicate that potential risk gains are often substantially enhanced by using a number of principal components restrictions that is approximately the same as the number of relatively small eigenvalues of $X'X$.

REFERENCES

Breusch, Trevor S. (1980) "Useful Invariance Results for Generalized Regression Models." *Journal of Econometrics* 13, 327-340.

Casella, G. (1977) "Minimax Ridge Estimation." Unpublished Ph.D. dissertation, Purdue University.

Casella, G. (1980) "Minimax Ridge Regression Estimation." *The Annuals of Statistics* 8, 1036-1056.

Casella, G. (1985) "Condition Numbers and Minimax Ridge Regression Estimators." *Journal of the American Statistical Association* 80, 753-758.

Conniffee, D. and J. Stone (1973) "A Critical View of Ridge Regression." *The Statistician* 22, 181-187.

Dempster, A. P., M. Schatzoff, and N. Wermuth (1977) "A Simulation Study of Alternatives to Least Squares (with Comments and Rejoinder)." *Journal of the American Statistical Association* 72, 77-106.

Draper, Norman R. and R. Craig Van Nostrand (1978) "Ridge Regression: Is It Worthwhile?" University of Wisconsin Statistics Department, Technical Report No. 501.

Farebrother, R. W. (1983) "An Examination of Recent Criticisms of Ridge Regression Simulation Designs." *Communications in Statistics, Series A* 12, 2549-2555.

Farebrother, R. W. and R. P. Thompson (1983) "Two Simulation Studies of a Class of Biased Estimators in the Standard Linear Model." University of Manchester discussion paper.

Fomby, Thomas B. and David K. Guilkey (1978) "On Choosing the Optimal Level of Significance for the Durbin-Watson Test and the Bayesian Alternative." *Journal of Econometrics* 8, 203-213.

Fomby, Thomas B., R. C. Hill and S. R. Johnson (1978) "An Optimality Property of Principal Components Regression." *Journal of the American Statistical Association* 73, 191-193.

Gibbons, Diane Galarneau (1978) "A Simulation Study of Some Ridge Estimators." General Motors Research Laboratories, Research Publication GMR-2659 (rev).

Gunst, Richard F. and Robert L. Mason (1977) "Biased Estimation in Regression: An Evaluation Using Mean Square Error." *Journal of the American Statistical Association* 72, 616-628.

Hill, R. C. and G. Judge (1987) "Improved Prediction in the Presence of Multicollinearity." *Journal of Econometrics* 35, 83-100.

Hill, R. C. and R. Ziemer (1983) "Small Sample Performance of the Stein-Rule in Nonorthogonal Designs." *Economics Letters* 10, 285–292.

Hill, R. C. and R. Ziemer (1984) "The Risk of General Stein-like Estimators in the Presence of Multicollinearity." *Journal of Econometrics* 25, 205–216.

Hoerl, A. E. and R. W. Kennard (1970a) "Ridge Regression: Biased Estimation for Nonorthogonal Problems." *Technometrics* 12, 55–67.

Hoerl, A. E. and R. W. Kennard (1970b) "Ridge Regression: Applications to Nonorthogonal Problems." *Technometrics* 12, 69–82.

Hoerl, A. E., Robert W. Kennard, and Kent F. Baldwin (1975) "Ridge Regression: Some Simulations." *Communications in Statistics, Series A* 4, 105–123.

Hoerl, Roger W., John H. Schuenmeyer, and Arthur E. Hoerl (1986) "A Simulation of Biased Estimation and Subset Selection Regression Techniques." *Technometrics* 28, 369–380.

James, W. and C. Stein (1961) "Estimation with Quadratic Loss." Pp. 361–379 in *Proceedings of the Fourth Berkeley Symposium on Mathematical Statisticss and Probability.* Berkeley: University of California Press.

Judge, George G. and M. E. Bock (1978) *The Statistical Implications of Pre-Test and Stein-Rule Estimators in Econometrics.* Amsterdam and New York: North-Holland Publishing.

Judge, George G., W. E. Griffiths, R. Carter Hill, Helmut Lütkepohl, and Tsoung-Chao Lee (1985) *The Theory and Practice of Econometrics,* 2nd ed. New York: Wiley.

Lawless, J. F. and P. Wang (1976) "A Simulation Study of Ridge and Other Regression Estimators." *Communications in Statistics, Series A* 5, 307–323.

McDonald, Gary C. and Diane I. Galarneau (1975) "A Monte Carlo Evaluation of Some Ridge Type Estimators." *Journal of the American Statistical Association* 70, 407–416.

Newhouse, Joseph P. and Samuel D. Oman (1971) "An Evaluation of Ridge Estimators." Rand Corporation, Report R-716-PR.

Pagel, Mark D. (1981) "Comment of Hoerl and Kennard's Ridge Regression Simulation Methodology." *Communications in Statistics, Series A* 10, 2361–2367.

Silvapulle, M. J. (1985) "An Examination of Criticisms of Ridge Regression Simulation Methodology." *Communications in Statistics, Series A* 14, 829–835.

Smith, Gary and Frank Campbell (1980) "A Critique of Some Ridge Regression Method (with Comments and Rejoinder)." *Journal of the American Statistical Association* 75, 74–103.

Stein, C. (1955) "Inadmissibility of the Usual Estimator for the Mean of a Multivariate Normal Distribution. Pp. 197–206 in *Proceedings of the Third Berkeley Symposium on Mathematical Statistics and Probability,* Vol. 1. Berkeley: University of California Press.

Strawderman, W. E. (1978) "Minimax Adaptive Generalized Ridge Regression Estimators." *Journal of the American Statistical Association* 73, 623–627.

Thisted, Ronald A. (1977) "Comment" on Dempster, A. P., Martin Schatzoff, and Nanny Wermuth, "A Simulation Study of Alternatives to Ordinary Least Squares." *Journal of the American Statistical Association* 72, 102–103.

Van Nostrand, R. Craig (1980) "Comment" on Smith, G. and F. Campbell, "A Critique of Some Ridge Regression Methods." *Journal of the American Statistical Association* 75, 92–94.

Wichern, Dean W. and Gilbert A. Churchill (1978) "A Comparison of Ridge Estimators." *Technometrics*, 20, 301–311.

Zellner, Arnold (1971) *An Introduction to Bayesian Inference in Econometrics.* New York: Wiley.

Zellner, Arnold (1980) "On Assessing Prior Distributions and Bayesian Regression Analysis with g-Prior Distributions." Paper presented to the Econometric Society Meeting, Denver, September.

COMPUTER ALGEBRA:
SYMBOLIC AND ALGEBRAIC COMPUTATION
IN ECONOMIC/ECONOMETRIC APPLICATIONS

K. J. Hayes, Joseph G. Hirschberg, and D. J. Slottje

I. INTRODUCTION

In the natural sciences, a quiet revolution has been taking place. Natural scientists have become increasingly reliant on the computer to manipulate symbols as well as numbers. Algebraic manipulation by the computer has allowed heretofore intractable problems in physics and mathematics to be reduced to expressions that are quickly solved. Curiously, social scientists—and particularly economists, those who might benefit most—have not seemed to take much interest in utilizing these advances. There have been some exceptions. Nerlove et al. (1979) used an early computer algebra program, FORMAC, to attempt to solve a dynamic

Advances in Econometrics, Volume 6, pages 51–89
Copyright © 1987 by JAI Press Inc.
All rights of reproduction in any form reserved.
ISBN: 0-89232-795-2

programming problem but found that the expansion became unwieldly. Since the problem was analyzed in 1971/72, it would probably be solvable with today's programs. While a number of papers have been written on the use of computer algebra in other applications, we believe this is the first to review the uses of these algorithms and their attendant software packages solely in an economic and econometric context.

The purpose of the present paper is to give a brief overview of several popular algorithms used for reducing the complexity of algebraic expressions and then to present actual examples where the algorithms are seen to simplify the problem. The problems of complicated algebraic expressions are universal to almost all applications in economics and econometrics. The micro and macro theorist must contend with the arduous task of evaluating comparative static results in much of his/her work. The bordered Hessian is frequently unwieldy and difficult to manipulate. The econometrician deals with messy variance–covariance matrices and manipulation of complex statistical distribution transformations as a routine matter in trying to ply his/her trade. Checking stability conditions and identifiability restrictions can pose particularly complex problems for the applied econometrician. The list goes on and on and holds special painful moments for most individuals doing rigorous economic research.

As Calmet and van Hulzen (1982) note, the pioneering work on use of the digital computer for algebraic computation was done almost 30 years ago. The systems have been classified by Calmet and van Hulzen as follows (p. 222):

RADICAL SYSTEMS can handle a single well defined class of expressions (e.g., polynomials, rational functions, truncated power series, truncated Poisson series). Such systems radically alter the form of an expression in order to get it into its internal (canonical) form, implying that the task of the manipulating algorithms is well defined and lends itself to efficient manipulation.

NEW LEFT SYSTEMS arose in response to some of the difficulties with radical systems, such as caused by the automatic expansion of expressions (think of $(x + y)^{1000}$). Expansion, for instance, is brought under user control. Such systems can usually handle a wide variety of expressions with greater ease, though with less power than a radical system, by using labels for nonrational (sub)expressions.

LIBERAL SYSTEMS rely on a very general representation of expressions and use simplification transformations which are close in spirit to the ones used in paper and pencil calculations. Therefore, a major disadvantage a liberal system has relative to a radical or new left system is its inefficiency, both in space and time requirements. An advantage might be that one can express problems more naturally.

CONSERVATIVE SYSTEMS are so unwilling to make inappropriate transformations that [such systems] essentially [force] a user to write his own simplification rules. Their designers state that all simplification is determined by context and thus can better be based on the theoretical concept of Markov-algorithms.

CATHOLIC SYSTEMS use more than one representation for expressions and have more than one approach to simplification. The designers of such systems want to give the user the ease of working with a liberal system, the efficiency and power of a radical system and the attention to context of a conservative system. An implied disadvantage is therefore [such a system's] size and organization.

While it is estimated that almost 50 of these computer algebra systems now exist, we will discuss only two in this paper. The two we will explore re MACSYMA and REDUCE. These are both intended for mainframe use. We have chosen to review these two since they are considered the "giants" in the field in the sense that they are catholic systems and are the two that are the most widely available. They are both general-purpose systems and allow the economist and econometrician more flexibility than other systems. The interested reauer should see Yun and Stoutemeyer (1980) for a review of other systems (from a computer scientists' perspective), including some for microcomputer use (e.g., MU-MATH).

The paper will proceed as follows: We introduce these algorithms in Section II, below. We begin with a brief history of how they were developed and then discuss their respective capabilities. In Section III we present some special economic/econometric problems and demonstrate how they can be solved using the computer algebra systems. Section IV compares and contrasts the performance of the different algorithms in simplifying actual problems, and Section V concludes the study.

II. DESCRIPTION OF COMPUTER ALGEBRA SYSTEMS

In this section we describe some characteristics of the two computer algebra systems analyzed in this paper. We note here that we are not evaluating the two systems in this section, but rather describing the systems based on Yun and Stoutemeyer's (1980) claims of what the systems can do. The two computer algebra systems examined in this paper are MACSYMA and REDUCE. In the next section we will present some actual economic/econometric applications. After exploring some actual econometric and economic applications, we will present our impressions of the efficacy of each of the respective computer algebra systems.

Yun and Stoutemeyer (1980) briefly explain the origin and some capabilities of each system. We now present excerpts from their comprehensive review. We begin with MACSYMA (p. 273), followed by REDUCE (p. 275):

MACSYMA

MACSYMA is an acronym for project MAC's SYmbolic MAnipulation system. MAC is an acronym variously expanded to Man And Computer or Multiple Access Computer. MACSYMA is an interactive LISP-based system designed by the MATH-LAB group at M.I.T. under the direction of J. Moses. (MATHLAB is also the name of a MACSYMA forerunner developed by C. Engleman of Mitre Corp.) MACSYMA syntax is about 2/3 ALGOL and 1/3 unique, with some evidence of LISP influence in the semantics. MACSYMA is implemented for the PDP-10 using the ITS operating system and for the Honeywell 60 series 68/80 using the MULTICS operating system. In its entirety, MACSYMA occupies about 250,000 (36-bit) words of storage on a PDP-10, but the system is highly integrated with the operating system so that a user can start with a basic nucleus of about 60,000 words, with additional portions automatically loaded as needed.

MACSYMA can treat general expressions, including fractional powers, elementary functions, a few special functions, and equations. Numerical coefficients can be floating-point, indefinite-precision integers, indefinite-precision rationals, or arbitrary-precision floating-point with indefinite-precsion exponents. There are two supplementary packages for tensor operations; and there are built-in functions for Taylor series, Poisson series, and matrix operations. There are built-in functions for differentiation, integration, complex arithmetic, greatest common divisors, polynomial factoring, partial fractions, continued fractions, simplification of radicals and trigonometric functions, closed-form summation to rational functions, Laplace transforms, and the solution of one or more linear or nonlinear algebraic or differential equations. There are complete facilities for extracting the parts of an expression, and there are facilities for explicit and automatic substitution for a wide variety of subexpressions. There are facilities for automatic or explicit saving and restoring expressions to and from secondary storage, and there are facilities for loading programs from files on secondary storage. The user may write recursive functions or subroutines with arguments and local variables. Also, there are facilities for redefining or extending the syntax. In other words, the user may redefine or establish new prefix, infix, and postfix operators, together with their precedence, properties such as linearity, commutativity, associativity, and simplification rules.

REDUCE

REDUCE is a LISP-based system designed by A. C. Hearn at the University of Utah. REDUCE syntax is about 4/5 ALGOL and 1/5 unique, with some evidence of LISP influence in the semantics. REDUCE is a good example of how to achieve portability using bootstrapping and macros. Versions are available for the PDP-10, the UNIVAC 1100 series, CDC7600, Burroughs 6700, and the IBM 360/370 computers, requiring about 60,000 36-bit words, 70,000 32-bit words, 40,000 60-bit words, 55,000 48-bit words, and 30,000 bytes of storage, respectively. REDUCE is interactive, [and] provides [that] sufficiently large memory partitions are available from a time-sharing operating system.

REDUCE has built-in simplification facilities for rational functions, fractional powers, and a few elementary functions. Expansions, the making of common denominators, and the removal of greatest common divisors are under user control. Numerical coefficients can be indefinite-precision integers, indefinite-precision rationals, or single-precision floating point. There are a variety of flags for controlling output style, including the option of FORTRAN-compatible output. There are built-in facilities for differentiation, integration, complex arithmetic, and high-energy physics. There is built-in matrix algebra, together with facilities for extracting the numerator and demoninator of a fraction, and polynomial coefficients of expression. There are built-in facilities permitting explicit substitution for indeterminates together with automatic substitution for indeterminates or a wide variety of subexpressions. REDUCE also has facilities for loading programs from secondary storage, and for explicitly saving and restoring expressions from secondary storage. The user can write recursive functions with arguments and local variables, and there are facilities for redefining or extending the syntax.

III. SOME APPLICATIONS

In this section we provide several examples of the usefulness of these techniques for simplifying algebraic expressions that are seemingly intractable on first perusal. The first application (Section III.A) comes from research in the applied welfare analysis literature. The usage of a differential equation algorithm in MACSYMA is demonstrated. The second example (Section III.B) uses REDUCE to solve a system of equations and to perform comparative statics. The third example (Section III.C) uses REDUCE to demonstrate the evaluation of the determinant for a covariance matrix. REDUCE and MACSYMA are both employed to evaluate the properties of the translog cost function in Section III.D.

A. Integration for Indirect Utility Functions

Since we can use a computer algebra system to find solutions to differential equations, one application is to derive compensating and equivalent variation measures from the market demand functions (Hausman, 1981). By using Roy's identity we can integrate back to the indirect utility function. Inverting the indirect utility function yields the expenditure function. Evaluating compensating or equivalent variation is straighforward using observed data points and parameter estimates. Confidence intervals can also be derived using the analysis of Zellner et al. (1965). We begin with a two good example. The demand function for good x_1:

$$x_1 = f(p, y, z),$$

where p is the price of x_1; y is total expenditure; and z is a vector of taste variables. Note that to ensure integrability p and y are deflated by the price of the second good. From Roy's identity we know that

$$x_1 = \frac{-(\partial v(p, y)/\partial p)}{\partial v(p, y)/\partial y}.$$

By solving this partial differential equation and holding utility constant, we can express this form as

$$\frac{dy(p)}{dp} = f(p, y, z). \tag{1}$$

The MACSYMA program used to solve (1) is given in Figure 1. Specifically, statement (c2) and the response (d2) defines the solution of the differential equation:

$$\frac{\partial y(p, z)}{\partial p} = g(p)y + q(p), \tag{2}$$

```
This is UNIX MACSYMA Release 304..
(c) 1976,1983 Massachusetts Institute of Technology.
All Rights Reserved.
Enhancements (c) 1983, Symbolics, Inc. All Rights Reserved.
Type describe(trade-secret); to see Trade Secret notice.

(c1)
(c2) F(G,Q) := %E**INTEGRATE(-G,P) *
(C + INTEGRATE(Q*%E**INTEGRATE(G,P),P)) ;

                integrate(- g, p)                      integrate(g, p)
(d2) f(g, q) := %e              (c + integrate(q %e               , p))

(c3) F(-D,(A*P+CONT)) ;

                              - d p          - d p
                a (d p + 1) %e        cont %e           d p
(d3)           (- ------------------- - ------------ + c) %e
                         2                  d
                        d

(c4) RATSIMP(%);

                        2   d p
                    c d  %e    - a d p - cont d - a
(d4)                ------------------------------
                                   2
                                  d

(c5) F(-D,(A*(((P**L)-1)/L) +CONT)) ;

                     /
                     [   l log(p) - d p
                 a I %e              dp
                     ]                           - d p          - d p
            d p  /                        a %e          cont %e
(d5)       %e    (--------------------- + --------- - ------------ + c)
                            l                d l           d

(c6) RATSIMP(%);

                    /
              d p [   l log(p) - d p              d p
         a d %e    I %e              dp + c d l %e    - cont l + a
                    ]
                    /
(d6)       -----------------------------------------------------------
                                    d l

(c7) F(-D,(A1*P+A2*(P**2)+A3*(1/P)+A4*(1/(P**2))+CONT));

                         /  - d p
                         [ %e
                 (a3 - a4 d) I ------- dp
                         ]   2
            d p          /  p
(d7) %e      (- -----------------------
                         d

      2  3         2              2                        2   - d p
  (a2 d  p  + (a1 d  + 2 a2 d) p  + (a1 d + 2 a2) p + a3 d ) %e
 - -----------------------------------------------------------------
                             3
                            d  p
```

Figure 1. The MACSYMA program to solve for the indirect utility
function.

```
        - d p
   cont %e
 - ------------ + c)
        d
```

(c8) RATSIMP(%);

```
                      /   - d p
         3      2    d p [ %e            3     d p       2  3
(d8) ((a4 d  - a3 d ) p %e    I ------- dp + c d   p %e      - a2 d  p
                          ]     2
                      /     p
```

```
            2                 2                  2              2   3
   + (- a1 d  - 2 a2 d) p  + (- cont d  - a1 d - 2 a2) p - a3 d  )/(d  p)
```

(c9) F(-D,(A1*SIN(P)+A2*COS(P)+A3*SIN(2*P)+A4*COS(2*P)+CONST));

```
               - d p
      d p a3 %e      (- d sin(2 p) - 2 cos(2 p))
(d9) %e      (-------------------------------------
                             2
                            d  + 4
```

```
        - d p                              - d p
   a4 %e      (2 sin(2 p) - d cos(2 p))  a1 %e      (- d sin(p) - cos(p))
 + ------------------------------------ + --------------------------------
                 2                                    2
                d  + 4                              d  + 1
```

```
        - d p                            - d p
   a2 %e      (sin(p) - d cos(p))  const %e
 + ------------------------------ - ------------- + c)
             2                          d
            d  + 1
```

(c10) RATSIMP(%);

```
          4        3       2
(d10) - ((a3 d  - 2 a4 d  + a3 d  - 2 a4 d) sin(2 p)
```

```
        4        3       2
 + (a4 d  + 2 a3 d  + a4 d  + 2 a3 d) cos(2 p)
```

```
        4       3       2
 + (a1 d  - a2 d  + 4 a1 d  - 4 a2 d) sin(p)
```

```
        4       3       2                    5       3            d p
 + (a2 d  + a1 d  + 4 a2 d  + 4 a1 d) cos(p) + (- c d  - 5 c d  - 4 c d) %e
```

```
          4            2                 5       3
 + const d  + 5 const d  + 4 const)/(d  + 5 d  + 4 d)
```

(c11) quit();

Figure 1. (Continued)

where z can be included in functions g and q. Thus, the solution is of the form:

$$y = e^{-\int g(p)\, dp}\left\{ C + \int q(p)\, e^{\int g(p)\, dp}\, dp \right\},$$

which can be written in the MACSYMA programming language [see (d2) in Figure 1].

$f(g, q) := \%e ** \text{integrate} (-g, p) *$
$(c + \text{integrate} ((q * \%e ** \text{integrate} (g, p)), p))$

The following examples were done using this program. The first example uses the linear demand equation. The result is given in (d4) of Figure 1. Since the solution is easily derived, the linear demand is not a very interesting example. The remainder of the examples are more complicated and discussed below. These are also defined by the output given in Figure 1. For example, consider the demand function in which price enters as a Box–Cox transformation [see (c5) of Figure 1]:

$$x_1 = \text{cont.} + \alpha\left(\frac{p^\lambda - 1}{\lambda}\right) + \delta y, \tag{3}$$

where cont. includes z and a coefficient for z. To find the expenditure function, we first put this in the form of (1):

$$\frac{dy(p)}{dp} = \text{cont.} + \alpha\left(\frac{p^\lambda - 1}{\lambda}\right) + \delta y.$$

This differential equation would be difficult or at least time consuming to solve without the use of a computer algebra routine. We can restate this in terms of (2), where

$$g(p) = -\delta \quad \text{and} \quad q(p) = \alpha\left(\frac{p^\lambda - 1}{\lambda}\right) + \text{cont.}$$

Making these substitutions in (2) and solving using MACSYMA yields

$$y(p) = e^{\delta p} - \frac{\alpha \int e^{\lambda \log(p) - \delta p} \, dp}{\lambda} + \frac{\alpha e^{-\delta p}}{\delta \lambda} - \frac{\text{cont } e^{-\delta p}}{\delta} + c . \tag{4}$$

Applying the function which simplifies expressions, RAT-SIMP(%), to (4) yields [(d6) in Figure 1]

$$y(p) = \frac{\alpha \delta e^{\delta p} \int e^{\lambda \log(p) - \delta p} \, dp + c \delta \lambda e^{\delta p} - \text{cont.} \lambda + \alpha}{\delta \lambda}. \tag{5}$$

If we choose $c = u_0$ as the initial level of the utility index, the indirect utility index can be expressed as

$$v(p, y) = \frac{y}{e^{\delta p}} \frac{\alpha \int e^{\lambda \log(p) - \delta p} \, dp}{\lambda} + \frac{\alpha \, e^{-\delta p}}{\delta \lambda} - \frac{\text{cont.} \, e^{-\delta p}}{\delta}, \quad (6)$$

and the expenditure function follows by interchanging the utility level with the income level:

$$e(p, \bar{u}) = e^{\delta p} \frac{\alpha \int e^{\lambda \log(p) - \delta p} \, dp}{\lambda} + \frac{\alpha \, e^{-\delta p}}{\delta \lambda} - \frac{\text{cont.} \, e^{-\delta p}}{\delta} + \bar{u}. \quad (7)$$

We can follow the same procedure to derive the expenditure function for a demand function in which prices enter in second-order Laurents expansion [see (c7) in Figure 1]:

$$x_1 = \text{cont.} + \alpha_1 p + \alpha_2 p^2 + \alpha_3 \frac{1}{p} + \alpha_4 \frac{1}{p^2} + \delta y. \quad (8)$$

The expenditure function for this form is found using MACSYMA and (2). In this case

$$g(p) = -\delta \quad \text{and} \quad q(p) = \alpha_1 p_1 + \alpha_2 p_1^2 + \alpha \frac{1}{3p} + \alpha_4 \frac{1}{p^2} + \text{cont.}$$

The result is

$$e(p, \bar{u}) = e^{\delta p} \left(\frac{-(\alpha_3 - \alpha_4 \delta) \int (e^{-\delta p}/p^2) \, dp}{\delta} \right.$$

$$- \frac{(\alpha_2 \delta^2 p^3 + \alpha_1 \delta^2 + 2\alpha_2 \delta)p^2 + (\alpha_1 \delta + 2\alpha_2)p + \alpha_3 \delta^2)e^{-\delta p}}{\delta^3 p}$$

$$\left. - \frac{\text{cont.} \, e^{-\delta p}}{\delta} + \bar{u} \right). \quad (9)$$

Another type of expansion is the Fourier (see Gallant, 1981). We can also derive the expenditure function for a demand function in which prices follow a Fourier series [see (c9) of Figure 1]:

$$x_1 = \text{cont.} + \alpha_1 \sin(p) + \alpha_2 \cos(p)$$
$$+ \alpha_3 \sin(2p) + \alpha_4 \cos(2p) + \delta y. \quad (10)$$

In this case

$$y(p) = -\delta \qquad \text{and} \qquad q(p) = \alpha_1 \sin(p) + \alpha_2 \cos(p)$$
$$+ \alpha_3 \sin(2p) + \alpha_4 \cos(2p) + \text{cont.}$$

The expenditure function for this demand function is found using (2):

$$e(p, \bar{u}) = e^{\delta p}\left(\frac{\alpha_3 e^{-\delta p}(-\delta \sin(2p) - 2 \cos(2p))}{\delta^2 + 4}\right.$$

$$+ \frac{\alpha_4 e^{-\delta p} (2 \sin(2p) - \delta \cos(2p))}{\delta^2 + 4}$$

$$+ \frac{\alpha_1 e^{-\delta p} (-\delta \sin(p) - \cos(p))}{\delta^2 + 1} \tag{11}$$

$$+ \frac{\alpha_2 e^{-\delta p} (\sin(p) - \delta \cos(p))}{\delta^2 + 1} - \frac{\text{cont. } e^{-\delta p}}{\delta} + \bar{u}\right).$$

This procedure can be very useful for the researcher who wishes to fit the data closely using a demand function which may not be derived ex ante from the utility function. Measures of welfare change and true cost-of-living indices can be **derived** based on the resulting integration.

B. Comparative Statics Uses

Another example where both MACSYMA and REDUCE are useful is in solving systems of equations and performing comparative statics and comparative dynamics. Both programs can perform the calculations; however, REDUCE does somewhat better at simplifying the expressions.

Consider the following two sector tax incidence problem from Atkinson and Stiglitz (1980). The "ˆ" notation is used to denote proportionate change. The following notation is used: the goods x and y have prices, p_x and p_y; the factors of production are k and l; the factor prices are denoted r and w, respectively. If we assume homotheticity, the elasticity of substitution between demands is σ_D, where $\sigma_D \geq 0$. Here θ_{li} (θ_{ki}) are factor share of labor (capital) in sector i and

$$\theta^* = \theta_{lx} - \theta_{ly} = \theta_{ky} - \theta_{kx}.$$

The share of the labor force (capital) in x and y is given by $x_{lx}(\lambda_{kx})$ and $\lambda_{ly}(\lambda_{ky})$. Also, $\lambda^* =: x_{lx} - \lambda_{kx} = \lambda_{ky} - \lambda_{ly}$. We denote the elasticity of substitution for the ith industry by σ_i. The tax incidence model contains three equations: a demand equation and two supply equations. The demand equation is given by

$$\hat{x} - \hat{y} = -\sigma_D(\hat{p}_x - \hat{p}_y).$$

The supply equations which relate good prices and factor prices are

$$\hat{p}_x - \hat{p}_y = \theta^*(\hat{w} - \hat{r}).$$

The second supply equation relates output to factor prices:

$$\lambda^*(\hat{x} - \hat{y}) = (\hat{w} - \hat{r})(a_x\sigma_x + a_y\sigma_y),$$

where $a_i = \theta_{ki}\lambda_{li} + \theta_{li}\lambda_{ki}$, and σ_i represents the elasticity of substitution between K and L in sector i. If we define partial factor taxes as T_{ki} and T_{li} and selective excise taxes as T_i, tax incidence analysis can be completed by including the appropriate tax in the three-equation model.

The example here is for a tax on K in sector X, the standard corporate income tax incidence analysis (Harberger, 1962). We first define the 3×3 matrix: the solution from REDUCE is given below:

$$\hat{x} - \hat{y} = (\theta_{kx}\lambda^*(\theta_{kx}\theta^* + \delta_x a_x))/(\sigma_y a_y + \alpha_x a_x + \lambda^*\theta^*\sigma_D); \quad (12)$$

$$\hat{p}_x - \hat{p}_y = (\theta_{kx}(\theta_{xx}\sigma_y a_y + \theta_{kx}\sigma_x a_x - \sigma_x a_x\lambda^*\sigma_D))/ \quad (13)$$
$$(\sigma_y a_y + \sigma_x a_x + \lambda^*\theta^*\sigma_D);$$

$$\hat{w} - \hat{r} = (-\theta_{kx}(\theta_{kx}\theta^* + \sigma_x a_x))/(\alpha_y a_y + \sigma_x a_x + \lambda^*\theta^*\sigma_D). \quad (14)$$

To do an analysis of the incidence of T_{KX}, the third element (14) is the important one. We note that our results are similar to the Harberger results. The denominator will always be positive. The sign of the numerator depends on the relative factor intensities of x and y. Here θ^* will be positive if x is relatively labor intensive, and in this case labor could bear some of the burden of the tax. This would depend on the relative size of the elasticity of substitution in x as well as the factor shares. Uses of income incidence can be determined from (12) and (13). In terms of the demand equation, the consumers of x reduce their consumption relative to y only if x is capital intensive and $\sigma_x a_x > \theta_{kx}\theta^*$. The impact on the relative price of x is ambiguous if x is relatively labor intensive [see (13)]. Only if x is capital intensive does the price of x increase.

In the next step the solutions are differentiated with respect to various variables. We will discuss only one example. In examining the third element of the solution we noted that **the** part of the tax borne by capital depended on the degree of substitutability between capital and labor in sector x as well as the level of factor shares and factor intensities. Using REDUCE, we differentiate the third element with respect to σ_x and get the following expression:

$$(a_y\lambda^*\theta_{ly}\sigma_D - 2a_y\theta^*T_{kx} + a_yT_{kx}\theta_{ky}\theta_{lx} - a_x\lambda^*T_{kx}\sigma_x\theta_{ly}\sigma_D$$

$$-2a_x\theta^*T_{kx}\sigma_x + a_xT_{kx}\sigma_x\lambda_{lx} + a_xT_{kx}\sigma_x\theta_{ky}\theta_{lx} + a_x\sigma_x\lambda_{lx}$$

$$-\lambda^*\theta^{*2}T_{kx}\sigma_D - \lambda^*\theta^*T_{kx}\sigma_x\lambda_{lx}\sigma_D + \lambda^*T_{kx}\sigma_xX_{lx}\sigma_D$$

$$+\lambda^*T_{kx}\sigma_x\lambda_{lx}\theta_{kx} - \lambda^*X_{ky}\theta_{ly}^2\sigma_D + \lambda^*\lambda_{lx}\theta_{ky}\theta_{lx}\sigma_D$$

$$-2\theta^*T_{kx}\sigma_y\lambda_{ky}\theta_{ly} + 2\theta^*T_{kx}\sigma_x\lambda_{lx}\theta_{kx} + 2\theta^*T_{kx}\lambda_{ky}\theta_{ly}$$

$$-\theta^*T_{kx}\lambda_{lx}\theta_{kx} + T_{kx}\sigma_y\lambda_{ky}\theta_{ly}\theta_{ky}\theta_{ky}\theta_{lx} - T_{ky}\sigma_x\lambda_{lx}^2\theta_{kx}$$

$$- T_{kx}\sigma_x\lambda_{lx}\theta_{kx}\theta_{kx}\theta_{ky} - T_{kx}\lambda_{ky}\theta_{ly}\theta_{ky}\theta_{lx} + T_{kx}\lambda_{lx}\theta_{kx}\theta_{ky}\theta_{lx}$$

$$+\sigma_y\lambda_{ky}\lambda_{ly}\theta_{ly} - \sigma_x\lambda_{lx}^2\theta_{kx})/(a_y^2 + 2a_y\lambda^*\theta^*\sigma_D + 2a_y\sigma_y\lambda_{ky}\theta_{ly}$$

$$-2a_y\lambda_{ky}\theta_{ly} + 2a_y\lambda_{lx}\theta_{kx} + a_x^2 + \sigma_x^2 + 2a_x\lambda^*\theta^*\sigma_x\sigma_D$$

$$+2a_x\sigma_y\sigma_x\lambda_{ky}\theta_{ly} - 2a_x\sigma_x\lambda_{lx}\theta_{kx} + 2a_x\sigma_x\lambda_{lx}\theta_{kx} + \lambda^{2*}\theta^{2*}\sigma_D^2$$

$$+2\lambda^*\theta^*\sigma_y\lambda_{ky}\theta_{ly}\sigma_D - 2\lambda^*\theta^*\sigma_x\lambda_{lx}\theta_k)_x\sigma_D - 2\lambda^*\theta^*\lambda_{ky}\theta_{ly}\sigma_D$$

$$+2\lambda^*\theta^*\lambda_{lx}\theta_{kx}\sigma_D - 2\lambda^*\sigma_x\theta_{ky}\theta_{lx} + 2\theta^*\sigma_y\sigma_x\lambda_{ky}\lambda_{lx} - 2\theta^*\sigma_y\lambda_{ky}\lambda_{lx}$$

$$+2\theta^*\lambda_{ky}\lambda_{lx} + \sigma_y^2\lambda_{xy}^2 - 2\sigma_y\sigma_x\lambda_{ky}\lambda_{lx}\theta_{ky}\theta_{lx} - 2\sigma_y\lambda_{ky}^2\theta_{ly}^2$$

$$+2\sigma_y\lambda_{ky}\lambda_{lx}\theta_{ky}\theta_{lx} + \sigma_x^2\lambda_{lx}^2\theta_{kx}^2 + 2\sigma_x\lambda_{ky}\lambda_{lx}\theta_{ky}\theta_{lx} - 2\sigma_x\lambda_{lx}^2\theta_{kx}^2$$

$$+\lambda_{ky}^2\theta_{ly}^* - 2\lambda_{ky}\lambda_{lx}\theta_{ky}\lambda_{lx}\theta_{ky}\theta_{lx} + \lambda_{lx}^2\theta_{kx}^2).$$

Unfortunately this expression is not easily signed without specific values for the function. We conclude that increasing the substitutability of labor for capital certainly increases the numerator. But it also increases the denominator, and thus a definitive answer can be given at this general level.

This procedure for solving a system of equations and differentiating the solutions has many potential uses. The procedure enables the researcher to perform comparative statics or comparative dynamics relatively quickly. Alternative specifications can easily be examined. Substitution of specific values for functions is straightforward if this is necessary for determining the sign of the solution or derivative.

C. The Evaluation of the Determinant of a Covariance Matrix

The multivariate normal log-likelihood function includes the determinant of the covariance matrix as a term in the expression. The log-likelihood of a normally distributed random vector ε with mean zero and covariance Ω is

$$\log(L) = \tfrac{1}{2}\log(2\Pi) - \tfrac{1}{2}\log(|\Omega|) - \tfrac{1}{2}(\varepsilon'\Omega^{-1}\varepsilon).$$

When computing the maximum likelihood estimates, we can use the algebraic result that the derivative of the log of the determinant of the covariance matrix with respect to the covariance matrix is the inverse of the covariance matrix:

$$\frac{\partial \log(|\Omega|)}{\partial \Omega} = \Omega^{-1}.$$

Thus in many cases the determinant of the likelihood need never be computed.

However, in studies where likelihood ratio tests are used and a common Ω matrix is not assumed, the need arises to determine the value of the likelihood function. For example, when considering the specification of a system of demand equations fit to time-series data, where the assumption of autoregressive parameters may vary by specification, one would need to compare likelihood values.

In econometrics it is not unusual to use covariance matrices of great size, often dimensioned as large as the number of observations or the number of observations times the number of equations. The example we use here employs Zellner's (1962) "Seemingly Unrelated Regressions (SUR)," with a first-order autoregressive parameter in each equation and across each equation, a simplification of the vector autoregressive process proposed by Guilkey and Schmidt (1973).

Thus in the two-equation case we have

$$y_1 = x_1 B_1 + \varepsilon_1$$
$$y_2 = x_2 B_2 + \varepsilon_2,$$

where the error structure is given by

$$\varepsilon_{1t} = \rho_{11}\varepsilon_{1t-1} + \rho_{12}\varepsilon_{2t-1} + u_1$$

$$\varepsilon_{2t} = \rho_{21}\lambda_{1t-1} + \rho_{22}\varepsilon_{2t-1} + u_2.$$

We define the total covariance of $E(\varepsilon\varepsilon') = \Omega$, where

$$\varepsilon = (\varepsilon_{11}, \varepsilon_{12}, \ldots, \varepsilon_{1T}, \varepsilon_{21}, \varepsilon_{21}, \ldots, \varepsilon_{2T})'$$

and

$T =$ number of observations for each equation;

and the covariance between the cross-equation errors u_1 and u_2 is given as

$$E[u_{(r)}u_{(t)}'] = \Sigma \qquad \text{if } t = r,$$

$$= 0 \qquad \text{if not.}$$

If we have known values for the ρ's and Σ, we can compute the generalized least squares (GLS) estimates of the parameters B by first finding a matrix P such that $P\Omega P' = [\Sigma \otimes I_t]$ and then performing the SUR estimation on the transformed dependent and independent variables. We write

$$\Omega^{-1} = P'(\Sigma^{-1} \otimes I_t)P,$$

where

$$P = \begin{bmatrix} P_{11} & P_{12} & \cdots & P_{1n} \\ P_{21} & P_{22} & \cdots & P_{2n} \\ P_{n1} & P_{n2} & \cdots & P_{nn} \end{bmatrix},$$

and

$$\underset{(T \times T)}{P_{ii}} = \begin{bmatrix} \alpha_{ii} & 0 & 0 & \cdots & 0 & 0 \\ -\rho_{ii} & 1 & 0 & \cdots & 0 & 0 \\ 0 & -\rho_{ii} & 1 & \cdots & 0 & 0 \\ \cdots\cdots\cdots\cdots\cdots\cdots\cdots\cdots\cdots \\ \cdots\cdots\cdots\cdots\cdots\cdots\cdots\cdots\cdots \\ 0 & 0 & 0 & \cdots & -\rho_{ii} & 1 \end{bmatrix},$$

$$\underset{(T \times T)}{P_{ij}} = \begin{bmatrix} \alpha_{ij} & 0 & 0 & \cdots & 0 & 0 \\ -\rho_{ij} & 0 & 0 & \cdots & 0 & 0 \\ 0 & -\rho_{ij} & 0 & \cdots & 0 & 0 \\ \cdots\cdots\cdots\cdots\cdots\cdots\cdots\cdots\cdots \\ \cdots\cdots\cdots\cdots\cdots\cdots\cdots\cdots\cdots \\ 0 & 0 & 0 & \cdots & -\rho_{ij} & 0 \end{bmatrix}.$$

This is a generalization of the standard autoregressive regression problem. With the matrix A as the matrix of first observation transformations, ($\alpha_{11} = \sqrt{1 - \rho_{11}^2}$ for the single-equation case):

$$A_{(n \times n)} = \begin{bmatrix} \alpha_{11} & \alpha_{12} & \cdots & \alpha_{1n} \\ \alpha_{21} & \alpha_{22} & \cdots & \alpha_{2n} \\ & & & \\ \alpha_{n1} & \alpha_{n2} & \cdots & \alpha_{nn} \end{bmatrix}.$$

Consequently we have a rather complex covariance for the error vector ε. Under the assumption of normality in the errors we can compute the value of the likelihood function only if we have a value for the determinant of the covariance matrix Ω. By the properties of Kronecker products (Graybill, 1983, p. 184), we can show that $|\Omega| = |P|^2 |\Sigma|^{-T}$; thus we still need the determinant of P, an $nT \times nT$ matrix.

Here P is a matrix with a special form that **may** have a simple solution to the determinant. Hirschberg (1986) **has** shown that for the case of no cross-equation autoregressive parameters, when $\rho_{ij} = 0$ (for $i \neq j$), the determinant of P becomes the product of the first observation transformation terms, the α_{ii}'s. Thus, although we could not locate the particular matrix theory result that pertained to the type of matrix we observe in P, we assumed that there might be reason to believe that P also conforms to a special case for which the determinant is a simple function of covariance parameters.

To derive this result we employ the REDUCE program because this program allows the definition of sparse matrices in a straightforward manner. In MACSYMA the definition of the matrix takes place either in an interactive mode in which each element is queried for or in one definition statement where all **zero** values need be specified as well. The REDUCE program allows **the** definition of a zero matrix of any size, and then each nonzero element can be defined separately.

What we propose is a constructive proof. We will specify some candidate P matrices and then use REDUCE to compute the analytic determinants to see if we can discern a pattern that may provide a general form of the determinant of P with respect to the elements of its constituent matrices. For the first case we set up a P matrix with four observations and two equations; thus the matrix is an

```
matrix P (8,8) ;
P(1,1) := a11  ;
P(1,5) := a12  ;
P(5,1) := a21  ;
P(5,5) := a22  ;
P(2,2) := 1 ;
P(3,3) := 1 ;
P(4,4) := 1 ;
P(6,6) := 1 ;
P(7,7) := 1 ;
P(8,8) := 1 ;
P(2,1) := -r11 ;
P(3,2) := -r11 ;
P(4,3) := -r21 ;
P(6,1) := -r21 ;
P(7,2) := -r21 ;
P(8,3) := -r21 ;
P(2,5) := -r12 ;
P(3,6) := -r12 ;
P(4,7) := -r12 ;
P(6,5) := -r22 ;
P(7,6) := -r22 ;
P(8,7) := -r22 ;
P ;
det(P) ;

a11*a22 - a21*a12

bye;
```

Figure 2. The REDUCE program to compute the determinant for the 8×8 P matrix (a two-equation and four-observation case).

8×8 matrix. Figure 2 is the REDUCE program that defined the 8×8 P matrix used.[1] Note that only the nonzero elements need to be entered. From this first case we find $|P| = |A|$. Because this result could be due to the two-equation example we chose, we have constructed a 12×12 P matrix that would result when three equations were included. This experiment (shown in Figure 3) also resulted in the determinant of P being the determinant of A.

Thus, when the estimated residuals and the estimated covariance matrix are used to compute the value of the likelihood function (the concentrated likelihood), we obtain the following result:

$$\hat{\varepsilon}'\hat{\Omega}^{-1}\hat{\varepsilon} = T - n,$$

where $\hat{\varepsilon}$ = vector of estimated residuals;

$\hat{\Omega}$ = estimated covariance matrix.

Thus the log-likelihood value for the model becomes

$$\log(L) = \tfrac{1}{2}\log(2\Pi) + \log(|\hat{A}|) - (T/2)\log(|\hat{\Sigma}|) + T - n,$$

```
matrix P(12,12);
P(1,1)  := a11  ;
P(1,5)  := a12  ;
P(5,1)  := a21  ;
P(5,5)  := a22  ;
P(1,9)  := a13  ;
P(5,9)  := a23  ;
P(9,9)  := a33  ;
P(9,5)  := a32  ;
P(9,1)  := a31  ;
P(2,2)  := 1  ;
P(3,3)  := 1  ;
P(4,4)  := 1  ;
P(6,6)  := 1  ;
P(7,7)  := 1  ;
P(8,8)  := 1  ;
P(10,10) := 1  ;
P(11,11) := 1  ;
P(12,12) := 1  ;
P(2,1)  := -r11  ;
P(3,2)  := -r11  ;
P(4,3)  := -r21  ;
P(6,1)  := -r21  ;
P(7,2)  := -r21  ;
P(8,3)  := -r21  ;
P(2,5)  := -r12  ;
P(3,6)  := -r12  ;
P(4,7)  := -r12  ;
P(6,5)  := -r22  ;
P(7,6)  := -r22  ;
P(8,7)  := -r22  ;
P(2,9)  := -r13  ;
P(3,10) := -r13  ;
P(4,11) := -r23  ;
P(6,9)  := -r23  ;
P(7,10) := -r23  ;
P(8,11) := -r23  ;
P(10,9) := -r33  ;
P(11,10) := -r33  ;
P(12,11) := -r33  ;
P(10,1) := -r31  ;
P(11,2) := -r31  ;
P(12,3) := -r31  ;
P(10,5) := -r32  ;
P(11,6) := -r32  ;
P(12,7) := -r32  ;
P ;
det(P) ;

- a11*a32*a23 + a11*a33*a22 + a31*a23*a12 - a31*a13*a22 + a32*a13*a21
- a33*a21*a12

bye;
```

Figure 3. The REDUCE program to compute the determinant for the 12×12 P matrix (a three-equation and four-observation case).

where $\hat{A}$ = matrix of first estimated observation transformations;

$\hat{\Sigma}$ = estimated cross-equation covariance matrix.

And in the case of no cross-equation autocorrelation we obtain a diagonal A, and the determinant of A is the **product** of the first observation transformations, as was shown in **Hirschberg (1986)**.

D. Properties of the Transcendental Logarithmic Cost Function

Christensen et al. (1971) introduced the transcendental logarithmic (TL) function form as the specification of a flexible cost, production, expenditure, or utility function. Essentially this function is a second-order Taylor series of the log of a scalar function in terms of the log of a vector of arguments. In the examples discussed here we will refer to the linear homogeneous TL cost function. We define this function as

$$\ln(C) = \sum_{i=1}^{n} \alpha_i \ln(p_i) + \tfrac{1}{2} \sum_{i=1}^{n} \sum_{j=1}^{n} \beta_{ij} \ln(p_i) \ln(p_j),$$

where α, β = vector and matrix of parameters;

p_i = price of input i;

C = total cost at the minimum cost level.

This specification has been used extensively in the estimation of demand equations when Shephard's lemma (1953) is applied. This lemma states that the demand for a particular commodity is the partial derivative of the cost function with respect to the price of that commodity:

$$x_i = \frac{\partial C(p)}{\partial p_i}.$$

The common form of estimation (see, for example, Christensen and Greene 1976 is by use of the cost-share equation. By using the result that the $\partial \ln(C)/\partial \ln(p_1)$ is equal to the cost share for $m_i = p_i x_i / C$, we obtain the TL cost-share equation for input i:

$$m_i = \alpha_i + \sum_{j=1}^{n} \beta_{ij}.$$

In this example we will investigate two issues in the use of the TL cost function: First we will look at the price elasticities of demand by using MACSYMA and REDUCE to derive the expression for the price elasticities in terms of the unrestricted parameters of the model and the prices, instead of the usual form in which an expression is used that involves the use of cost-share values. Then we use MACSYMA to solve for the eigenvalues of the B matrix. Diewart and Wales (1985) have shown that if B is negative semidefinite we have a sufficient condition for the Hessian of the TL cost function to be negative semidefinite—a necessary property of a theoretical cost function.

1. The Price Elasticities of the TL Cost Function

The commonly used method for estimating price elasticities for the TL estimated demand relationships employs the following formula:

$$\eta_{ij} = m_j + \frac{\beta_{ij}}{m_i} - \delta_{ij},$$

where η_{ij} = elasticity for x_i with respect to p_j;

        $m_j = p_j x_j / C$ = cost share for x_j;

        δ_{ij} = Kronecker delta ($\delta_{ij} = 1$ iff $i = j$).

Unfortunately this expression assumes that the m_i's and m_j's are known, when in fact they are functions of all the x's, the terms that are assumed to be stochastic. Thus, to use this function, an assumption needs to be made when estimating the variances of n_{ij}—that the m_i's and m_j's are fixed. However, these elasticities are often employed for the prediction of the reaction to future price changes when no x's are observed. If we insert the estimated cost shares in this equation, we end up with a nonlinear function of the estimated parameters of the cost function. Thus, we propose to solve for the price elasticities in terms of the parameters in B and α by applying MACSYMA and reducing the expressions. Once these have been derived, we can then compute the derivatives of η_{ij} with respect to the parameters in B and α in order to use a first-order Taylor series expansion to estimate the variance of the elasticities from the estimated asymptotic covariance of these parameters.

Employing Shephard's lemma and the definition of the price elasticity, we can derive the price elasticity using the following relationship:

$$\eta_{ij} = \left[\frac{\partial^2 C}{\partial p_i\, \partial p_j}\right]\left[\frac{p_j}{\partial C / \partial p_i}\right].$$

To use MACSYMA for this problem (the program appears in Figure 4), we first define the matrix B in terms of another set of parameters g_{ij} [see statement (d11) in Figure 4) and the vector α in terms of a vector a [see statement (d43) in Figure 4 (*aa* is used for α)].

```
This is UNIX MACSYMA Release 304.
(c) 1976,1983 Massachusetts Institute of Technology.
All Rights Reserved.
Enhancements (c) 1983, Symbolics, Inc. All Rights Reserved.
Type describe(trade-secret); to see Trade Secret notice.

(c1)
(c2) b11 : g11;

(d2)                              g11

(c3) b12 : g12;

(d3)                              g12

(c4) b13 : -g11 - g12 ;

(d4)                       - g12 - g11

(c5) b22 : g22 ;

(d5)                              g22

(c6) b21 : g12;

(d6)                              g12

(c7) b23 : -g12 - g22 ;

(d7)                       - g22 - g12

(c8) b31 : -g11 - g12 ;

(d8)                       - g12 - g11

(c9) b32 : -g12 - g22 ;

(d9)                       - g22 - g12

(c10) b33 : g11 + g12 + g12 + g22 ;

(d10)                 g22 + 2 g12 + g11

(c11) b : matrix([b11,b12,b13],[b21,b22,b23],[b31,b32,b33]);
```

Figure 4. The MACSYMA program to solve for the derivatives of the elasticities of the three good TL cost function and the eigenvalues of the matrix of own-price parameters.

```
                        [     g11          g12          - g12 - g11      ]
                        [                                                 ]
(d11)                   [     g12          g22          - g22 - g12      ]
                        [                                                 ]
                        [ - g12 - g11   - g22 - g12   g22 + 2 g12 + g11 ]
```

(c12) eigenvalues(b) ;

Batching the file /usr/src/macsyma/share/eigen.mac
Batching done.

$$(d40) \quad [[- \sqrt{g22^2 + (2\,g12 - g11)\,g22 + 4\,g12^2 + 2\,g11\,g12 + g11^2} + g22$$

$$+ g12 + g11,\ \sqrt{g22^2 + (2\,g12 - g11)\,g22 + 4\,g12^2 + 2\,g11\,g12 + g11^2} + g22$$

$$+ g12 + g11,\ 0],\ [1,\ 1,\ 1]]$$

(c41) ratsimp(%) ;

$$(d41) \quad [[- \sqrt{g22^2 + (2\,g12 - g11)\,g22 + 4\,g12^2 + 2\,g11\,g12 + g11^2} + g22$$

$$+ g12 + g11,\ \sqrt{g22^2 + (2\,g12 - g11)\,g22 + 4\,g12^2 + 2\,g11\,g12 + g11^2} + g22$$

$$+ g12 + g11,\ 0],\ [1,\ 1,\ 1]]$$

(c42) lp : matrix([log(p1),log(p2),log(p3)]);

$$(d42) \qquad\qquad\qquad [\ \log(p1)\ \ \log(p2)\ \ \log(p3)\ ]$$

(c43) aa : matrix([a1,a2,(1-a1-a2)]) ;

$$(d43) \qquad\qquad\qquad\qquad [\ a1\ \ a2\ \ - a2 - a1 + 1\ ]$$

(c44) lcost : (aa.transpose(lp) + (lp . b .transpose(lp))/2) ;

$$(d44) \quad (\log(p3)\ ((g22 + 2\,g12 + g11)\,\log(p3) + (- g22 - g12)\,\log(p2)$$

$$+ (- g12 - g11)\,\log(p1)) + \log(p2)\ ((- g22 - g12)\,\log(p3) + g22\,\log(p2)$$

$$+ g12\,\log(p1)) + \log(p1)\ ((- g12 - g11)\,\log(p3) + g12\,\log(p2) + g11\,\log(p1)))$$

$$/2 + (- a2 - a1 + 1)\,\log(p3) + a2\,\log(p2) + a1\,\log(p1)$$

(c45) logcontract(%) ;

$$(d45) \quad (\log(p3^2) + g12\ (2\,\log^2(p3) - \log(p2^2)\,\log(p3) + \log(p1)\,\log(\tfrac{p2^2}{p3^2}))$$

$$+ g22\ (\log^2(p3) - \log(p2^2)\,\log(p3) + \log^2(p2))$$

$$+ g11\ (\log^2(p3) - \log(p1^2)\,\log(p3) + \log^2(p1)) + a2\,\log(\tfrac{p2^2}{p3^2}) + a1\,\log(\tfrac{p1^2}{p3^2}))/2$$

Figure 4. (*Continued*)

(c46) cost : exp(lcost) ;

(d46) expt(%e, (log(p3) ((g22 + 2 g12 + g11) log(p3) + (- g22 - g12) log(p2)

+ (- g12 - g11) log(p1)) + log(p2) ((- g22 - g12) log(p3) + g22 log(p2)

+ g12 log(p1)) + log(p1) ((- g12 - g11) log(p3) + g12 log(p2) + g11 log(p1)))

/2 + (- a2 - a1 + 1) log(p3) + a2 log(p2) + a1 log(p1))

(c47) xa1 : logcontract(ratsimp(diff(cost,p1))) ;

$$\text{(d47)} \quad \left(g12 \log\left(\frac{p2}{p3}\right) + g11 \log\left(\frac{p1}{p3}\right) + a1\right) p3$$

$$\text{expt}\left(\%e, \left(g12 \left(2 \log^2(p3) - \log(p2^2) \log(p3) + \log(p1) \log\left(\frac{p2^2}{p3^2}\right)\right)\right.\right.$$

$$+ g22 (\log^2(p3) - \log(p2^2) \log(p3) + \log^2(p2))$$

$$\left.\left.+ g11 (\log^2(p3) - \log(p1^2) \log(p3) + \log^2(p1)) + a2 \log\left(\frac{p2^2}{p3^2}\right) + a1 \log\left(\frac{p1^2}{p3^2}\right)\right)/2\right)$$

/p1

(c48) xa2 : logcontract(ratsimp(diff(cost,p2))) ;

$$\text{(d48)} \quad \left(g22 \log\left(\frac{p2}{p3}\right) + g12 \log\left(\frac{p1}{p3}\right) + a2\right) p3$$

$$\text{expt}\left(\%e, \left(g12 \left(2 \log^2(p3) - \log(p2^2) \log(p3) + \log(p1) \log\left(\frac{p2^2}{p3^2}\right)\right)\right.\right.$$

$$+ g22 (\log^2(p3) - \log(p2^2) \log(p3) + \log^2(p2))$$

$$\left.\left.+ g11 (\log^2(p3) - \log(p1^2) \log(p3) + \log^2(p1)) + a2 \log\left(\frac{p2^2}{p3^2}\right) + a1 \log\left(\frac{p1^2}{p3^2}\right)\right)/2\right)$$

/p2

(c49) xa3 : logcontract(ratsimp(diff(cost,p3))) ;

$$\text{(d49)} \quad - \left(g22 \log\left(\frac{p2}{p3}\right) + g11 \log\left(\frac{p1}{p3}\right) + g12 \log\left(\frac{p1\ p2}{p3^2}\right) + a2 + a1 - 1\right)$$

Figure 4. (*Continued*)

```
                          2               2                      p2
expt(%e, (g12 (2 log (p3) - log(p2 ) log(p3) + log(p1) log(---))
                                                             2
                                                            p3


            2               2            2
+ g22 (log (p3) - log(p2 ) log(p3) + log (p2))


            2               2            2        p2      2      p1   2
+ g11 (log (p3) - log(p1 ) log(p3) + log (p1)) + a2 log(---) + a1 log(---))/2)
                                                         2            2
                                                        p3           p3


(c50) n11 : logcontract(ratsimp(diff(xa1,p1)*p1/xa1 ) ) ;


                        2                   2
                      p3        2     p2   p2      p1
(d50) (g12 (g11 (log(p3) log(---) + log(p1 ) log(--) + log(---) log(--))
                             2                    p3     2     p3
                            p2                         p3


       2          4
     p3        p2        2         p3        2     p1
+ log(---) + a1 log(---)) + g11  (log(p3) log(---) + log(p1 ) log(--))
      2            4                          2                    p3
     p2          p3                          p1


       2          4                  2
     p3        p1            2     p2   p2      2
+ g11 (log(---) + a1 log(---) + 2) + g12  log(---) log(--) + 2 a1  - 2 a1)
           2            4                      2     p3
          p1          p3                      p3


       2          2
     p2        p1
/(g12 log(---) + g11 log(---) + 2 a1)
          2            2
         p3           p3

  .        (for brevity we skip the other own-price elasticity).
  .
  .


(c53) n12 : logcontract(ratsimp(diff(xa1,p2)*p2/xa1 ) ) ;


                     p3               p2
(d53) (g22 (g12 (log(p3) log(--) + log(p2) log(--))
                     p2               p3


               p3               p1        p2
+ g11 (log(p3) log(--) + log(p2) log(--)) + a1 log(--))
               p1               p3        p3


       2        p3               p2
+ g12  (log(p3) log(--) + log(p1) log(--))
                p2               p3


               p3               p1        p2        p1
+ g12 (g11 (log(p3) log(--) + log(p1) log(--)) + a2 log(--) + a1 log(--) + 1)
                    p1               p3        p3        p3
```

Figure 4. (*Continued*)

74

```
        p1                     p2                 p1
 + a2 g11 log(--) + a1 a2)/(g12 log(--) + g11 log(--) + a1)
        p3                     p3                 p3
.
.
.
(The listing concludes with the other crossprice elasticities).

end.
```

Figure 4. (*Continued*)

This is done because of the symmetry and homogeneity restrictions imposed on the matrix *B* as implied by the economic theory of cost functions:

$$\sum_{i=1}^{n} \beta_{ij} = 0, \quad \text{for all } i, \quad \text{and} \quad \beta_{ij} = \beta_{ji}, \quad \text{where } j \neq i;$$

$$\sum_{i=1}^{n} \alpha_1 = 1.$$

Using the matrix multiplication functions in MACSYMA, we define the log of the cost as the sum of the vector of the log of the prices times the vector α plus $\frac{1}{2}$ times the quadratic term formed by the vector of the log of the prices and the matrix *B* [see statement (c44) in Figure 4 ("·" is used to denote matrix multiplication)]. We define cost as the exponentiation of this term [statement (c46)]. To determine the demand for input 1 we differentiate the cost function in (d46) by the price of input 1 (via Shephard's lemma) and obtain (d47) as the demand equation. Now to derive the own-price elasticity we differentiate the demand function with respect to the price of input 1 (c50), resulting in (d50).[2] We also performed this derivation using the REDUCE program. These results are given in Figure 5. The two programs are essentially the same, the only difference being in the substitutions made by the programs and the format of the results. For example, statement (c50) in Figure 4 is equivalent to the statement in Figure 5 that provides the own-price elasticity for the first input (n11).

Toevs (1980, 1982) used a first-order Taylor series expansion to estimate the variance of the elasticities of substitution which have a similar form to the price elasticities given for both a TL production function and a TL cost function. The Allen partial elasticities

(*Text continues on page 84*)

```
REDUCE 3.2, 15-Apr-85 ...
gcd := on;

GCD := ON

num := 72;

NUM := 72

linelength (num:=72) ;

115

b11 := g11;

B11 := G11

b12 := g12;

B12 := G12

b13 := -g11 - g12 ;

B13 :=  - (G12 + G11)

b22 := g22 ;

B22 := G22

b21 := g12;

B21 := G12

b23 := -g12 - g22 ;

B23 :=  - (G12 + G22)

b31 := -g11 - g12 ;

B31 :=  - (G12 + G11)

b32 := -g12 - g22 ;

B32 :=  - (G12 + G22)

b33 := g11 + g12 + g12 + g22 ;

B33 := 2*G12 + G11 + G22

  b := mat((b11,b12,b13),(b21,b22,b23),(b31,b32,b33));

  *** B declared MATRIX

  B(1,1) := G11

  B(1,2) := G12

  B(1,3) :=  - (G12 + G11)

  B(2,1) := G12

  B(2,2) := G22
```

Figure 5. The REDUCE program to solve for the derivatives of the elasticities of the three good TL cost function.

```
B(2,3) :=  - (G12 + G22)

B(3,1) :=  - (G12 + G11)

B(3,2) :=  - (G12 + G22)

B(3,3) := 2*G12 + G11 + G22


lp := mat((log(p1),log(p2),log(p3)));

*** LP declared MATRIX

LP(1,1) := LOG(P1)

LP(1,2) := LOG(P2)

LP(1,3) := LOG(P3)


aa := mat((a1,a2,(1-a1-a2)));

*** AA declared MATRIX

AA(1,1) := A1

AA(1,2) := A2

AA(1,3) :=  - A2 - A1 + 1


lcost :=  trace (aa*tp(lp) ) + trace ( lp * b *tp(lp) ) / 2 ;
                2
LCOST := (LOG(P1) *G11 + 2*LOG(P1)*LOG(P2)*G12 - 2*LOG(P1)*LOG(P3)*

                                                                2
           G12 - 2*LOG(P1)*LOG(P3)*G11 + 2*LOG(P1)*A1 + LOG(P2) *G22

              - 2*LOG(P2)*LOG(P3)*G12 - 2*LOG(P2)*LOG(P3)*G22 + 2*LOG(

                      2                2                2
             P2)*A2 + 2*LOG(P3) *G12 + LOG(P3) *G11 + LOG(P3) *G22 - 2

             *LOG(P3)*A2 - 2*LOG(P3)*A1 + 2*LOG(P3))/2

 cost := exp(lcost) ;

 COST :=

                  2
              (LOG(P1) *G11 + 2*LOG(P1)*LOG(P2)*G12 + 2*LOG(P1)*A1
        SQRT(E)

                   2                           2
               + LOG(P2) *G22 + 2*LOG(P2)*A2 + 2*LOG(P3) *G12 +

                   2                2
             LOG(P3) *G11 + LOG(P3) *G22 + 2*LOG(P3))
                                                         /
         (LOG(P1)*LOG(P3)*G12 + LOG(P1)*LOG(P3)*G11 + LOG(P2)*LOG(
        E
```

Figure 5. (Continued)

P3)*G12 + LOG(P2)*LOG(P3)*G22 + LOG(P3)*A2 + LOG(P3)*A1)

xa1 := df(cost,p1) ;

XA1 := (

$$
\begin{array}{l}
\quad (LOG(P1)^2*G11 + 2*LOG(P1)*LOG(P2)*G12 + 2*LOG(P1)*A1 \\
SQRT(E)
\end{array}
$$

+ LOG(P2)^2*G22 + 2*LOG(P2)*A2 + 2*LOG(P3)^2*G12 +

LOG(P3)^2*G11 + LOG(P3)^2*G22 + 2*LOG(P3))
                                              (LOG(P1)

G11 + LOG(P2)*G12 - LOG(P3)*G12 - LOG(P3)*G11 + A1))/(

  (LOG(P1)*LOG(P3)*G12 + LOG(P1)*LOG(P3)*G11 + LOG(P2)*LOG
E

  (P3)*G12 + LOG(P2)*LOG(P3)*G22 + LOG(P3)*A2 + LOG(P3)*

  A1)
      *P1)

xa2 := df(cost,p2) ;

XA2 := (

$$
\begin{array}{l}
\quad (LOG(P1)^2*G11 + 2*LOG(P1)*LOG(P2)*G12 + 2*LOG(P1)*A1 \\
SQRT(E)
\end{array}
$$

+ LOG(P2)^2*G22 + 2*LOG(P2)*A2 + 2*LOG(P3)^2*G12 +

LOG(P3)^2*G11 + LOG(P3)^2*G22 + 2*LOG(P3))
                                              (LOG(P1)

G12 + LOG(P2)*G22 - LOG(P3)*G12 - LOG(P3)*G22 + A2))/(

  (LOG(P1)*LOG(P3)*G12 + LOG(P1)*LOG(P3)*G11 + LOG(P2)*LOG
E

  (P3)*G12 + LOG(P2)*LOG(P3)*G22 + LOG(P3)*A2 + LOG(P3)*

  A1)
      *P2)

xa3 := df(cost,p3) ;

XA3 := (

$$
\begin{array}{l}
\quad (LOG(P1)^2*G11 + 2*LOG(P1)*LOG(P2)*G12 + 2*LOG(P1)*A1 \\
SQRT(E)
\end{array}
$$

+ LOG(P2)^2*G22 + 2*LOG(P2)*A2 + 2*LOG(P3)^2*G12 +

Figure 5. (*Continued*)

78

$$\text{LOG(P3)}^2 \text{*G11} + \text{LOG(P3)}^2 \text{*G22} + 2\text{*LOG(P3)})$$

$$*(- \text{LOG(P1}$$

$$)\text{*G12} - \text{LOG(P1)*G11} - \text{LOG(P2)*G12} - \text{LOG(P2)*G22} + 2\text{*LOG(}$$

$$\text{P3)*G12} + \text{LOG(P3)*G11} + \text{LOG(P3)*G22} - \text{A2} - \text{A1} + 1))/($$

$$(\text{LOG(P1)*LOG(P3)*G12} + \text{LOG(P1)*LOG(P3)*G11} + \text{LOG(P2)*LOG}$$

E

$$(\text{P3)*G12} + \text{LOG(P2)*LOG(P3)*G22} + \text{LOG(P3)*A2} + \text{LOG(P3)*}$$

A1)

$$*\text{P3})$$

n11 := df(xa1,p1)*p1/xa1 ;

$$\text{N11} := (\text{LOG(P1)}^2\text{*G11} + 2\text{*LOG(P1)*LOG(P2)*G12*G11} - 2\text{*LOG(P1)*LOG(}$$

$$\text{P3)*G12*G11} - 2\text{*LOG(P1)*LOG(P3)*G11}^2 + 2\text{*LOG(P1)*G11*A1} -$$

$$\text{LOG(P1)*G11} + \text{LOG(P2)}^2\text{*G12}^2 - 2\text{*LOG(P2)*LOG(P3)*G12}^2 - 2\text{*}$$

$$\text{LOG(P2)*LOG(P3)*G12*G11} + 2\text{*LOG(P2)*G12*A1} - \text{LOG(P2)*G12} +$$

$$\text{LOG(P3)}^2\text{*G12}^2 + 2\text{*LOG(P3)}^2\text{*G12*G11} + \text{LOG(P3)}^2\text{*G11}^2 - 2\text{*LOG(}$$

$$\text{P3)*G12*A1} + \text{LOG(P3)*G12} - 2\text{*LOG(P3)*G11*A1} + \text{LOG(P3)*G11}$$

$$+ \text{G11} + \text{A1}^2 - \text{A1})/(\text{LOG(P1)*G11} + \text{LOG(P2)*G12} - \text{LOG(P3)*G12}$$

$$- \text{LOG(P3)*G11} + \text{A1})$$

n12 := df(xa1,p2)*p2/xa1 ;

$$\text{N12} := (\text{LOG(P1)}^2\text{*G12*G11} + \text{LOG(P1)*LOG(P2)*G12}^2 + \text{LOG(P1)*LOG(P2)*}$$

$$\text{G11*G22} - \text{LOG(P1)*LOG(P3)*G12}^2 - 2\text{*LOG(P1)*LOG(P3)*G12*G11}$$

$$- \text{LOG(P1)*LOG(P3)*G11*G22} + \text{LOG(P1)*G12*A1} + \text{LOG(P1)*G11*}$$

$$\text{A2} + \text{LOG(P2)}^2\text{*G12*G22} - \text{LOG(P2)*LOG(P3)*G12}^2 - 2\text{*LOG(P2)*}$$

$$\text{LOG(P3)*G12*G22} - \text{LOG(P2)*LOG(P3)*G11*G22} + \text{LOG(P2)*G12*A2}$$

$$+ \text{LOG(P2)*A1*G22} + \text{LOG(P3)}^2\text{*G12}^2 + \text{LOG(P3)}^2\text{*G12*G11} +$$

$$\text{LOG(P3)}^2\text{*G12*G22} + \text{LOG(P3)}^2\text{*G11*G22} - \text{LOG(P3)*G12*A2} - \text{LOG(}$$

$$\text{P3)*G12*A1} - \text{LOG(P3)*G11*A2} - \text{LOG(P3)*A1*G22} + \text{G12} + \text{A2*A1})$$

$$/(\text{LOG(P1)*G11} + \text{LOG(P2)*G12} - \text{LOG(P3)*G12} - \text{LOG(P3)*G11} + \text{A1}$$

$$\vdots$$

Figure 5. (*Continued*)

79

(For brevity we skip the other price elasticities).

```
n11g11 := df(n11,g11) ;

                3    2              2                              2
N11G11 := (LOG(P1) *G11  + 2*LOG(P1) *LOG(P2)*G12*G11 - 2*LOG(P1) *

                         2              2              2
         LOG(P3)*G12*G11 - 3*LOG(P1) *LOG(P3)*G11  + 2*LOG(P1) *

                     2    2
         G11*A1 + LOG(P1)*LOG(P2) *G12  - 2*LOG(P1)*LOG(P2)*LOG(

              2
         P3)*G12  - 4*LOG(P1)*LOG(P2)*LOG(P3)*G12*G11 + 2*LOG(P1)

                             2    2
         *LOG(P2)*G12*A1 + LOG(P1)*LOG(P3) *G12  + 4*LOG(P1)*

                 2                        2    2
         LOG(P3) *G12*G11 + 3*LOG(P1)*LOG(P3) *G11  - 2*LOG(P1)*

                                                              2
         LOG(P3)*G12*A1 - 4*LOG(P1)*LOG(P3)*G11*A1 + LOG(P1)*A1

               2              2                2    2
         - LOG(P2) *LOG(P3)*G12  + 2*LOG(P2)*LOG(P3) *G12  + 2*

              2
         LOG(P2)*LOG(P3) *G12*G11 - 2*LOG(P2)*LOG(P3)*G12*A1 +

                       3    2              3
         LOG(P2)*G12 - LOG(P3) *G12  - 2*LOG(P3) *G12*G11 -

              3    2              2                2
         LOG(P3) *G11  + 2*LOG(P3) *G12*A1 + 2*LOG(P3) *G11*A1 -

                           2              2    2
         LOG(P3)*G12 - LOG(P3)*A1  + A1)/(LOG(P1) *G11  + 2*LOG(

         P1)*LOG(P2)*G12*G11 - 2*LOG(P1)*LOG(P3)*G12*G11 - 2*

                           2                              2
         LOG(P1)*LOG(P3)*G11  + 2*LOG(P1)*G11*A1 + LOG(P2) *

              2                              2
         G12  - 2*LOG(P2)*LOG(P3)*G12  - 2*LOG(P2)*LOG(P3)*G12*

                                    2    2              2
         G11 + 2*LOG(P2)*G12*A1 + LOG(P3) *G12  + 2*LOG(P3) *

                       2    2
         G12*G11 + LOG(P3) *G11  - 2*LOG(P3)*G12*A1 - 2*LOG(P3)

              2
         *G11*A1 + A1 )

n11g12 := df(n11,g12) ;

                2              2              2              2
N11G12 := (LOG(P1) *LOG(P2)*G11  - LOG(P1) *LOG(P3)*G11  + 2*LOG(P1

              2
         )*LOG(P2) *G12*G11 - 4*LOG(P1)*LOG(P2)*LOG(P3)*G12*G11
```

Figure 5. (Continued)

80

$$- 2*LOG(P1)*LOG(P2)*LOG(P3)*G11^2 + 2*LOG(P1)*LOG(P2)*$$

$$G11^2*A1 + 2*LOG(P1)*LOG(P3)^2*G12*G11 + 2*LOG(P1)*LOG(P3)^2$$

$$*G11^2 - 2*LOG(P1)*LOG(P3)*G11^2*A1 + LOG(P2)^3*G12^2 - 3*$$

$$LOG(P2)^2*LOG(P3)*G12^2 - 2*LOG(P2)^2*LOG(P3)*G12*G11 + 2*$$

$$LOG(P2)^2*G12*A1 + 3*LOG(P2)*LOG(P3)^2*G12^2 + 4*LOG(P2)*$$

$$LOG(P3)^2*G12*G11 + LOG(P2)*LOG(P3)^2*G11^2 - 4*LOG(P2)*LOG$$

$$(P3)*G12*A1 - 2*LOG(P2)*LOG(P3)*G11*A1 - LOG(P2)*G11 +$$

$$LOG(P2)*A1^2 - LOG(P3)^3*G12^2 - 2*LOG(P3)^3*G12*G11 -$$

$$LOG(P3)^3*G11^2 + 2*LOG(P3)^2*G12*A1 + 2*LOG(P3)^2*G11*A1 +$$

$$LOG(P3)*G11 - LOG(P3)*A1^2)/(LOG(P1)^2*G11^2 + 2*LOG(P1)*$$

$$LOG(P2)*G12*G11 - 2*LOG(P1)*LOG(P3)*G12*G11 - 2*LOG(P1$$

$$)*LOG(P3)*G11^2 + 2*LOG(P1)*G11*A1 + LOG(P2)^2*G12^2 - 2*$$

$$LOG(P2)*LOG(P3)*G12^2 - 2*LOG(P2)*LOG(P3)*G12*G11 + 2*$$

$$LOG(P2)*G12*A1 + LOG(P3)^2*G12^2 + 2*LOG(P3)^2*G12*G11 +$$

$$LOG(P3)^2*G11^2 - 2*LOG(P3)*G12*A1 - 2*LOG(P3)*G11*A1 +$$

$$A1^2)$$

```
n11g22 := df(n11,g22) ;

N11G22 := 0

n11a1  := df(n11,a1) ;
```

$$N11A1 := (LOG(P1)^2*G11^2 + 2*LOG(P1)*LOG(P2)*G12*G11 - 2*LOG(P1)*LOG$$

$$(P3)*G12*G11 - 2*LOG(P1)*LOG(P3)*G11^2 + 2*LOG(P1)*G11*A1$$

$$+ LOG(P2)^2*G12^2 - 2*LOG(P2)*LOG(P3)*G12^2 - 2*LOG(P2)*LOG$$

$$(P3)*G12*G11 + 2*LOG(P2)*G12*A1 + LOG(P3)^2*G12^2 + 2*$$

Figure 5. (*Continued*)

$$\text{LOG(P3)}^2 \text{*G12*G11 + LOG(P3)}^2 \text{*G11}^2 \text{ - 2*LOG(P3)*G12*A1 - 2*}$$

$$\text{LOG(P3)*G11*A1 - G11 + A1}^2 \text{)/(LOG(P1)}^2 \text{*G11}^2 \text{ + 2*LOG(P1)*}$$

$$\text{LOG(P2)*G12*G11 - 2*LOG(P1)*LOG(P3)*G12*G11 - 2*LOG(P1)}$$

$$\text{*LOG(P3)*G11}^2 \text{ + 2*LOG(P1)*G11*A1 + LOG(P2)}^2 \text{*G12}^2 \text{ - 2*}$$

$$\text{LOG(P2)*LOG(P3)*G12}^2 \text{ - 2*LOG(P2)*LOG(P3)*G12*G11 + 2*}$$

$$\text{LOG(P2)*G12*A1 + LOG(P3)}^2 \text{*G12}^2 \text{ + 2*LOG(P3)}^2 \text{*G12*G11 +}$$

$$\text{LOG(P3)}^2 \text{*G11}^2 \text{ - 2*LOG(P3)*G12*A1 - 2*LOG(P3)*G11*A1 +}$$

$$\text{A1}^2 \text{)}$$

```
n11a2   := df(n11,a2) ;

N11A2 := 0

n11p1   := df(n11,p1) ;
```

$$\text{N11P1 := (G11*(LOG(P1)}^2 \text{*G11}^2 \text{ + 2*LOG(P1)*LOG(P2)*G12*G11 - 2*LOG(P1}$$

$$\text{)*LOG(P3)*G12*G11 - 2*LOG(P1)*LOG(P3)*G11}^2 \text{ + 2*LOG(}$$

$$\text{P1)*G11*A1 + LOG(P2)}^2 \text{*G12}^2 \text{ - 2*LOG(P2)*LOG(P3)*G12}^2$$

$$\text{- 2*LOG(P2)*LOG(P3)*G12*G11 + 2*LOG(P2)*G12*A1 +}$$

$$\text{LOG(P3)}^2 \text{*G12}^2 \text{ + 2*LOG(P3)}^2 \text{*G12*G11 + LOG(P3)}^2 \text{*G11}^2$$

$$\text{- 2*LOG(P3)*G12*A1 - 2*LOG(P3)*G11*A1 - G11 + A1}^2 \text{))}$$

$$\text{/(P1*(LOG(P1)}^2 \text{*G11}^2 \text{ + 2*LOG(P1)*LOG(P2)*G12*G11 - 2*LOG(P1}$$

$$\text{)*LOG(P3)*G12*G11 - 2*LOG(P1)*LOG(P3)*G11}^2 \text{ + 2*LOG(}$$

$$\text{P1)*G11*A1 + LOG(P2)}^2 \text{*G12}^2 \text{ - 2*LOG(P2)*LOG(P3)*G12}^2$$

$$\text{- 2*LOG(P2)*LOG(P3)*G12*G11 + 2*LOG(P2)*G12*A1 +}$$

$$\text{LOG(P3)}^2 \text{*G12}^2 \text{ + 2*LOG(P3)}^2 \text{*G12*G11 + LOG(P3)}^2 \text{*G11}^2$$

$$\text{- 2*LOG(P3)*G12*A1 - 2*LOG(P3)*G11*A1 + A1}^2 \text{))}$$

```
n11p2   := df(n11,p2) ;
```

Figure 5. (*Continued*)

82

```
                    2     2
N11P2 := (G12*(LOG(P1) *G11  + 2*LOG(P1)*LOG(P2)*G12*G11 - 2*LOG(P1

                                                         2
          )*LOG(P3)*G12*G11 - 2*LOG(P1)*LOG(P3)*G11  + 2*LOG(

                     2     2                        2
          P1)*G11*A1 + LOG(P2) *G12  - 2*LOG(P2)*LOG(P3)*G12

          - 2*LOG(P2)*LOG(P3)*G12*G11 + 2*LOG(P2)*G12*A1 +

                 2     2             2              2     2
          LOG(P3) *G12  + 2*LOG(P3) *G12*G11 + LOG(P3) *G11

                                                       2
          - 2*LOG(P3)*G12*A1 - 2*LOG(P3)*G11*A1 - G11 + A1 ))

                     2     2
          /(P2*(LOG(P1) *G11  + 2*LOG(P1)*LOG(P2)*G12*G11 - 2*LOG(P1

                                                         2
          )*LOG(P3)*G12*G11 - 2*LOG(P1)*LOG(P3)*G11  + 2*LOG(

                     2     2                        2
          P1)*G11*A1 + LOG(P2) *G12  - 2*LOG(P2)*LOG(P3)*G12

          - 2*LOG(P2)*LOG(P3)*G12*G11 + 2*LOG(P2)*G12*A1 +

                 2     2             2              2     2
          LOG(P3) *G12  + 2*LOG(P3) *G12*G11 + LOG(P3) *G11

                                                       2
          - 2*LOG(P3)*G12*A1 - 2*LOG(P3)*G11*A1 + A1 ))

n11p3   := df(n11,p3) ;

                    2           2         2   3
N11P3 := ( - LOG(P1) *G12*G11  - LOG(P1) *G11  - 2*LOG(P1)*LOG(P2)*

          2             2
          G12 *G11 - 2*LOG(P1)*LOG(P2)*G12*G11  + 2*LOG(P1)*LOG(P3)

          2                          2
          *G12 *G11 + 4*LOG(P1)*LOG(P3)*G12*G11  + 2*LOG(P1)*LOG(P3

          3                              2
          )*G11  - 2*LOG(P1)*G12*G11*A1 - 2*LOG(P1)*G11 *A1 -

              2   3          2     2
          LOG(P2) *G12  - LOG(P2) *G12 *G11 + 2*LOG(P2)*LOG(P3)*

          3                  2
          G12  + 4*LOG(P2)*LOG(P3)*G12 *G11 + 2*LOG(P2)*LOG(P3)*G12

          2              2
          *G11  - 2*LOG(P2)*G12 *A1 - 2*LOG(P2)*G12*G11*A1 -

              2   3          2     2            2         2
          LOG(P3) *G12  - 3*LOG(P3) *G12 *G11 - 3*LOG(P3) *G12*G11

              2   3              2
          - LOG(P3) *G11  + 2*LOG(P3)*G12 *A1 + 4*LOG(P3)*G12*G11*
```

Figure 5. (*Continued*)

83

```
                     2                          2      2
     A1 + 2*LOG(P3)*G11 *A1 + G12*G11 - G12*A1    + G11   - G11*

      2                    2      2
     A1 )/(P3*(LOG(P1) *G11   + 2*LOG(P1)*LOG(P2)*G12*G11 - 2*

                                                                  2
          LOG(P1)*LOG(P3)*G12*G11 - 2*LOG(P1)*LOG(P3)*G11

                              2      2
          + 2*LOG(P1)*G11*A1 + LOG(P2) *G12  - 2*LOG(P2)*

               2
          LOG(P3)*G12  - 2*LOG(P2)*LOG(P3)*G12*G11 + 2*LOG

               2      2                    2
          (P2)*G12*A1 + LOG(P3) *G12  + 2*LOG(P3) *G12*G11

               2      2
          + LOG(P3) *G11  - 2*LOG(P3)*G12*A1 - 2*LOG(P3)*

               2
          G11*A1 + A1 ))

       bye;
 *** END OF RUN
```

Figure 5. (Continued)

of substitution for a TL cost function are given as

$$\sigma_{ij} = \frac{\eta_{ij}}{m_j}.$$

Anderson and Thursby (1986) employ an approximation for the ratio of normally distributed random variables to also derive the variance of the elasticity of substitution. However, our findings indicate that the elasticities are more complex fuctions than simple ratios of the estimated parameters of the cost function and that the best we can hope for is the use of a Taylor series expansion of these nonlinear functions of the cost function parameters.[3] We have estimated the first-order derivatives of the own-price elasticity for the first input with respect to the cost function parameters (see Figure 5). These equations can then be used to linearize the elasticity expressions so that the variance can be computed in the same vein as Toevs suggested, though these expressions are much more complex than those he provided for the elasticities expressed in terms of the cost shares. Furthermore REDUCE can provide output in FORTRAN language form that can be inserted into a FORTRAN program.

2. The Curvature Restrictions on the TL Cost Function

One of the theoretical properties of a cost function is its concavity in the input prices. Since they are unlike the conditions of homogeneity and symmetry, we cannot impose these conditions through the use of linear restrictions on the parameters of the cost function. This condition requires that the Hessian of the cost function with respect to the prices of the inputs is negative semidefinite and that the first derivatives are positive (the estimated demand for the inputs). Here we will concentrate on the Hessian condition. If all the eigenvalues (latent or characteristic roots) of the Hessian are nonpositive (negative or zero), we then have the negative semidefiniteness of the equation.

Diewart and Wales (1985) have shown that a sufficient condition for the Hessian of the TL cost function to be negative semidefinite is that the matrix of cross-price terms B be negative semidefinite. They also note that this is possibly an overly restrictive condition— that the Hessian may be negative semidefinite when the B matrix is not. In the present example we will employ MACSYMA's EIGEN macro, providing the MACSYMA code that enables us to derive the analytic eigenvalues of a matrix. The code employed works as follows: First the determinant of $(B - \lambda I)$ is derived, where λ is a scalar and I the identity matrix. Then the SOLVE function, which determines roots of a polynomial, is used to find the values of λ that set the determinant to zero. The EIGEN macro in MACSYMA can also provide the eigenvectors of the matrix.

In Figure 4 at statement (c12) we invoke the EIGEN macro to determine the eigenvalues of the matrix B defined in statement (d11). Statement (d40) is the resulting vector of eigenvalues for B. Note we could have determined the global conditions if we took the second-order derivative of the cost function with respect to the prices and then solved for eigenvalues of this matrix. We attempted to solve this problem, but we found the expression for the Hessian became so cumbersome that the problem could not be solved in the memory of the system to which we had access. We feel that such a solution is possible, but the complexity would overwhelm our present discussion.

When we examine the resulting eigenvalues [(d40) in Figure 4] we find that only two are nonzero. We can write them in the following form:

$$\lambda_1 = A - B$$
$$\lambda_2 = A + B,$$

where $A = g_{11} + g_{12} + g_{22}$;

$$B = \text{sqrt}(g_{22}^2 + (2g_{12} - g_{11})g_{22} + 4g_{12}^2 + 2g_{11}g_{12} + g_{11}^2).$$

We require that both λ_1 and λ_2 be negative; thus $|B| \le |A|$ because $B \ge 0$.[4] Consequently, the only condition that need hold is that $\lambda_2 \le 0$. In conclusion, we find that this single nonlinear inequality restriction need be applied to have a sufficient condition for global concavity of the three-input TL cost function.[5]

IV.   CONCLUSIONS

Clearly there are some very important uses for these computer algebra programs. The differentiation, integration, factorization, and differential equation routines may well be attractive to many economists. Obviously the results are exact, and there is none of the statistical error related with numerical solutions. With MACSYMA, the user can generate FORTRAN expressions. This allows for the merging of symbolic and numerical analysis. For the theorist, the computer algebra programs enables the user to focus on the analytics of a problem. In fact, many seemingly insolvable problems may be solved by these programs, reducing the analyst's dependence on generalizations from the data.

In general, we found the manual for the REDUCE program to be quite poor. The chapters were diverse in style and lacked examples in many cases. The MACSYMA guide, on the other hand, was far more useful due to its example orientation.

One of the features of MACSYMA is the ability to produce output that can be interpreted by the typesetting routines to drive a laser printer. However, the RATSIMP procedure in MACSYMA has a tendency to construct algebraic expressions that are too long for insertion on a single line; thus most of the output which appears in the figures of this paper could not be translated for the laser printer.

An area of interest for future research in this field could be the development of more sophisticated matrix algebra processing, thus allowing for the inclusion of the rules of matrix algebra and matrix differentiation. Such a package or extension of one of the existing computer algebra languages could then be employed with such matrix language numeric routines as APL, GAUSS, or SAS's IML routines.

NOTES

1. The option ECHO: OFF is used so the matrix definition statements are not echoed by the program.
2. Note that we use the two MACSYMA functions **RATSIMP** and LOG-CONTRACT to simplify the expressions reported. Otherwise MACSYMA would not combine similar expressions, nor would it combine the sums of logs as the logs of the products.
3. Krinsky and Robb (1986) propose an alternative pseudo-bootstrap approach that can be employed instead of the linearization suggested here.
4. We can show $B \geq 0$ because this is the square root of a quadratic expression from the pre- and postmultiplication of a positive definite matrix:

$$B = g'Qg, \qquad Q = \begin{bmatrix} 1 & 2 & -1 \\ 0 & 4 & 2 \\ 0 & 0 & 1 \end{bmatrix}, \qquad g = (g_{11}, g_{12}, g_{22})'.$$

$Det(Q) = 4$; thus $B \geq 0$.
5. In an investigation of the four-input case the resulting eigenvalues were much more complex functions of the equivalent parameters in **g**.

REFERENCES

Anderson, R. G. and J. Thursby (1986) "Confidence Intervals of Elasticity Estimators in Translog Models." *Review of Economics and Statistics* 647–656.
Atkinson, A. B. and J. E. Stiglitz (1980) *Lectures on Public Economics.* New York: McGraw-Hill.
Barnett, W. A. (1985) "The Minflex-Laurents Translog Flexible Functional Form." *Journal of Econometrics* (1982) 30, 33–45.
Calmet, J. and J. A. van Hulzen (1982) "Computer Algebra Applications," Pp. 245–258. B. Buchberger, G. E. Collins, and R. Loos (eds.), in *Computing Supplementum*, Vol. 4. New York: Springer-Verlag.
Christensen, L. R. and W. H. Green (1976) "Economics of Scale in U.S. Electric Power Generation." *Journal of Political Economy* 84, 655–676.

Christensen, L. R., D. W. Jorgenson, and L. J. Lau (1971) "Conjugate Duality and the Transcendental Logarithmic Function." *Econometrica* 39, 255-256.

Diewart, W. E. and T. J. Wales (1985) "Flexible Functional Forms and Global Curvature Conditions." Working Paper No. 85-19, Department of Economics, University of British Columbia.

Davenport, J. (1979) "Integration of Algebraic Functions." Pp. 415-425 in Edward W. Ng (ed.), *Symbolic and Algebraic Computation, Eurosam '79*, Vol. 72 of *Lecture Notes in Computer Science* (G. Goos and J. Harmanis, eds.). New York: Springer-Verlag.

Gallant, A. N. (1981) "On the Bias in Flexible Functional Forms and an Essentially Unbiased Form: The Fourier Flexible Form." *Journal of Econometrics* 15, 211-245.

Graybill, F. A. (1983) *Matrices with Applications in Statistics*, 2nd edition, Wadsworth Publishing Company, Belmont, California.

Guilkey, D. R. and D. Schmidt (1973) "Estimation of Seemingly Unrelated Regressions with Vector Autoregressive Errors." *Journal of the American Statistical Association* 68, 642-647.

Harberger, A. C. (1962) "The Incidence of the Corporation Income Tax." *Journal of Political Economy* 70, 215-240.

Hausman, J. A. (1981) "Exact Consumer's Surplus and Deadweight Loss." *American Economics Review* 71, 662-676.

Hirschberg, J. G. (1986) "A Comparison of Three Flexible Cost Functions Using Establishment Level Electricity Use Data." Modeling Research Group Working Paper No. M8607, University of Southern California.

Krinsky, Itzhale and A. Leslie Robb (1986) "On Approximating the Statistical Properties of Elasticities." *Review of Economics and Statistics* 68, 715-719.

Leon, J. and V. Pless (1979) "CAMAC 1979." Pp. 249-257 in Edward W. Ng (ed.), *Symbolic and Algebraic Computation, Eurosam '79*, Vol. 72 of *Lecture Notes in Computer Science* (G. Goos and J. Hartmanis, eds.). New York; Springer-Verlag.

Nerlove, M., D. Grether and J. Carvalho (1979) *Analysis of Economic Time Series: A Synthesis*. New York: Academic Press.

Pavelle, Richard (1985) "MACSYMA: Capabilities and Applications to Problems in Engineering and the Sciences." Pp. 180-232. In Bruno Buchberger (eds), *Eurocal '85*, Vol. 203 of *Lecture Notes in Computer Science* (O. Goos and J. Hartmanis, eds.). New York: Springer-Verlag.

Pavelle, Richard, Michael Rothstein, and John Fitch (1981) "Computer Algebra." *Scientific American* 245 (Dec.), 136-152.

Shephard, R. W. (1953) *Cost and Production Functions*. Princeton, NJ: Princeton University Press.

Rich, A. and D. Stoutemeyer (1979) "Capabilities of the MUMATH-78 Computer Algebra System for the Intel-8080 Microprocessor." Pp. 242-257 in Edward W. Ng (ed.), *Symbolic and Algebraic Computation, Eurosam '79*, Vol. 72 of *Lecture Notes in Computer Science* (G. Goos and J. Hartmanis, eds.). New York: Springer-Verlag.

Toevs, A. L. (1980) "Approximate Variance Formulas for the Elasticities of Substitution Obtained from Translog Production Functions." *Economic Letters* 15, 155-160.

Toevs, A. L. (1982) "Approximate Variance Formulas for the Elasticities of Substitution Obtained from the Translog Cost Functions." *Economic Letters* 10, 107–113.

Wolfram, Stephen. "Computer Software in Science and Mathematics." *Scientific American* 251 (Sept.), 188–229.

Yun, D. Y. Y. and R. D. Stoutemeyer (1980) "Symbolic Mathematical Computation." Pp. 235–310 in J. Belzer, A. G. Holzman, and A. Kent (eds.), *Encyclopedia of Computer Science and Technology*, Vol. 15. New York: Dekker.

Zellner, A. (1962) "An Efficient Method of Estimating Seemingly Unrelated Regressions and Tests of Aggregation Bias." *Journal of the American Statistical Association* 57, 348–368.

Zellner, A., D. Huang and A. Chau (1965) "Further Analysis of the Short-Run Consumption Function." *Econometrica* 33, 571–588.

MONTE CARLO EXPERIMENTATION USING PC-NAIVE

David F. Hendry and Adrian J. Neale

I. INTRODUCTION

Experimentation using Monte Carlo techniques has proved invaluable in developing a quantitative understanding of the finite sample properties of econometric estimators and test statistics. The simulation approach has spawned a considerable literature over the years both concerning the methodology of Monte Carlo itself (for an exposition see Hendry, 1984) as well as many applications (see Sowey, 1973, for a partial list). This chapter is primarily concerned with simulation methodology and, in particular, efficient Monte Carlo experimentation for teaching and research.

There are five themes to the analysis. First, for classroom demonstrations, the range of cases open to investigation within a program should cover most of those in common use by allowing

Advances in Econometrics, Volume 6, pages 91–125
Copyright © 1987 by JAI Press Inc.
All rights of reproduction in any form reserved.
ISBN: 0-89232-795-2

for a suitably general data generation process (DGP). Secondly, asymptotic outcomes should be available for comparison with their finite sample counterparts, for stationary processes at least, and hence population moments and functions thereof (such as model parameters and variances) should be calculated numerically. Next, the comparative advantages of a microcomputer can be exploited via a menu-driven editor for direct alteration of experimental designs and by screen graphics which can immediately portray the simulation findings in a readily understood form. This idea interacts with the fourth theme in which the comparative disadvantage of current personal computer (PC) technology (i.e., speed for pre-80386/7 microchips) is offset by adopting *recursive* techniques. In that mode, *every* feasible sample size can be calculated for less than twice the cost of a conventional experiment at the largest sample size studied. Behavior over all sample sizes can be graphed immediately, including plotting against a second method or an asymptotic outcome. Finally, the properties of recursive estimation and testing procedures themselves can be examined (such as those incorporated in PC-GIVE[1]), including tests for structural change (e.g., the sizes of *sequences* of Chow tests).

Monte Carlo techniques are typically justified as a means of solving deterministic problems when the theoretical solution is analytically intractable or the labor costs involved are high relative to the capital cost of computer simulation. Against this, one must balance the inherent imprecision and specificity of simulation, although the use of antithetic variates and control variables and the formulation of response surfaces help minimize such drawbacks. Careful design of the Monte Carlo experiments can also help reduce specificity through the formulation of a parameter space $(\theta:T)$ of sufficient generality relative to the required uses. This issue is discussed elsewhere, however, and is not our present concern (see Hammersley and Handscomb, 1964, p. 59; Hendry, 1984). Here, we are primarily interested in the role of T, the sample size, and the associated use of recursive estimation techniques to increase the information obtained about any given point in θ.

The role of Monte Carlo (abbreviated to MC as necessary below) in a live teaching environment is emphasised relative to its research role since the present version of PC-NAIVE is indeed naive in many ways (the acronym stands for **N**umerical **A**nalysis of **I**nstrumental **V**ariables **E**stimators). For example, variance reduction methods have yet to be implemented, but the structure of the program allows these to be incorporated jointly with recursion and asymptotic analysis in due course as briefly discussed below.

The five themes above are discussed in the context of PC-NAIVE in Section II, followed in Section III by illustrations of more conventional methods. Section IV then describes the advantages for finite sample Monte Carlo studies of adopting recursive methods, the relevant algorithms being analyzed in Section V. Illustrative applications are discussed in Section VI, and Section VII concludes the chapter.

II. AN OVERVIEW OF PC-NAIVE

PC-NAIVE is a menu-driven Monte Carlo program for the numerical analysis of PC-GIVE estimators for IBM^{TM} PCs, ATs, and compatibles.[2] The program is written in FORTRAN 77, so is fast and accurate, and it can exploit a math coprocessor. Problems are designed, simulated, and analyzed *interactively.*

Input is controlled by an interactive editor which presents a sequence of menus covering various facets of the design of each experiment. The desired input number is typed directly into a highlighted box, alternatives are selected via the "return" key, and movement between boxes is controlled by the "arrow" keys. The function keys F1–F10 control which menus are offered.

Since a considerable amount of information is required from the user, PC-NAIVE takes this information from an input file but uses the editor to construct or change the structure of the DGP and other input information. The editor operates via a series of screen menus, each dealing with logically distinct groups of information. The currently active specifications may be changed by selecting the desired box and inputting the revised values. While some error protection is provided, guarding against the input of nonsensical values, the user must check rank conditions for identification and stationarity (if required) and whether the first two moments of the estimators exist.

A menu-driven program provides an interactive environment without the investment in familiarization with a command structure, and later retention of its language. Thus, menus allow ease of design of an experiment at the presimulation stage, as well as flexibility and speed in selecting results for postsimulation analysis. Conversely, such a program is limited to the facilities directly provided by its authors.

The initial screen menu takes the form shown in Table 1 (abbreviated to fit on the page, and preceded by the algebraic form of the DGP equations shown in (1)-(3) below).

When studying *finite sample behavior,* simulation efficiency can be increased by using *recursive Monte Carlo methods* to simultaneously compute outcomes at all sample sizes up to the largest of interest. There is little increase in cost over direct methods, but duplication of experiments at different sample sizes is eliminated, reducing the number of experiments needed for a given level of specificity. Indeed, recursive Monte Carlo methods can be viewed as a technique for variance reduction by minimizing uncertainty between the outcomes at successive sample sizes. Less obviously, recursive estimation linked to graphic output also helps reduce the consumption costs entailed in the analysis of MC results by providing graphic analogs of response surfaces for fixed θ but varying intensively over T and tying the numerical findings to asymptotic analyses. In a classroom environment, such techniques aid the demonstration of most theoretical results, and examples of this analysis and interpretation of econometric results are shown below.

Thus, we believe that four features make PC-NAIVE useful for classroom demonstrations of econometric methods:

1. The flexibility of interactive analysis and the fact that the demonstrator can prepare examples in advance, thus avoiding the need to formulate the experiment from scratch in the classroom
2. The exploitation of computer graphics so that students can literally *see* results immediately—learning seems more rapid when theory and application are combined, directly linking the (usual) econometric theory with a (less usual) quantitative demonstration
3. The use of recursive methods to support feature 2, above, by providing detailed analyses of results as a function of T
4. The combination of features that can be built into an artificial numerical DGP, together with the wide range of

Table 1

PRIMARY INFORMATION

No. of Models	1	No. Est Meths	1	Est Eq	INVARIANT	No. Z Vars	1
Replications	100	Est Meth. 1	OLS	Y1 Meas Err	NO	Z Vars	STOCHASTIC
No. Generated	4	Est Meth. 2	—	Y2 Meas Err	NO	Z DGP	INVARIANT
Obs Discard	20	Constant	NO	Y2 Model	INV	COMFAC Test	NO
Correlogram	4	No. Transfs	0	Power LR Test	NO	LM AR Test	NO
Auto Design	NO	IEX	0	ARCH Errors	NO	Use Z_{t-1}	NO
IWRITE	0	Recurs Init	0	Co-Intgn Tests	NO		

Location of Further Instruments

Inst 1		Inst 2	5	Inst 3	6	Inst 4	7	0

←↕→   Selects   or   F1 Next Menu   F3 Restart   F6 QUIT   F9 Help statistics available, enhances the coverage of econometrics and brings formulas to "life"

The notion of conducting classroom simulations as a didactic device is by no means new, and Hammersley and Handscomb (1964, p. 7) report a case from early in this centry in which students of statistics were required to pour lead shot down boards studded with pins that would deflect the shot, which collected in boxes at the bottom of the board. The object of the exercise was to see if the shot collected from each box conformed to the theoretical predictions. Here the analogy ceases, as the students' exercise was labor intensive whereas present methods are capital intensive.

The DGP used by PC-NAIVE is defined as

$$By_t + Dy_{t-1} + Cz_t = u_t \tag{1}$$

$$u_t = Ru_{t-1} + \varepsilon_t \qquad \varepsilon_t \sim IN(0, \Sigma) \tag{2}$$

$$z_t = \Lambda z_{t-1} + v_t \qquad v_t \sim IN(0, \Omega), \tag{3}$$

where $E(\varepsilon_t \ v_s') = 0 \ \forall t, s$.

Two endogenous and up to three exogenous variables (strictly or strongly exogenous, according to design) are allowed, so writing the DGP in scalar form yields

$$y_{1t} = b_{12}y_{2t} + \sum_{i=1}^{2} d_{1i}y_{it-1} + \sum_{k=1}^{3} c_{1k}z_{kt} + u_{1t} \tag{4}$$

$$y_{2t} = b_{21}y_{1t} + \sum_{i=1}^{2} d_{2i}y_{it-1} + \sum_{k=1}^{3} c_{2k}z_{kt} + u_{2t} \tag{5}$$

$$z_{kt} = \lambda_k z_{kt-1} + v_{kt} \qquad (k = 1, 3), \tag{6}$$

where $E(v_{kt}v_{js}) = \delta_{ts}\omega_{jk}$, and

$$\begin{bmatrix} u_{1t} \\ u_{2t} \end{bmatrix} = \begin{bmatrix} r_{11} & r_{12} \\ r_{21} & r_{22} \end{bmatrix} \begin{bmatrix} u_{1t-1} \\ u_{2t-1} \end{bmatrix} + \begin{bmatrix} \varepsilon_{1t} \\ \varepsilon_{2t} \end{bmatrix}, \tag{7}$$

where $E(\varepsilon_{jt}\varepsilon_{js}) = \delta_{ts}\sigma_{ij}$, and δ_{ij} is the Kronecker delta.

Thus, a wide range of problems can be incorporated within this DGP including simultaneity; dynamics; weak or strong exogeneity (see Engle et al., 1983); autoregressive, intercorrelated and cross-serially correlated errors; omitted or falsely included variables; and collinearity. In addition, but notationally awkward to show, the DGP allows for measurement errors, structural breaks, and nonstationarity, as well as most combinations of all these. The user also has control over a variety of other features, including the options of defining a second model so that the encompassing and nonnested hypothesis tests discussed in Ericsson (1983) can be examined or inducing autoregressive conditional heteroscedasticity (ARCH) (for a Monte Carlo application see Engle et al., 1985). Dickey–Fuller (1979) and Durbin–Watson tests for cointegration can be computed (see Granger, 1986; Engle and Granger, 1987); and the z_t variables can either be stochastic or held fixed across replications.

Once the structure of the DGP has been defined, an experiment also requires the formulation of the equations to be estimated (these need not coincide with any equation in the DGP and may include a constant and/or trend, as well as other regressors transformed prior to estimation), the estimation method[s] to be used [which are currently ordinary least squares (OLS) and two-stage least squares (TSLS) and their recursive generalizations], the largest sample size to be used, the number of observations retained for forecast tests, and the number of times each experiment is to be replicated. Currently, the maximum-permissible-sized problem [due to storage constraints, assuming 512K RAM (random access memory)] allows 200 observations and 500 replications. The constructed time-series data from any one replication can be saved to an output file for subsequent analysis, random numbers can be generated from a user-selectable "seed" or input to the program from a data bank of standard normal variates starting from a position in the bank selected by the user, and in each case the user has control over the number of initial normal random variates discarded at each replication before data variables are constructed.

If the model is stationary, then the population moments and asymptotic values of the coefficients of each model, their associated standard errors, equation standard errors, R^2, etc. can be computed. From (1)–(3), the system can be written in companion form as

$$f_t = K f_{t-1} + \eta_t,$$

where

$$\eta_t = \begin{bmatrix} B^{-1}(\varepsilon_t - C v_t) \\ v_t \\ 0 \end{bmatrix}, \tag{8}$$

and $f'_t = (y'_t \quad z'_t \quad y'_{t-1})$, where $E(\eta_t\eta'_t) = \Psi$ and (K, Σ, Ω), with K depending on (B, C, D, R). From (8), the moments of f_t can be calculated as

$$M = E(f_t f'_t) = K M K' + \Psi \qquad \text{and} \qquad M_1 = E(f_t f'_{t-1}) = K M.$$
$$(9)$$

Irrespective of the exact formulation of any linear model of a subset of f_t, the plims of its parameters and their estimated standard errors, equation standard errors, etc. are all functions of $(M M_1)$, and hence are readily calculated (see Hendry, 1982). This applies to rival models even if these are nonnested.

With the problem of interest completely defined, numerical simulation can proceed, possibly involving multiple jobs where each job comprises a different point in the parameter space $(\theta : T)$. Random numbers are used for the ε_t and v_t, and hence for constructing y_{it} and z_{kt} (and also for any measurement errors—if this option has been selected). The basic random numbers are rectangularly distributed random variates from a multiplicative congruential method; if desired, standard normal random variates can be constructed using the Box–Muller method.

On completion of a Monte Carlo run, the random numbers are analyzed and an output menu offers access to the stored simulation findings (shown below). The output of PC-NAIVE is both numerical (e.g., average biases, standard errors) and graphic (e.g., histograms of frequency distributions), and items can be repeated so that several kinds of cross-comparisons can be made. Averages over replications of estimators and test statistics can be plotted against the associated sample size as well as pictorial histograms of the distributions of estimators and tests across replications at a given sample size, with interpolations approximating the density functions.

Finally, and implicit in the above discussion, a high degree of error protection is essential. Not only should a program be protected against crashing (embarrassing in a live demonstration!), but also against accidental user input of nonsensical parameters.

The next section discusses the functioning of PC-NAIVE in conventional MC, and in Section VI we return to illustrate the use of PC-NAIVE in its more powerful recursive mode.

III. DESKTOP AND CLASSROOM EXPERIMENTATION

Let us consider a first-order autoregressive model which serves the dual purposes of illustrating the output produced by PC-NAIVE and acting as a stylized example of conventional Monte Carlo methods, for later contrast with the gains offered by recursion. The structure of this DGP[3] is

$$y_t = \alpha y_{t-1} + \varepsilon_t, \quad \text{for } t = 1, \ldots, T_i, \tag{10}$$

where

$$\varepsilon_t \sim \text{IN}(0, \sigma_\varepsilon^2), \quad \text{with } |\alpha| < 1, \tag{11}$$

and

$$y_0 \sim N(0, \sigma_\varepsilon^2 / (1 - \alpha^2)), \tag{12}$$

when T_i is the sample size to be used in the ith experiment. Thus, the parameter space of interest comprises

$$\{\theta = (\alpha, \sigma_\varepsilon^2 \mid |\alpha| < 1, \quad \sigma_\varepsilon^2 > 0); \quad T_i\}.$$

The objective of the Monte Carlo is to calculate $E(\hat{\alpha})$ (assumed intractable analytically) and contrast its value with plim $\hat{\alpha}$ where for a given sample size T

$$\hat{\alpha} = \sum_{t=1}^{T} y_t y_{t-1} \bigg/ \sum_{t=1}^{T} y_{t-1}^2. \tag{13}$$

A sequence of points in θ and T are selected on which to carry out numerical simulation of the estimator (13), and any one set of points [for instance, $\theta_1 = (\alpha = 0.85, \quad \sigma_\varepsilon^2 = 1); \quad T = 60$] defines a single experiment which is replicated N times by generating pseudorandom numbers for ε_t and thereby generating y_t. A single experiment with PC-NAIVE was run at θ_1 ($\sigma_\varepsilon^2 = 1.0$ without loss of generality), with $N = 400$, each replication taking approximately 2 sec on an AT with a maths coprocessor running at 8 MHz. This time includes the data generation, parameter estimation, and the calculation of auxiliary statistics, as well as any necessary disk access.

The *output menu* of PC-NAIVE appears on completion of the replications as shown in Table 2.

Table 2

OUTPUT MENU

```
1.   Biases
2.   Standard Errors
3.   t Values
4.   Forecast/Stability Tests
5.   Autocorrelation Tests
6.   Encompassing Tests
7.   DGP and Model
8.   Data Moments
9.   Population Parameter Values
10.  Review Stored Results
11.  Graph the Data/Recursions
12.  Review Random Numbers
13.  Change Screen Color
14.  Change Default Graph Colors
15.  Terminate Output
```

Choose an Option:

In the example just considered, interest focuses on the bias of $\hat{\alpha}$ (option 1) and the t statistic (option 3)—although one could also examine the estimated standard error (SE) (option 2), the performance of the Durbin–Watson statistic, and tests for cointegration (option 5); or recall the DGP (option 7, also available from the "return" key); or graph the data used in the last replication (option 11); or analyze the first four moments and the correlation properties of the random numbers used (option 12). Since no observations were retained for forecast tests and no second nonnested model was selected, options 4 and 6 are inapplicable in the present context. The population data moments and the plims of the sample statistics are shown by options 8 and 9.

Selecting option 1 yields information on the mean bias (over replications), the standard error of the bias (and hence whether BIAS/(SE OF BIAS) differs significantly from zero using a t distribution), the standard deviation of the bias [i.e., the correct sampling standard deviation (SD) of $\hat{\alpha}$], and the frequency distribution of $\hat{\alpha}$ over replications in classes of 0.5 SD, as shown in the tabulation [the asymptotic $\sigma_{\hat{\alpha}}$ for $T = 60$ is 0.069, and the mean estimated SE = 0.074].

DIRECT SIMULATION Using
ORDINARY LEAST SQUARES (OLS)

VARIABLE	BIAS	SE OF BIAS	SD	ROOT MSE
YA1	−.0313	.0039	.0771	.0833

FREQUENCY DISTRIBUTION OF Estimator

PARAMETER 1

INTERVAL IS 0.5σ = 0.0386   CENTERED ON: 0.0

−∞	−2.5	−2	−1.5	−1	−0.5	0	0.5	1	1.5	2	2.5	∞
	20	8	24	40	65	99	69	57	18	0	0	0

Graphing the (scaled) frequency distribution, as in Figure 1a (where a cubic interpolant has been fitted; see Mazzarino, 1986), reveals negative skewness in the distribution. The cumulative distribution function is plotted in Figure 1b against a cumulative normal with the same mean and variance. Analogously, one can examine the distribution of the *t* statistic, first around zero and then around the true parameter, as shown in the second tabulation.

ANALYSIS of REGRESSION *t* Values Around ZERO

VARIABLE	MEAN	SD	H_0 REJECTED
YA1	11.600	3.140	400 (100%)

FREQUENCY DISTRIBUTION of *t* Statistics

INTERVAL IS 0.5σ = 1.5702   CENTERED ON: 11.600

∞	−2.5	−2	−1.5	−1	−0.5	0	0.5	1	1.5	2	2.5	∞
0	2	19	41	64	95	70	47	25	22	10	5	

ANALYSIS of REGRESSION *t* Values Around TRUE Parameter

VARIABLE	MEAN	SD	H_0 REJECTED
YA1	−0.2587	0.9571	19 (4.75%)

σ has MEAN .9861   and   SE .0092

Figures 2a and 2b show some little evidence of positive skewness in the distribution of the *t* values for H_0: $\alpha = 0$. Since these results apply to only one point in the parameter space and one sample size, further experiments are needed to build up a complete picture of the performance of the estimator and its *t* statistic.

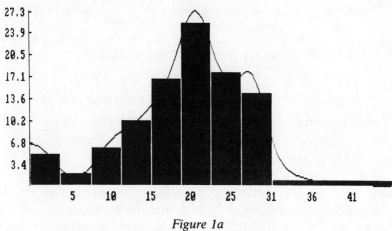

Figure 1a

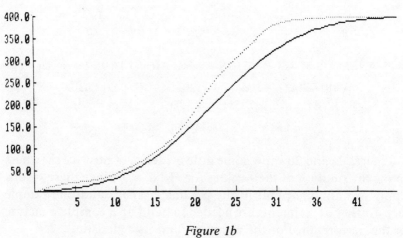

Figure 1b

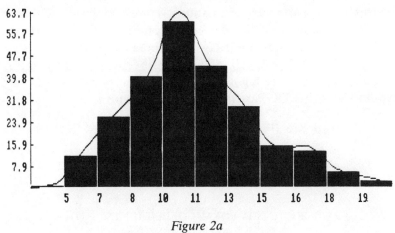

Figure 2a

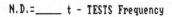

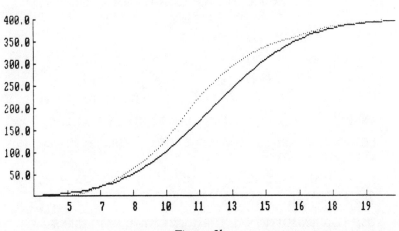

Figure 2b

The second example is a classroom demonstration of simultaneity bias in OLS and its relative absence in GIVE (Generalized Instrumental Variables Estimation), contrasting this with their relative variances. Consider the complete DGP with two endogenous variables, their lags and three exogenous regressors, denoted YA, YB, ZA, ZB, and ZC, respectively, with a suffix 1 denoting a first-order lag. Option 7 in the output menu (Table 2) would show this DGP as in the third tabulation.

COEFFICIENTS OF STRUCTURE: $By(t) + Cy(t-1) + Dz(t) = u(t)$

YA	YB	YA1	YB1	ZA	ZB	ZC
−1.00	.50	.50	.00	.00	1.00	.00
−0.40	−1.00	.00	.75	1.00	.00	1.00

REDUCED FORM COEFFICIENTS: $y(t)$
$$= \Pi(1)y(t-1) + \Pi(2)z(t) + v(t)$$

YA1	YB1	ZA	ZB	ZC
.42	.31	.42	.83	.42
−.17	.63	.83	−.33	.83

AUTOCORRELATIONS AND SDs of Z's:

ZA	ZB	ZC
.75	.50	.50
1.00	1.00	1.00

Z's ARE STOCHASTIC: CORRELATION $(ZB, ZC) = .80000$

CORRELATION (ERRORS Generating ZB;
ERRORS Generating ZC) = .80000

ERROR PROCESS is $u(t) = Ru(t-1) + e(t)$

$\text{CORR}(e(1, t), e(2, t)) = -0.5$

$$R = \begin{bmatrix} .000 & .000 \\ .000 & .000 \end{bmatrix} \qquad \begin{matrix} \text{SD1} = 1.000 \\ \text{SD2} = 1.000 \end{matrix}$$

400 REPLICATIONS WITH INITIAL RANDOM NUMBER = 1306

EQUATIONS ARE ESTIMATED USING 50 OBSERVATIONS and 0 FORECASTS

MAIN MODEL IS YA ON   YB YA1 ZB CNST

WITH YB ENDOGENOUS FOR TSLS

USING AS ADDITIONAL INSTRUMENTAL VARIABLES
YB1 ZA ZC

Hence we have a model in which $YB1$, ZA, and ZC are excluded from the first equation defining YA (so it is overidentified) while ZB is excluded from the equation for YB, but nevertheless ZB and ZC are highly correlated. This stationary DGP was replicated 400 times using both OLS and GIVE, with the two estimation methods being applied to the same random numbers to minimize the variance of interestimator comparisons. Asymptotic data moments were computed together with the plims of the estimators and their SEs, and these produce the following output. Although the mean of the data process is zero, a constant was included in the estimated equation. Note how the asymptotic values immediately indicate the likely severity and direction of bias in OLS to be expected in the numerical simulations for reasonable sample sizes, but the asymptotic SEs are inconsistent for the SDs of the limiting distributions (as in the fourth tabulation).

ASYMPTOTIC ANALYSIS

MODEL 1 OLS:		YA ON	YB	YA1		ZB	CNST
Population Statistics:			R^2 = .8986			σ = 0.9489	
Betas:	.3673	.5558	.9969	.0000			
SEs:	.0589	.0551	.1269	.1212			

MODEL 1 GIVES		YA ON	YB	YA1		ZB	CNST
Population Statistics:			R^2 = .8874			σ = 1.0000	
Betas:	.5000	.5000	1.0000	.0000			
SEs:	.0690	.0594	.1337	.1277			

The experiment took approximately 3.4 sec per replication, which is less than double the time taken for the first example despite there now being both two estimators and four regressors involved. This highlights the costs incurred in generating random normal variates and the pure efficiency gains in using the same random numbers for both estimators independently of the lower variance obtained for interestimator comparisons. As in the first example, we can obtain histograms of the distributions of the estimated parameters of both estimators, along with the associated distributions of the t statistics, but here we simply tabulate (in Table 3) the summary results (for the primary equation of interest, YA).

Table 3

DIRECT SIMULATION—ANALYSES OF BIAS

	OLS			VARIABLE	GIVE			
RMSE	SD	SE BIAS	BIAS		BIAS	SE BIAS	SD	RMSE
0.148	0.059	.0030	−0.136	YB	0.018	.0042	0.083	0.085
0.066	0.052	.0026	0.042	$YA1$	−0.007	.0032	0.063	0.064
0.129	0.125	.0063	0.031	ZB	0.010	.0070	0.141	0.141
0.152	0.152	.0076	−0.012	CNST	0.003	.0084	0.167	0.168

ANALYSIS OF REGRESSION t VALUES AROUND TRUE PARAMETER

	OLS			VARIABLE	GIVE		
H_0 REJ %	SD	MEAN			MEAN	SD	H_0 REJ %
0.5875	0.9927	−2.2222		YB	0.0556	1.0317	0.035
0.105	0.9502	0.7751		$YA1$	−0.0345	1.0056	0.04
0.04	0.9593	0.2205		ZB	0.0732	0.9993	0.05
0.035	0.9768	−0.0621		CNST	0.0084	0.9961	0.0425
—	0.0089	0.8921		σ	1.0125	0.0119	—

Having viewed PC-NAIVE in conventional mode, we turn next to the use of recursive procedures for improving its efficiency and the communicability of the results.

IV. RECURSIVE MONTE CARLO TECHNIQUES

The previous section deliberately isolated T from the rest of the parameter space θ, given the fundamental role which T (or perhaps $\sqrt{T}$) plays in MC work on finite sample distributions, especially in the estimation of response surfaces for the reduction of specificity. Frequently it would be desirable to formulate response surfaces based on many different values T_i for each selected point in θ. In conventional MC, this has typically required a separate experiment for each combination of T_i and θ_j which can be expensive (for example, $T_i = 25, 64, 100, 196$). Using a recursive estimation technique for $\hat{\alpha}$ then for any point θ_j we estimate α not just for the chosen sample of size T (equal to the largest sample entertained) but also for every intermediate sample size from the smallest sample size available i_0 (equal to the number of observations used to initialize the recursive algorithm) through to T, thus yielding $M = T - i_0 + 1$ outcomes. The cost of each experiment is increased, but for many applications this will be relatively negligible (e.g., about *two* experiments at T for OLS; see Section VI) and is much cheaper than conducting M separate conventional experiments—although one would not wish to adopt such a design outside of a recursive mode. While we only consider the class of *linear dynamic simultaneous equations estimators* (and test statistics derived therefrom), it should be possible to extend the recursive estimator to other classes of model, such as the *estimator-generating equation* class (discussed in Hendry, 1976).

Although random number generators may be good at producing rectangularly distributed random variates, successive values of such numbers may be correlated. For the multiplicative congruential generator

$$\xi_i = a\xi_{i-1}(\text{modulo } m), \tag{14}$$

so that ξ_i is the remainder when $a\xi_{i-1}$ is divided by m; then an approximate result due to Greenberger (1961/62) shows that the correlation between successive numbers generated by (14) lies between the bounds

$$E(\xi_i, \xi_{i-1}) \approx \frac{1}{a} - \frac{6}{am}\left(1 - \frac{1}{m}\right) \pm \frac{a}{m}. \tag{15}$$

This intercorrelation applies to all MC work whether conventional or recursive, but in conventional MC choosing different "seeds" to start the generator (14) helps ensure independence across experiments.

In a recursive framework, it may be objected that the technique cannot produce results from M separate experiments since while the numbers used are random they are not independent over T_i for a given θ_j (cf. the discussion of common random numbers in Hendry, 1985), although they will be independent for a given T_i, or over T_i, across θ_j and θ_k (assuming different seeds are used in different experiments). In the present context, however, this is not a problem and in fact acts as a variance-reducing technique.

For given θ_j, the main interest is in the properties of the estimators/test statistics as T_i varies. By using the same stream of random numbers as T_i varies, the estimate of the effect $T_j - T_i$ $(j > i)$ will have lower variance than if separate independent streams of random numbers are used. The difference between two unbiased estimates remains an unbiased estimate of the difference, even if the estimates are dependent, but the variance of the estimated difference will be smaller if there is positive dependence: if sampling variation leads to over(under)estimation in the first estimate, the dependence leads to a similar over(under)estimation in the second estimate. The effect of moving from T_i to T_j is not swamped by gross sampling variation in T_i and T_j, as it might be if separate streams of random numbers were used. Thus, positive dependence can be beneficial. An analogy can be drawn here with the common practice, when studying two or more estimators, of using the same data to analyze all the different estimators in order to increase the precision of interestimator comparisons.

Any gains which recursive estimation procedures offer apply to all models obtainable from the DGP including most types of misspecifications, as well as the properties of test statistics to detect such misspecifications. Also, with the use of recursive procedures, "post-estimation-sample forecast tests" are virtually redundant since forecast test statistics can now be computed recursively for any desired length of forecast within the sample T. These are issues which could have been studied in a conventional MC, albeit at a greater cost than recursive MC offers. The latter, however, also allows us to consider problems which conventional techniques can only handle very poorly (i.e., those which would typically involve considerably more specificity and uncertainty). One obvious example is the performance of estimators and tests when a "structural break" occurs in the DGP. At its broadest interpretation, a "structural break" means introducing parameter variation into the DGP, from a simple "blip" effect in a coefficient of the DGP (such that at one point in the sample a coefficient changes value and subsequently reverts to its former value) through similar step and trend changes in coefficients, parameter variation schemes of the random walk form, as well as nonlinear parameter changes over time, for evaluating the usefulness of linear models as local approximations to nonlinear DGPs. Indeed, the study of parameter variation was the sine qua non of early work with recursive least squares (RLS) estimators (Brown et al., 1975), and it is only natural to extend this to recursive MC.

From the teaching perspective, allied to the use of graphic computer techniques, recursive procedures provide instant classroom demonstrations of properties of estimators and tests, either under correct or incorrect specifications, as T varies from very small to fairly large, including possibly the asymptotic outcomes. This is the feature which will probably commend them most strongly in practice.

V. RECURSIVE ESTIMATION ALGORITHMS

While the method of RLS is well known and has been popularized by (inter alia) Phillips and Harvey (1974) and Brown et al. (1975), RLS has previously been suggested primarily for the analysis of specific problems such as serial correlation (cf. Phillips and Harvey, 1974); parameter stability (Brown et al., 1975); and functional form misspecification (Harvey and Collier, 1977). Here, we derive recursive MC procedures as a general replacement for full sample estimation and, to guard against rounding-error accumulation, suggest a more direct technique for updating parameter estimates than is typically used. An extension of recursive estimation to GIVE is also provided (denoted RIV), which offers similar computational advantages to those provided by RLS.[4]

The recursive estimators are based on the matrix inversion lemma (see, for example, Harvey, 1984):

We let $D = [A + B' C B]^{-1}$; then by using $DD^{-1} = I$ it may be verified that

$$D = A^{-1} - A^{-1}B' H^{-1} BA^{-1}, \tag{16}$$

where

$$H = [C^{-1} + B A^{-1} B'] \tag{17}$$

for nonsingular matrices A and C of order k and m, respectively, and where B is $k * m$. Thus, we update the inverse of a cross-product matrix $(X'_{T-1}X_{T-1})^{-1}$ by adding one further observation to form $(X'_T X_T)^{-1}$, where X_T is of dimension $(T * k)$ so that

$$(X'_T X_T) = \sum_{t=1}^{T} x_t x'_t = (X'_{T-1}X_{T-1}) + x_T x'_T \tag{18}$$

and x'_t denotes the $(1 * k)$ vector comprising the tth row of X_T. Then in (16), A becomes $(X'_{T-1}X_{T-1})$; B is the vector x_T; C is the unit scalar; and D is $(X'_T X_T)^{-1}$. Thus,

$$(X'_T X_T)^{-1} = (X'_{T-1}X_T - 1)^{-1} - \frac{\phi_T \phi'_T}{1 + \phi'_T x_T}, \tag{19}$$

where

$$\phi_T = (X'X)^{-1}_{T-1} x_T.$$

Once an initial inverse has been computed on, say, the first i_0 observations to yield $(X'_{i_0}X_{i_0})^{-1}$, adding a further observation requires only k scalar divisions and $k(2k + 1)$ multiplication operations to form the new inverse, $(X'_{i_0+1}X_{i_0+1})^{-1}$, with *no further matrix inversion*; this process may be applied recursively until all observations have been included. As noted, for econometric estimators this result has been applied to the OLS estimator by a number of authors. However, its applicability extends to GIVE. We denote the general linear model by

$$y = W\delta + u, \tag{20}$$

where y is a $T * 1$ vector of observations on the dependent variable such that T is the largest sample size desired in the case of MC or the largest available for empirical research. Similarly, W is a $T * n$ full rank matrix of observations on n explanatory variables such that w_t is the $1 * n$ vector corresponding to the tth row of

W; δ is $n * 1$ vector of coefficients; and u is a $T * 1$ vector of stochastic disturbances distributed normally with zero mean and constant variance σ_u^2. Now W and δ may be partitioned conformably as

$$W = [Y : X] \quad \text{and} \quad \delta' = [\alpha' : \beta'], \quad (21)$$

where Y is a $T * m$ matrix of endogenous variables, and X is a $T * k$ matrix of at least weakly exogenous regressors (see Engle et al., 1983), with corresponding parameter vectors α and β of dimension $m * 1$ and $k * 1$, respectively. A $T * p$ matrix of instruments V is required additional to those in X (so that there are no redundancies) such that $p > m$ and the $T * (k + p)$ matrix Z can be partitioned as

$$Z = [X : V]. \quad (22)$$

If we take the RLS case first ($\alpha = 0$), recursions proceed from an initial estimate based on the first i observations ($k + 1 \leq i \leq T$):

$$\hat{\beta}_i = (X_i'X_i)^{-1}X_i'y_i, \quad (23)$$

where X_i denotes the matrix X, comprising the first i observations only, and y_i denotes the vector of i observations on the dependent variable so that

$$X_i'y_i = \sum_{j=1}^{i} x_y'y_j = \sum_{j=1}^{i-1} x_j'y_j + x_i'y_i. \quad (24)$$

Here y_i is the ith component of the vector y_T. The product $X_i'y_i$ is updated at $i + 1$, $i + 2$, etc. exactly as $X_T'y_T$ would be to compute OLS estimates on the full sample (except that intermediate estimates are now used), and each technique requires one call to a matrix inversion routine so there is an equivalent computational burden between OLS and RLS in computing these terms. If i is too close to $k + 1$, then $\det|X_i'X_i|$ may be close to zero and inversion will be inaccurate, so an initialization period of $k + 10$, say,[5] is advisable.

The inverse matrix is updated via the matrix inversion lemma described above. Forming $(X_T'X_T)$ for OLS involves Tk^2 operations,[6] whereas updating $(X_j'X_j)^{-1}$ for RLS involves $2k^2 + k$ operations for each j, where $j = i + 1, \ldots, T$. Thus, the additional burden for RLS varies inversely with the choice of i but is of the order of two OLS regressions. In practice, as users of PC-GIVE have found, the time delay is often unnoticeable: heuristically, one method updates $(X'X)$ and then inverts, whereas the other inverts and then updates.

To form $\hat{\beta}_j$ given $(X'_j X_j)^{-1}$ and $X'_j y_j$ requires a further k^2 operation $(j = i, \ldots, T)$, and thus to directly form RLS parameter estimates by this method imposes $(T - i)k^2$ operations more than OLS. For example, if $T = 100$, $k = 10$, and $i = 20$, the cost increase of RLS over OLS is a little over 50%, but instead of obtaining one estimate of the vector β based on the full sample, one obtains $T - i + 1 = 81$ sequences of estimates, $\tilde{\beta}$, which is a large increase in information. Similar considerations apply to estimates of sequences of residual sums of squares, which are available virtually costlessly, and, *if they are computed*, sequences of parameter and equation standard errors, and other test statistics for autocorrelation, heteroscedasticity, parameter stability, etc. However, the latter will increase computational time.[7]

Recursive estimates are usually updated by

$$\hat{\beta}_{i+1} = \hat{\beta}_i + \frac{\phi_{i+1} \nu_{i+1}}{1 + x_{i+1}\phi_{i+1}} \tag{25}$$

where ν_{i+1} is the innovation in going from i to $i + 1$:

$$\nu_{i+1} = y_{i+1} - x'_{i+1}\hat{\beta}_i, \tag{26}$$

which only imposes $2(T - i)k$ operations more than OLS. However, Eqs. (25) and (26) allow rounding error to build up more rapidly than the direct method of updating (23) described earlier. Using that technique in PC-GIVE produces estimates of β_T which are equal to 10 decimal places to those of OLS in most problems, using double-precision arithmetic in both cases. The form in (25) would also require storing the parameter estimates in double precision for accuracy, whereas the "brute force" method permits storage in single precision, a useful consideration given present memory constraints on MS-DOS microcomputers.

Let us move now to consider recursive GIVE estimators. While there are going to be similarities to RLS, the estimator

$$\hat{\delta}_T = [X'_T Z_T (Z'_T Z_T)^{-1} Z'_T X_T]^{-1} X'_T Z_T (Z'_T Z_T)^{-1} Z'_T y_T \tag{27}$$

is not in a convenient form for recursive updating of $[X'_j Z_j (Z'_j Z_j)^{-1} Z'_j X_j]^{-1}$ compared to recursive updating in (19). Note that C in (17) is no longer a scalar; it cannot be set to

$Z_j(Z_j'Z_j)^{-1}Z_j'$ (which is singular), and using $B = Z_j'X_j$ in (14) would involve the expensive inversion of a $k * k$ matrix at each j. However, $(Z_j'Z_j)^{-1}$ is updated easily in a manner analogous to $(X_j'X_j)^{-1}$ for RLS, and $(X_j'X_j)$ is the upper-left-hand submatrix of $(Z_j'Z_j)$.

One solution to finding a recursive GIVE estimator would be to compute reduced form coefficients separately for the full sample and, using these, to construct instruments for a second-stage regression that proceeds recursively in an identical fashion to RLS. This would not produce GIVE estimates for each subsample size, however, as the instruments would contain information based on the whole sample not used in the GIVE estimator, although the two estimators would coincide at the final full sample point. While such an estimator might be of interest in its own right, we now derive a fully recursive estimator identical to GIVE in subsamples, so that recursive MC techniques can compare the properties of different estimators at every sample size.

First, we rewrite the estimator in (27) as, say,

$$\hat{\delta}_j = \begin{bmatrix} Y_j'Z_j(Z_j'Z_j)^{-1}Z_j'Y_j & Y_j'X_j \\ X_j'Y_j & X_j'X_j \end{bmatrix}^{-1} \begin{bmatrix} Y_j'Z_j(Z_j'Z_j)^{-1}Z_j'y_j \\ X_j'y_j \end{bmatrix} \quad (28)$$

$$= \Omega_j^{-1}\Phi_j,$$

based on $i \le j \le T$ observations. The matrix to be inverted, Ω_j, can be rewritten in partitioned form:

$$\Omega_j = \begin{bmatrix} P_j & R_j \\ R_j' & Q_j \end{bmatrix}, \quad (29)$$

where P_j is of dimension $m * m$; R_j is $m * k$; and Q_j is $k * k$. Then, by partitioned inversion:

$$\Omega_j^{-1} = \begin{bmatrix} H_j^{-1} & \vdots & -H_j^{-1}R_jQ_j^{-1} \\ -Q_j^{-1}R_j'H_j^{-1} & \vdots & Q_j^{-1} + Q_j^{-1}R_j'H_j^{-1}R_jQ_j^{-1} \end{bmatrix}, \quad (30)$$

where $H_j = (P_j - R_jQ_j^{-1}R_j')$.

At all observations $(i \le j \le T)$ this formulation requires the inversion of Q_j, that is, the inversion of $(X_j'X_j)$, but this can be achieved in the same manner as for RLS. Also, the inversion of $(P_j - R_jQ_j^{-1}R_j')$ is of dimension $m * m$, and thus is likely to be small. Indeed, for the DGP in PC-NAIVE, H_j will be a *scalar* and hence is very cheap to invert! Moreover, $(Z_j'Z_j)^{-1}$ is a component of P_j, and this term may be updated either by direct application of the matrix inversion lemma or by partitioned inversion (by virtue of $[X_j'X_j]$, whose inverse is already computed, being a subcomponent of $[Z_j'Z_j]$). Thus, direct application of the matrix inversion lemma involves only a few more operations and little extra storage.

Despite some computational demands for computing Ω_j^{-1}, most of the terms required for forming Φ_j are available, other than $Z_j'Y_j$ and its subcomponent $X_j'Y_j$, which are anyway cheap to update recursively, as discussed in (24), above. Then $\hat{\delta}_j$ may be obtained by repeated application of (16) for all j ($i \le j \le T$). We have found in practice that full sample estimates of δ_T by RIV are equal to those obtained from GIVE to at least the first four decimal places. However, RIV is noticeably slower, as one might expect, because of updating (in effect) both the reduced form and the structural $\hat{\delta}_j$. Finally, for recursive estimates of parameter and equation standard errors, the sequences of residual sums of squares (RSS) are required and can be obtained by recomputing the residuals for all observations as $\hat{\delta}_j$ changes, although this is relatively expensive:

$$\text{RSS}_j = (y_j - W_j\hat{\delta}_j)'(y_j - W_j\hat{\delta}_j). \tag{31}$$

In conventional MC analysis of econometric estimators and test statistics, the main interest is in the first two moments of the simulation results, which are computed over the N replications per experiment. With recursive MC, the focus becomes the first two moments at each of the T_i observations per replication. These can be obtained by also using recursive updating formulas for the simulation mean and SD (analogously for other moments)

$$\mu_{i+1} = (i+1)^{-1}[i\mu_i + \pi_{i+1}] \tag{32}$$

for the mean μ of a variable π, and for the SD

$$\sigma_{i+1}^2 = ([i-1]/i)\sigma_i^2 + (i+1)^{-1}[\pi_{i+1} - \mu_i]^2. \tag{33}$$

Interestingly, control variables also have recursive forms which could be used at each subsample. We let $M_{xx} = E(x_tx_t')$; then

$$\tilde{\tilde{\beta}}_t = \tilde{\tilde{\beta}}_{t-1} + M_{xx}^{-1}x_t\nu_t \tag{34}$$

(where ν_t is the equation error) is a control variable for RLS, and equivalent formulae 5 follow for RIV. The cost of calculating (34) is trivial.

VI. PC-NAIVE IN RECURSIVE MODE

We now reconsider the two MC experiments of Section III using the recursive simulation option in PC-NAIVE. The first experiment, involving a first-order autoregressive model with 60 observations and 400 replications is rerun using the RLS estimator, starting from the same random number seed and retaining the first 15 observations in each replication to initialize the algorithm. The full sample estimates (i.e., for $T = 60$) are virtually identical to those already reported, but we can exploit graphic techniques to consider the properties of the estimator for all T ($15 \le T \le 60$). Whereas the OLS estimator in Section III took 2 sec per replication, RLS increases the average time per replication to 2.9 sec, which is relatively cheap. Figure 3 graphs the estimated mean bias $\hat{E}(\hat{\alpha} - \alpha)$ in the estimator $\hat{\alpha}$ with $\pm 2\hat{\sigma}_{\hat{\alpha}}$ and $\pm 2\sigma_{\alpha}$ around the bias over the entire sample range $T = 15, \ldots, 60$ (where $\hat{\sigma}_{\hat{\alpha}}$ is the mean estimated SE). Although it must be remembered that every track is a sample statistic subject to MC variability, Figure 3 demonstrates four important features:

1. The persistent downward bias in $\hat{\alpha}$ at all available sample sizes

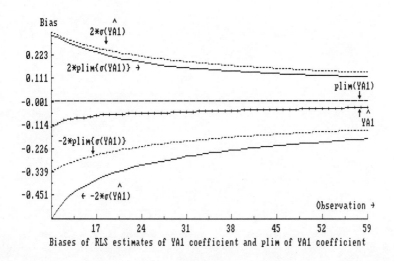

Biases of RLS estimates of YA1 coefficient and plim of YA1 coefficient

Figure 3

2. The decline in bias as T increases, although the relative size of $\hat{\sigma}_{\hat{\alpha}}$ somewhat camouflages this
3. The fall in $\hat{\sigma}_{\hat{\alpha}}$ as the sample size increases
4. The closeness of σ_{α} to its finite sample counterpart

As indicated in Section III, it is interesting to consider what happens to the estimator when a structural break occurs in the DGP, and with recursive procedures this becomes feasible. Thus, another experiment was run corresponding to that just described except that a "step" change was introduced into the DGP. From *sample sizes 30 to 39* the autoregressive parameter changes from $\alpha = 0.85$ by an amount of 0.15 to $\alpha = 1.0$; and at $T = 40, \ldots, 60$, α reverts to 0.85. Figure 4 graphs the bias of the estimator $\pm 2\hat{\sigma}_{\hat{\alpha}}$ and $\pm 2\sigma_{\alpha}$ (calculated for $\alpha = 0.85$). The bias diminishes from $T = 30$ (as expected with an increase in α in the DGP) and remains near zero even when α reverts to 0.85. The mean estimated SE also falls from the shock point and again remains near σ_{α}. Thus, the estimator seems relatively robust to this type of "on-off" structural change (at least in this experiment; further experiments at other points in the parameter space θ are needed to confirm or otherwise the extent of this phenomenon).

Next, we consider the power of alternative forms of Chow test to detect this structural change and evaluate three types. First, a

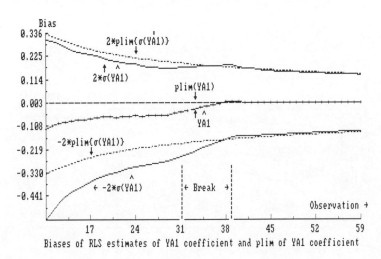

Biases of RLS estimates of YA1 coefficient and plim of YA1 coefficient

Figure 4

one-step-ahead test where at all available sequences $(T, T + 1)$ a Chow test of parameter constancy is calculated between the estimates based on the first T observations and those based on the first $T + 1$ observations. The number of times that the hypothesis of constancy is rejected (using the conventional single test 95% critical value) is recorded over the 400 replications. The second Chow test, denoted an $N\uparrow$ test, is calculated for constancy between the initial estimate (here based on $T = 15$ observations) and all subsequent sample sizes $(T = 16, \ldots, 60)$, and similarly records the number of rejections. These two tests are computed cheaply within the recursive estimation algorithm, based on the sequences of residual sums of squares. Thirdly, the $N\downarrow$ test evaluates the hypothesis that elements in the sequence of estimates of $\hat{\alpha}$ from $(T = 15, \ldots, 59)$ are equal to the estimate based on $T = 60$ observations. The number of rejections of constancy of these tests is very low for the structural break under study (around 7.5%), with little to choose between the one-step, $N\uparrow$ and $N\downarrow$ tests.

Only one point in the parameter space ($\alpha = 0.85$) was considered here, and further work is required on the properties of estimators and tests in the presence of structural breaks (including other blip effects, step and trend changes in parameters, random walk parameters, the point in the sample at which they occur, etc.); the choice of a step change was illustrative rather than realistic to highlight some of the additional information to be gleaned from using recursive MC techniques.

Returning to the second example of Section III, the simultaneous equations model, reveals further insights recursive techniques can yield. We concentrate on the biases of the two estimators recursive least squares (RLS) and recursive instrumental variables (RIV) as the sample size varies, and focus on the coefficients of YB and $YA1$. Replicating the experiment as in Section III, except for the use of RLS and RIV estimators (retaining the first 20 observations in each replication to initialize the algorithms), the graphic output from PC-NAIVE is shown in Figures 5–8. In Section III the mean time taken per replication was 3.4 sec, and now, using RLS and RIV, this has increased to 5.9 sec per replication. This is somewhat higher than the time increase incurred in the first example above, but it is relatively cheap considering the extra information obtained: compare the cost of having to run a further 30 separate conventional experiments to get equivalent output.

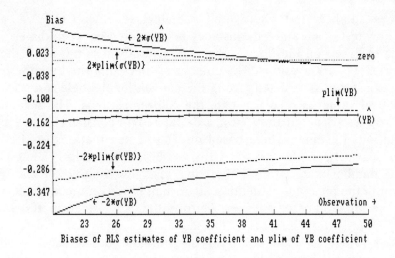

Biases of RLS estimates of YB coefficient and plim of YB coefficient

Figure 5

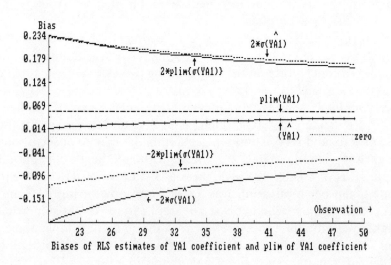

Biases of RLS estimates of YA1 coefficient and plim of YA1 coefficient

Figure 6

118

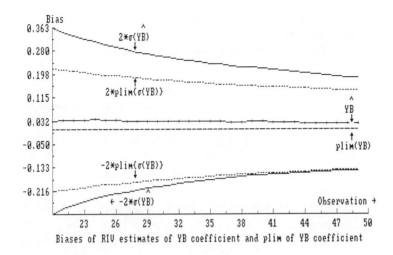

Biases of RIV estimates of YB coefficient and plim of YB coefficient

Figure 7

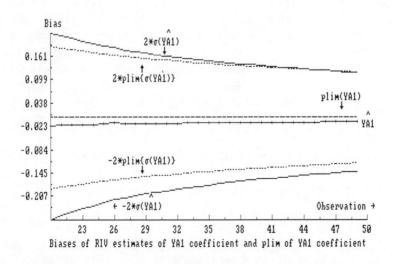

Biases of RIV estimates of YA1 coefficient and plim of YA1 coefficient

Figure 8

119

Figure 5 plots the sequence as T increases of the mean OLS bias in the estimate of the YB coefficient along with both $\pm 2\hat{\sigma}$ and the plim of the estimate and twice its asymptotic standard error (recalibrated to T). Figure 6 is the equivalent plot for the $YA1$ coefficient, while in Figures 7 and 8 the equivalent outcomes for the RIV estimator are plotted noting that in live examples the figures would distinguish lines by color. For the purposes of classroom demonstration, we believe that such illustrations are very helpful. Figures 5 and 6 demonstrate the extent of OLS bias, the fact that this bias does not decline much as the sample size increases but nevertheless the parameters remain constant, and the remarkable accuracy of the plims in predicting both the extent of the bias and the size of the SEs for all but the smallest sample sizes. Except for points close to nonstationarity, such a phenomenon often occurs. By comparison, Figures 7 and 8 show very little estimated bias when using RIV; note that this does decline with sample size, and again there is a close correspondence between both the mean estimates of the parameters and their plims and the mean estimates of the SEs and their plims (again, except at the smallest sample size).

Program PC-NAIVE also allows us to look at these features from a different perspective. We can plot the mean OLS bias and twice the mean SE of the YB coefficient along with the equivalent statistics estimated by RIV. This is shown in Figure 9, while Figure 10 produces the same analysis for the $YA1$ coefficient. The main addition to the interpretation provided by Figures 5–8 is that the RIV parameter SEs are distinctly larger than those for OLS so that the OLS parameter estimate may often fall within two RIV parameter SEs, although such features will be dependent on the DGP. Further, Figures 9 and 10 also highlight that the mean RIV parameter bias declines as the sample size increases whereas that for the OLS does not.

The final example is a topical follow-up to the Banerjee et al. (1986) MC study of biases in static estimates of cointegrating regression. The DGP is

$$y_{1t} = 0.1y_{2t} + 0.9y_{1t-1} + \varepsilon_{1t}, \qquad \varepsilon(\varepsilon_{it}^2) = 1, \qquad (35)$$

$$y_{2t} = \qquad 1.0y_{2t-1} + \varepsilon_{2t}, \qquad \varepsilon(\varepsilon_{it}\varepsilon_{js}) = 0 \qquad \forall\, t, s. \quad (36)$$

Thus, the long-run result is $y_1 = y_2$ and the static equation is the

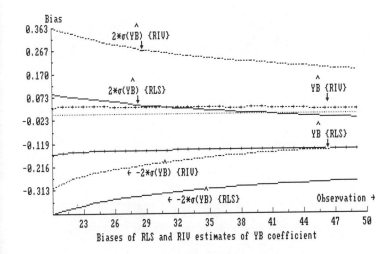

Figure 9

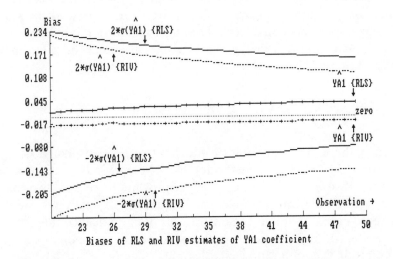

Figure 10

121

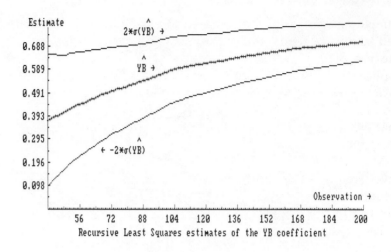

Figure 11

stochastic analog $y_{1t} = \gamma y_{2t} + U_t$. The RLS track of $\hat{\gamma}$ from $T = 40$ to 200 based on 400 replications (each of which took 6.2 sec on average) is shown in Figure 11. The SE lines in this illustration are a poor reflection of the current uncertainty in $\hat{\gamma}$, and later versions of PC-NAIVE will use the sampling standard deviation instead, based on (32) and (33). Nevertheless, the very slow convergence of $\hat{\gamma}$ to unity is obvious, as is the large downward bias at all the sample sizes considered. The analytical formulas in Banerjee et al. (1986) predict this type of outcome, although those authors only simulated three values of T.

VII. CONCLUSION

Clearly there are many other topics that could be pursued using recursive Monte Carlo methodology. The previous section was merely illustrative of the approach and of the increased information available from a single experiment for a relatively small increase in cost. For live demonstrations of numerical counterparts of asymptotic theoretical results and of the possible uses of asymptotic theory in finite samples, the recursive mode has many advantages. Combined with automatic graphing of outcomes over sample size variations, many interesting finite sample phenomena can be illustrated. Moreover, since across-replication phenomena are not then of primary interest, a relatively small number of replications is needed so that long elapsed times are avoidable. Where greater accuracy is important, the additional cost of recursion remains small in relation to the information provided, given that the focus of small sample studies of econometric methods is variation over sample size.

Moreover, recursive methods have a comparative advantage for investigating such problems as parameter change of the rejection frequencies of sequences of tests where power functions (over T) can be directly graphed.

The recursive calculations can be blended with traditional variance reduction methods and, as noted, when the population moments are available, with control variables; CVs can be calculated recursively for virtually no additional cost, but the computer programming is nontrivial and has not been implemented in PC-NAIVE to date! However, when combined with interactive editing, and three-dimensional graphics of changes in frequency distributions over T, recursive computation afforced by variance reduction methods offer an appealing prospect for exploiting the next generation of microcomputers.

Computation time for the range of problems so far studied has been roughly proportional to sample size, with less than twice as much time needed for recursive than for direct computation, and less than proportional to the number of methods or included regressors. These provide reasonable guidelines for the design of experiments for demonstrations. Finally, the efficiency of an interactive Monte Carlo program is also high for rapid exploration of a parameter space in a pilot study, where relatively few replications are required per experiment (especially if asymptotic outcomes are known) to highlight interesting regions for more detailed analyses.

ACKNOWLEDGMENTS

This research has been financed in part by the ESRC under grant B0022012. Developments to PC-NAIVE have been supported by the ESRC over many years including under grant HR8789 and the programme has benefited from valuable contributions from Robin W. Harrison, Frank Srba, and Neil R. Ericsson; PC-NAIVE is part of the AUTOREG Library.

NOTES

1. PC-GIVE Copyright © David F. Hendry, 1986, for Generalized Instrumental Variables Estimation and PC-NAIVE (© David F. Hendry and Adrian J. Neale, 1986) are part of the AUTOREG Library (see Hendry and Srba, 1980).

2. IBM is the registered trademark of the International Business Machines Corporation.

3. For convenience and simplicity we adopt the example considered in Hendry (1984).

4. After the time of writing the authors became aware of an RIV estimator introduced by Phillips (1977).

5. A second complication that we ignore here concerns the presence of dummy variables which may require special treatment if the indicator is always off—or always on in the presence of a constant in the sample up to i.

6. Operations count multiplication and division but discount the relatively cheap ADD and MOV operations.

7. The recursive computation of parameter and equation SEs is cheap since all the main variables are already available and the residual sum of squares (RSS) is cheaply updated via the innovations.

REFERENCES

Banerjee, A., J. J. Dolado, D. F. Hendry, and C. W. Smith (1986) "Exploring Equilibrium Relationships in Econometrics Through Static Model: Some Monte Carlo Evidence." *Oxford Bulletin of Economics and Statistics* 48, 253-277.

Brown, R. L., J. Durbin, and J. M. Evans (1975) "Techniques for Testing the Constancy of Regression Relationships Over Time (with Discussion)." *Journal of the Royal Statistical Society, Series B* 37, 149-192.

Dickey, D. A. and W. A. Fuller (1979) "Distribution of the Estimators for Autoregressive Time Series with a Unit Root." *Journal of the American Statistical Association* 74, 427-431.

Engle, R. F. and C. W. J. Granger (1987) "Cointegration and Error Correction: Representation, Estimation and Testing." Discussion paper, University of California, San Diego; to appear in *Econometrica.*

Engle, R. F., D. F. Hendry, and J.-F. Richard (1983) "Exogeneity," *Econometrica* 51, 277-304.

Engle, R. F., D. F. Hendry, and D. Trumbull (1985) "Small Sample Properties of ARCH Statistics and Tests." *Canadian Journal of Economics* 18(1), 66–93.

Ericsson, N. R. (1983) "Asymptotic Properties of Instrumental Variables Statistics for Testing Non-nested Hypotheses." *Reivew of Economic Studies* 50, 287–304.

Fuller, W. A. (1976) *Introduction to Statistical Time Series.* New York: Wiley.

Granger, C. W. J. (1986) "Recent Developments in Cointegration." *Oxford Bulletin of Economics and Statistics* 48, 213–228.

Greenberger, M. (1961/62) "An *a priori* Determination of Serial Correlation in Computer-Generated Random Numbers." *Mathematical Computing* 15, 383–389; and corrigenda, ibid. 16, 126.

Hammersley, J. M. and D. C. Handscomb (1964) *Monte Carlo Methods.* London: Methuen.

Harvey, A. C. (1984) *Times Series Models.* Oxford: Philip Allan Publishers.

Harvey, A. C. and P. Collier (1977) "Testing for Functional Misspecification in Regression Analysis." *Journal of Econometrics* 6, 103–119.

Hendry, D. F. (1976) "The Structure of Simultaneous Equations Estimators." *Journal of Econometrics* 4, 51–88.

Hendry, D. F. (1982) "A Reply to Professors Maasoumi and Phillips." *Journal of Econometrics* 19, 203–213.

Hendry, D. F. (1984) "Monte Carlo Experimentation in Econometrics." In Z. Griliches and M. D. Intriligator (eds.), *Handbook of Econometrics*, Vol. 2. Amsterdam and New York: North-Holland Publishing.

Hendry, D. F. (1987) *Users Manual for* PC-GIVE, *Version 4.2.* Oxford, England: Oxford Institute of Economics and Statistics.

Hendry, D. F. and F. Srba (1980) "AUTOREG: A Computer Program Library for Dynamic Econometric Models with Autoregressive Errors." *Journal of Econometrics* 12, 85–102.

Maasoumi, E. and P. C. B. Phillips (1982) "On the Behaviour of Inconsistent Instrumental Variable Estimators." *Journal of Econometrics* 19, 183–201.

Mazzarino, G. (1986) "Fitting of Distribution Curves to Grouped Data." *Oxford Bulletin of Economics and Statistics* (Practitioners Corner) 48(2), 189–200.

Phillips, G. D. A. (1977) "Recursions for the Two-Stage Least-Squares Estimators." *Journal of Econometrics* 6, 65–77.

Phillips, G. D. A. and A. C. Harvey (1974) "A Simple Test for Serial Correlation in Regression Analysis." *Journal of the American Statistical Association* 69, 935–939.

Sowey, E. R. (1973) "A Classified Bibliography of Monte Carlo Studies in Econometrics." *Journal of Econometrics* 1, 377–395.

MODELING MULTICOLLINEARITY
AND EXTRAPOLATION IN
MONTE CARLO EXPERIMENTS
ON REGRESSION

R. Carter Hill

I. INTRODUCTION

This paper examines two aspects of designing Monte Carlo experiments when the purpose of the Monte Carlo is to study properties of estimators for linear and nonlinear regression models. The first aspect considered is multicollinearity. Specifically, what are the alternative ways of representing multicollinear design matrices and what are the implications of each choice for both linear and nonlinear regression models? The second aspect treated is important for the evaluation of the predictive properties of regression

Advances in Econometrics, Volume 6, pages 127–155
Copyright © 1987 by JAI Press Inc.
All rights of reproduction in any form reserved.
ISBN: 0-89232-795-2

estimators. That is, how does extrapolation affect the accuracy of various predictors? Extrapolation in this context means the multivariate analog of moving away from the sample mean values in a simple linear regression model. Measures of extrapolation are defined that include not only distance between in-sample and out-of-sample data ellipsoids but also rotation and elongation, which allow for changes in collinearity patterns.

The plan of the paper is as follows: In Section II the question of what is multicollinearity in linear models is explored in some detail. Part of this discussion is an inquiry into the debate surrounding centering and/or scaling the data. In Section III the lessons of Section II are applied to designing procedures for modeling multicollinearity in the linear regression model. In Section IV the question of what is multicollinearity in nonlinear models is considered. Section V contains an analysis of how multicollinearity affects prediction both within sample and out-of-sample, which forms a basis for designing Mone Carlo experiment to study the predictive ability of alternative rules. Section VI summarizes the paper.

II. MULTICOLLINEARITY IN THE LINEAR STATISTICAL MODEL

Economists, like other scientists, use the scientific method and endeavor to obtain empirical evidence that either supports or refutes economic hypotheses that are obtained by a deductive process. Economic research, in general, and econometric research, in particular, are usually hampered, however, by an inability to carry out controlled experiments. Thus economists and other nonexperimental scientists may encounter more problems than are encountered by those who can perform controlled experiments. Examples of these problems include uncertainty about the error process, the relevant explanatory variables, and multicollinearity. Multicollinearity is associated with the fact that economists observe but do not set or control the values of the explanatory variables that produce or condition values of the dependent variable. More specifically, economic variables are often related in general ways, and a multicollinearity problem is said to exist when the statistical results are ambiguous because of interrelationships among the explanatory variables. The statistical ambiguity arises because, when explanatory variables have linear associations, their coefficients' estimates tend to have large sampling errors and thus the actual estimates may be far from the true parameter values. To see this, recall that a variable's coefficient is interpreted as the effect of a one-unit change in an independent variable on the dependent variable, all other things held constant. If, in a sample, variation in one or more other explanatory variables is closely linked, the resulting variation in the dependent variable cannot be accurately attributed to a specific source.

This situation is associated with the following negative consequences of least squares (LS) estimation: First, the direct result is that the separate effects of explanatory variables involved may not be estimated precisely and estimated coefficients may have incorrect signs or unreasonable magnitudes. Second, given the above, coefficients may not appear significantly different from zero and may be excluded from the analysis, not because the associated variable has no effect, but because the sample is inadequate to isolate it. This situation may occur despite possibly high R^2 or F values, indicating a model that fits the data well. Third, estimated coefficients may be sensitive to the addition or deletion of a few observations or the deletion of an apparently insignificant variable. All of these problems are common symptoms of multicollinearity and the large variances that the LS estimators of individual parameters may have as a result. In the following sections the concept of multicollinearity is defined more precisely. The reader will see that it is a slippery concept indeed.

Multicollinearity will now be defined and its statistical consequences investigated. Let the linear regression model be

$$\mathbf{y} = X\boldsymbol{\beta} + \mathbf{e}, \tag{2.0}$$

where $\mathbf{y}$ is a $(T \times 1)$ vector of observations; X is a nonstochastic $(T \times K)$ matrix of observations on explanatory variables; $\boldsymbol{\beta}$ is a $(K \times 1)$ vector of unknown regression coefficients; and $\mathbf{e}$ is a $(T \times 1)$ vector of normally and independently distributed random disturbances with zero means and constant variances σ^2. It will be useful to write $X = (\mathbf{x}_1, \mathbf{x}_2, \ldots, \mathbf{x}_K)$ where $\mathbf{x}_i$ is the ith column of X.

A. Exact or Perfect Multicollinearity

Exact or perfect multicollinearity is said to exist when the X matrix has rank less than K. This occurs when one or more exact relations exist among the columns of X. That is, there are one *or more* relations of the form

$$X\mathbf{c} = \mathbf{x}_1 c_1 + \mathbf{x}_2 c_2 + \cdots + \mathbf{x}_K c_K = \mathbf{0}, \qquad (2.1)$$

where $\mathbf{c} = (c_1, \ldots, c_K)'$ is a vector of constants c_i, not all of which are zero. Alternatively, assuming c_1 is not zero (if it is zero rearrange the column of X so it is not),

$$\mathbf{x}_1 = \mathbf{x}_2(-c_2/c_1) + \cdots + \mathbf{x}_K(-c_K/c_1)$$

so that the first variable can be written as an exact linear combination of the rest, and thus the columns of X are linearly dependent. This could happen, for example, if $T < K$, if too many dummy variables are included with an intercept, of if there are real, physical constraints relating the explanatory variables. An example of the latter case might be an output equation in which some of the inputs are always used in a fixed proportion. The case of perfect multicollinearity is easy to define but does not occur very often in practice. In the next subsection we consider the usual case where X is of full rank K but relations like (2.1) hold almost exactly.

B. Near Exact Multicollinearity and Auxiliary Regressions

We will now consider the case where the linear relationship between the columns of X is not an exact one, only nearly so, so that there exist one or more relations of the form

$$X\mathbf{c} = \mathbf{x}_1 c_1 + \mathbf{x}_2 c_2 + \cdots + \mathbf{x}_K c_K \doteq \mathbf{0}, \qquad (2.2)$$

where $\doteq$ means "almost equal to." Suppose $c_1 \neq 0$ so that

$$\mathbf{x}_1 \doteq \mathbf{x}_2(-c_2/c_1) + \mathbf{x}_3(-c_3/c_1) + \cdots + \mathbf{x}_K(-c_K/c_1) \qquad (2.3)$$

or

$$\mathbf{x}_1 = \mathbf{x}_2 d_2 + \mathbf{x}_3 d_3 + \cdots + \mathbf{x}_K d_K + \mathbf{v}_1, \qquad (2.4)$$

where $d_i = -c_i/c_1$, and $\mathbf{v}_1$ is just the difference between the left- and right-hand sides of (2.3). Relations like (2.4), where one regressor is written as a linear function of the other regressors plus the difference (or error), are called "auxiliary regressions" since they have the form of a regression equation. By examining (2.4) it should be intuitively clear that the better the fit of this auxiliary regression of x_1 on the other $(K - 1)$ regressors, the more nearly (2.2) holds and the more "severe" the multicollinearity. In fact, if (2.4) fit *exactly* [so that the sum of squared errors (SSE) is zero], then (2.2) would hold exactly, X would not have full rank and the multicollinearity would be perfect.

To make these notions precise so that we can pinpoint the statistical consequences of multicollinearity, let us make use of the following matrix result: Partition $X = (x_1 X_2)$, where x_1 is the first column of X (which might be any regressor by rearrangment of the columns of X) and X_2 contains the other $(K - 1)$ columns of X. If

$$N = I - X_2(X_2'X_2)^{-1}X_2',$$

then

$$(X'X)^{-1} = \frac{1}{x_1'Nx_1}$$

$$\times \begin{bmatrix} 1 & -x_1'X_2(X_2'X_2)^{-1} \\ -(X_2'X_2)^{-1}X_2'x_1 & x_1'Nx_1(X_2'X_2)^{-1} \\ & + (X_2'X_2)^{-1}X_2'x_1x_1'X_2(X_2'X_2)^{-1} \end{bmatrix}.$$

$$(2.5)$$

This result can be confirmed by multiplying $(X'X)^{-1}$ by

$$X'X = \begin{bmatrix} x_1'x_1 & x_1'X_2 \\ X_2'x_1 & X_2'X_2 \end{bmatrix}.$$

This result is useful because as noted in Section I the effect of multicollinearity is to make the sampling errors of the LS estimators large. If $b = (X'X)^{-1}X'y$ is the LS estimator then $cov(b) = \sigma^2(X'X)^{-1}$ measures the sampling variability of the LS estimator. If we use (2.5), the variance of b_1 is

$$var(b_1) = \frac{\sigma^2}{x_1'Nx_1}.$$

The term $x_1'Nx_1$ is the SSE from LS estimation of the auxiliary regression (2.4). To prove this, note that N is idempotent, so

$$x_1'Nx_1 = x_1'NNx_1$$
$$= (x_1 - \hat{x}_1)'(x_1 - \hat{x}_1) = \hat{v}_1'\hat{v}_1.$$

Where $\hat{\mathbf{v}}_1$ is a vector of LS residuals given by

$$\hat{\mathbf{v}}_1 = \mathbf{x}_1 - \hat{\mathbf{x}}_1 = \mathbf{x}_1 - X_2(X_2'X_2)^{-1}X_2'\mathbf{x}_1$$
$$= \mathbf{x}_1 - X_2\hat{\mathbf{d}}_1,$$

where $\hat{\mathbf{d}}_1 = (\hat{d}_2, \hat{d}_3, \ldots, \hat{d}_K)'$ is the vector of LS estimates of the coefficients in (2.4).

Consequently the variance of b_1 is

$$\text{var}(b_1) = \frac{\sigma^2}{\hat{\mathbf{v}}_1'\hat{\mathbf{v}}_1}, \tag{2.6}$$

which depends on σ^2 and the variation in $\mathbf{x}_1$ *not* explained by the linear influence of the other regressors. Thus the better the fit of the auxiliary regression (2.4) the larger $\text{var}(b_1)$, since the better the fit the smaller the SSE $\hat{\mathbf{v}}_1'\hat{\mathbf{v}}_1$.

The covariance between b_1 and the other LS estimators $b_2, \ldots, b_K$ are the remaining elements in the first column of $\sigma^2(X'X)^{-1}$. If we use (2.5) again, they are

$$\begin{bmatrix} \text{cov}(b_1, b_2) \\ \text{cov}(b_1, b_3) \\ \vdots \\ \text{cov}(b_1, b_K) \end{bmatrix} = \frac{-\sigma^2(X_2'X_2)^{-1}X_2'\mathbf{x}_1}{\mathbf{x}_1'N\mathbf{x}_1} = \frac{-\sigma^2\hat{\mathbf{d}}_1}{\hat{\mathbf{v}}_1'\hat{\mathbf{v}}_1}. \tag{2.7}$$

Thus $\text{cov}(b_1, b_j) = -\sigma^2\hat{d}_j/\hat{\mathbf{v}}_1'\hat{\mathbf{v}}_1$. The covariance between b_1 and b_j is larger (in absolute value) the greater the effect of x_j on x_1, as measured by $\hat{d}_j$, and the better the fit of the auxiliary regression.

The exposition above, using the notion of auxiliary regressions, is an intuitive one and clearly reveals the nature of the "multicollinearity problem." If $\mathbf{x}_1$ is a near-exact function of the other $(K-1)$ regressors, then the associated parameter β_1 will have an LS estimator whose variance is directly proportional to the severity of the multicollinearity as measured by $1/\hat{\mathbf{v}}_1'\hat{\mathbf{v}}_1$. And the larger the variance of b_1, and those of the LS estimators $b_2, \ldots, b_K$, the more likely the negative consequences listed in the introduction of Section II. This all fits together with the description in that introduction because the fit of the auxiliary regressions measures the degree of linear association between the explanatory variables.

C. Near-Exact Multicollinearity in the Principal Components Model

While the analysis of near-exact multicollinearity presented above is useful, it does not provide a framework for a complete and systematic analysis of multicollinearity and its effects. A more general framework is provided by considering a transformation of the regression model (2.0) into the principal components form of the model. This transformation is based on the characteristic vectors of the $X'X$ matrix.

Let P be the orthogonal $(K \times K)$ matrix whose columns, $\mathbf{p}_i$, are the characteristic vectors of $X'X$. Then

$$\mathbf{y} = X\boldsymbol{\beta} + \mathbf{e} = (XP)(P'\boldsymbol{\beta}) + \mathbf{e} = Z\boldsymbol{\theta} + \mathbf{e}, \qquad (2.8)$$

since $PP' = P'P = I$ (and where $Z = XP$, and $\boldsymbol{\theta} = P'\boldsymbol{\beta}$). The matrix Z is called the matrix of principal components. Its columns, $\mathbf{z}_i$, are linear combinations of the columns of X with the weights given by the elements of $\mathbf{p}_i$. That is, the ith principal component is

$$\mathbf{z}_i = X\mathbf{p}_i = \mathbf{x}_1 p_{1i} + \mathbf{x}_2 p_{2i} + \cdots + \mathbf{x}_K p_{Ki}, \qquad (2.9)$$

where p_{ji} is the element in the jth row and ith column of P. The principal components have the property that $\mathbf{z}_i'\mathbf{z}_i = \lambda_i$, where λ_i is the ith characteristic root of $X'X$. To see this, we let

$$\mathbf{z}_i'\mathbf{z}_i = \mathbf{p}_i'X'X\mathbf{p}_i = \mathbf{p}_i'(\lambda_i\mathbf{p}_i) = \lambda_i\mathbf{p}_i'\mathbf{p}_i = \lambda_i. \qquad (2.10)$$

Since $X'X\mathbf{p}_i = \lambda_i\mathbf{p}_i$, by the definition of characteristic roots and vectors and $\mathbf{p}_i'\mathbf{p}_i = 1$. Also $\mathbf{z}_i'\mathbf{z}_j = 0$, for $i \neq j$, since

$$\mathbf{z}_i'\mathbf{z}_j = \mathbf{p}_i'X'X\mathbf{p}_j = \mathbf{p}_i'(\lambda_j\mathbf{p}_j) = \lambda_j\mathbf{p}_i'\mathbf{p}_j = 0$$

because $\mathbf{p}_i'\mathbf{p}_j = 0$. Thus

$$Z'Z = (XP)'(XP) = P'X'XP$$

$$= \Lambda = \mathrm{diag}(\lambda_1, \lambda_2, \ldots, \lambda_K), \qquad (2.11)$$

where the diagonal matrix Λ contains the characteristic roots of $X'X$ on the diagonal, which as a convention are ordered so that $\lambda_1 \geq \lambda_2 \geq \ldots \geq \lambda_K$. The characteristic roots are real since $X'X$ is symmetric and are nonnegative since $X'X$ is positive semidefinite. The number of zero roots is equal to the number of exact linear dependencies among the columns of X, as we will see below. If X is of full rank K, then $X'X$ is positive definite and all the characteristic roots are positive. The LS estimator of $\boldsymbol{\theta}$ in the principal components model is

$$\hat{\theta} = (Z'Z)^{-1}Z'y = \Lambda^{-1}Z'y$$

has covariance matrix

$$\text{cov}(\hat{\theta}) = \sigma^2 \Lambda^{-1}.$$

Consequently,

$$\text{var}(\hat{\theta}_i) = \sigma^2/\lambda_i. \tag{2.12}$$

Thus the smaller the characteristic root λ_i, the less precisely the ith coefficient θ_i can be estimated. This is important because the size of the characteristic roots of $X'X$ relate directly to the multicollinearity problem. We also see that, in this transformed model, not all the θ_i's can be estimated equally well. Some may be associated with large λ_i's, and others with small ones. The latter then can be estimated only relatively imprecisely.

To see how the magnitude of the characteristic roots of $X'X$ relates to the multicollinearity problem, let us suppose that $\lambda_i = 0$ on the right side of (2.10). Then it must be true that

$$X\mathbf{p}_i = p_{1i}\mathbf{x}_1 + p_{2i}\mathbf{x}_2 + \cdots + p_{Ki}\mathbf{x}_K = 0. \tag{2.13}$$

Hence, if any λ_i is zero, we have identified a relation like that in (2.1) and perfect multicollinearity exists. If, instead, λ_i is a small nonnegative number, then (2.13) holds only approximately and the variance of $\hat{\theta}_i$ in (2.12) may be large. Thus the existence of some relatively small characteristic roots implies the existence of some near-exact relations like that in (2.2) and therefore implies that multicollinearity exists. Thus, in the transformed model, multicollinearity is completely revealed in the magnitudes of the characteristic roots of $X'X$. For every $\lambda_i = 0$, there is an exact linear dependency among the columns of X. For every $\lambda_i \doteq 0$ there is a near-exact linear dependency among the columns of X. It is extremely important to note that multicollinearity reveals itself in the principal components model as a lack of variation in some of the regressors. More will be said about this in Section III.

Whereas the effects of multicollinearity are easy to see in the transformed model, we must consider the effects on the original model. Since $\mathbf{b} = P\hat{\theta}$, it follows that

$$\text{cov}(\mathbf{b}) = \sigma^2 P\Lambda^{-1}P' = \sigma^2 \sum_{i=1}^{K} \lambda_i^{-1}\mathbf{p}_i\mathbf{p}_i' \tag{2.14}$$

and

$$\text{var}(b_j) = \sigma^2 \sum_{i=1}^{K} p_{ji}^2/\lambda_i \tag{2.15}$$

This expression shows that the variance of a particular b_j will depend, in general, on all the characteristic roots λ_i and the magnitudes of the elements in the characteristic vectors.

A transformation that is related to the principal components transformation and which can be used in much the same way is the singular value decomposition. The $(T \times K)$ matrix X can be written as

$$X = U\Lambda^{1/2}P', \tag{2.16}$$

where U is a $(T \times K)$ matrix whose columns are the characteristic vectors of the matrix XX' which are associated with nonzero roots; $\Lambda^{1/2}$ is the diagonal matrix containing the square roots of the characteristic roots of $X'X$ on the diagonal (and which in this context are called the singular values of X matrix); and P is the matrix whose columns are the orthonormal characteristic vectors of $X'X$. See Vinod and Ullah (1981, p. 5) for use of this decomposition in the linear statistical model.

D. The Centering–Noncentering and Scaling Debate

One issue that must be faced when examining problems related to multicollinearity is what to do about the intercept variable, if one is present. In the literature on diagnosing multicollinearity there is a continuing debate about whether the data should be centered, and/or scaled in some way, prior to computing measures of multicollinearity. In this subsection we will simply state the problem.

A normal way to think about the multicollinearity problem is to visualize a scatter diagram representing T observations in a $(K - 1)$-dimensional observation space. In this context "good" data are orthonormal, so that the data scatter is spherical about the means of the $(K - 1)$ nonconstant regressors. Multicollinear data, on the other hand, are visualized as falling in an ellipsoid, and the more elgonated the ellipsoid the worse the multicollinearity. This view of multicollinearity follows from the geometry of principal components analysis. If we assume a model with two

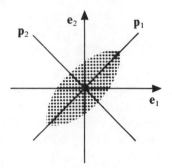

Figure 1. Multicollinear data scatter.

nonconstant regressors which are multicollinear, then the scatter of the centered data might resemble Figure 1.

Following Anderson (1984, Chap. 11) we know that the principal components of these data arise by viewing the data relative to a new set of axes defined by the characteristic vectors of the cross-product matrix formed from the centered regressors. The first principal component is the data projected onto the axis in the direction of the characteristic vector associated with the first characteristic root. This result follows from finding the linear combination of the variables that exhibits the greatest variability, *as defined by the sum of its squared elements.* The largest characteristic root λ_1 is the sum of squares of the first principal component and the associated characteristic vector points along the major axis of the data ellipse, and is labeled p_1 in Figure 1. The second principal component is orthogonal to the first and has variability λ_2. The relevant axis is in the direction p_2 in Figure 1, the minor axis of the data ellipse. A broader view of data scatter would present the data ellipse in Figure 1 as in Figure 2. Figure 1 is the projection of the ellipsoidal data disk onto the x_2-x_3 plane.

If the principal components are computed from the data matrix that includes a constant term and the two uncentered regressors, then the directions of greatest, second greatest, and least variability are measured with respect to variability about the origin, point O in Figure 2. The principal components in Figure 1 measure the variability of the data as measured from point A in Figure 2, the point representing the mean values of all three regressors. When the data is not centered, the characteristic vector p_1 will simply point out toward the data disk (and pass near its center) and λ_1

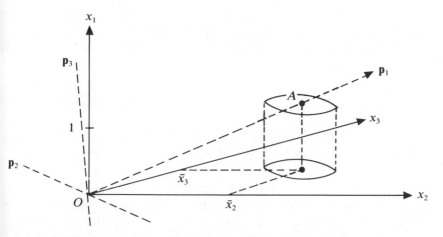

Figure 2. Data scatter in K-dimensional space.

will measure its distance from the origin. Given the data scatter as represented in Figure 2, the direction of second greatest variability is lateral and the direction of least variability is vertical, simply reflecting the fact that the data scatter is flat in three-dimensional space. The disagreement about whether or not to center the data prior to evaluating multicollinearity diagnostics is a debate about where the variability in the data should be measured from. Those that advocate centering note that diagnosing uncentered data, as in Figure 2, can lead to great differences in the magnitudes of the characteristic root of the cross-product matrix $X'X$ constructed from the uncentered data simply because the data are far from the origin and because we know that they are flat in K-dimensional space. Those that argue against centering note that if $K \geq 4$ then centering the data prior to diagnosing multicollinearity will mask the presence of linear dependencies in the data that involve the constant term and three or more other variables. While we do not wish to make a claim about which position is "right," we note that relatively unequal amounts of variation in variables or linear combinations in variables causes just as much difficulty for ordinary least squares (OLS) estimation as pairwise correlation between regressors and is not uncommon and should not be ignored. On the other hand, the demeaning effect on collinearity diagnostics of measuring the distance of the data from the origin is a real problem.

A related issue is that of scaling the data prior to evaluating the severity of multicollinearity. In order to compare the severity of multicollinearity in our data set with that in another, some scaling convention must be adopted since the choice of units of measurement affect the variability of the data and thus the measured degree of multicollinearity. A common choice of a scaling factor, for both centered and uncentered data, is to divide each explanatory variable by its length—that is, the square root of the sum of its squared elements—and thus the explanatory variables are scaled to unit length. In the centered data case this results in a cross-product matrix that is $(T - 1)$ times a correlation matrix. A measure of total variability in the data is tr $X'X$, which is $(K - 1)$ or K in the centered or uncentered data case, respectively. Based on these normalizations, various authors have suggested critical magnitudes for collinearity diagnostic measures. We will resist this impulse, as the severity of multicollinearity must be measured against the purpose to which the empirical results will be put, which varies by researcher.

III. MODELING MULTICOLLINEARITY IN THE LINEAR STATISTICAL MODEL

Given what has been said about multicollinearity in the foregoing sections, the discussion of how to construct multicollinear data is quite straightforward. For each way of describing multicollinearity there is an implicit scheme for generating such data artificially. We will consider in turn schemes that produce data that are generally intercorrelated, that exhibit near-exact linear dependencies, and that have unequal variation in all directions in the observation spaces.

A. Generating Data That Exhibit General Intercorrelations

When one is simulating macroeconomic or dynamic data, a reasonable approach for generating regressors values is to assume that a regressor x_t follows an autoregressive process:

$$x_t = \rho x_{t-1} + u_t, \tag{3.1}$$

where ρ is the autoregression parameter, and $u_t \sim N(0, \sigma^2)$ is a random disturbance. Following this scenario, a design matrix X could be constructed by specifying a separate autocorrelation process for each regressor variable, by taking lagged values of a single autoregressive process as separate variables, or by extending (3.1) to be a vector autoregressive process:

$$\mathbf{x}_t = R\mathbf{x}_{t-1} + \mathbf{u}_t. \tag{3.2}$$

Where $\mathbf{x}_t$ is a $(K \times 1)$ vector of observations on K variables at time T; R is a $(K \times K)$ matrix of autocorrelation parameters; and $\mathbf{u}_t \sim N(0, \Sigma)$, where Σ is a $(K \times K)$ matrix of contemporaneous covariances.

The problem with this approach to specifying multicollinear data is that controlling the degree of multicollinearity when one is using a model more complicated than (3.1) is a difficult task. Nonetheless, in general dynamic models this approach would produce "realistic" data with known properties.

B. The Use of Auxiliary Relations

In this approach we incorporate near-exact linear dependencies among some of the columns of X. We assume X is to be partitioned as $X = [W, Z]$, where W and Z have column dimensions K_1 and K_2, respectively, and $K_1 + K_2 = K$. Let us define $W = VCD^{-1/2}$. Where V is any nonstochastic $(T \times K_1)$ matrix of rank K_1, C is a matrix whose columns are the orthonormal characteristic vectors of $V'V$; and $D^{-1/2}$ is the diagonal matrix whose nonzero elements are the reciprocals of the square roots of $V'V$. Thus W is orthonormal, $W'W = I_{K_1}$. Now we let

$$Z = W\Phi + U, \tag{3.3}$$

where Φ is a $(K_1 \times K_2)$ parameter matrix, and U is a $(T \times K_2)$ matrix of independent and identically distributed random vectors $\mathbf{u}'_t$ which have contemporaneous covariance matrix Ω. In the simplest case, $\mathbf{u}'_t$ might have a multivariate normal distribution with contemporaneous covariance $\Omega = \text{diag}(\omega_{11}, \omega_{22}, \ldots, \omega_{K_2 K_2})$. Then the degree of collinearity is regulated by manipulating the variances ω_{ii}. As $\omega_{ii} \to 0$, the associated linear dependency among the columns of X becomes more nearly exact.

This design produces some "well-behaved" regressors, W, and some, in Z, that are linearly related to the variables in W. There is no reason, of course, why W must be orthogonal. Also, it may incorporate an intercept or an intercept might be appended to the X matrix after its construction, depending upon the viewpoint regarding the intercept that is chosen. Also, once the X matrix is generated, each regressor can be scaled to unit length. This is a desirable step to take so that results from one experiment to the next control for the total amount of variation in the data, as measured by tr $X'X$.

C. Use of the Singular Value Decomposition

As noted in Section II.C, the singular value decomposition, Eq. (2.16), allows a matrix to be broken down into components that reflect the orientation of the implied data scatter ellipsoid as well as measures of the variability of the data along the major and minor axes of the data ellipsoid. Let us be more specific about this decomposition. Any $(T \times K)$ matrix X can be decomposed as

$$X = U\Lambda^{1/2}P', \tag{3.4}$$

where $\Lambda^{1/2} = \text{diag}(\lambda_1^{1/2}, \ldots, \lambda_K^{1/2})$ is the diagonal matrix with diagonal elements, called singular values, $\lambda_i^{1/2}$, which are the square roots of the characteristic roots of $X'X$. The matrix P is the $(K \times K)$ matrix whose columns are the orthonormal characteristic vectors of $X'X$, and U is the $(T \times K)$ matrix whose elements are determined given Λ, P, and X as

$$U = XP\Lambda^{-1/2}.$$

It is useful to note that $U'U = I$. The crucial components of the decomposition are thus P and Λ, which have the same interpretation that they did in our discussion of principal components. The characteristic roots λ_i are the sums of squared values of the projections of the data on axes in the directions $\mathbf{p}_i$. While not noted above, the elements of the P matrix have interesting interpretations themselves.

In Figure 3, since $\mathbf{p}_1$ has unit length, the cosine of the angle θ_1 is p_{11}, that is, p_{11} is the cosine of the angle between $\mathbf{p}_1$ and $\mathbf{e}_1$. Similarly p_{21} is the cosine of the angle θ_2, the angle between $\mathbf{e}_2$ and $\mathbf{p}_1$. In general p_{ij} is the cosine of the angle between $\mathbf{e}_i$ and $\mathbf{p}_j$. The larger the cosince p_{ij}, the closer $\mathbf{e}_i$ is to $\mathbf{p}_j$. Thus the elements of P specify the amount of *rotation* between the standard basis

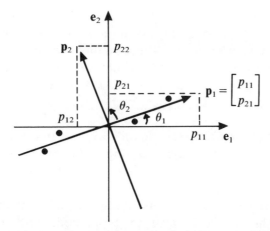

Figure 3. The geometry of principal components.

vectors e_i for the X-data space and the basis vectors p_i that span the principal components observation space.

With this geometric understanding of the singular value decomposition, its use as a method of generating multicollinear data is clear. Begin with a $T \times K$ matrix X. It may be a real data matrix or an artificially generated data matrix that is perhaps orthonormal. Perform a singular value decomposition of it. Your are now at liberty to *set* the variability in a *new* data matrix by specifying the magnitudes of the singular values or characteristic roots yourself. The characteristic root spectrum can range from $\lambda_i = 1$, for $i = 1, \ldots, K$, which would yield an orthonormal data matrix, to an array of values where the relative magnitudes are much different, indicating severe multicollinearity. It is a good practice to keep the total variability in the data,

$$\text{tr } X'X = \sum_{i=1}^{K} \lambda_i,$$

constant even though the characteristic root spectra are altered to maintain comparability across experiments. If *only* the characteristic roots are altered, the orientation of the data ellipsoid is left unaffected. That is, altering the characteristic roots changes the elongation of the data ellipsoid but leaves the direction of its major and minor axes unaffected as long as the ranks of the characteristic roots remains the same, so that $\lambda_1 \geq \lambda_2 \cdots \geq \lambda_K$ even after alteration.

On the other hand, changing the orientation of the ellipsoid can be achieved by altering the magnitudes of the elements of P, remembering to preserve its orthogonality. The matrix P is $(K \times K)$ and thus has K^2 elements. There are $K(K + 1)/2$ orthogonality conditions ($\mathbf{p}'_i\mathbf{p}_i = 1$ and $\mathbf{p}'_i\mathbf{p}_j = 0$, for $i \neq j$), leaving $K(K - 1)/2$ "free" elements. As a practical matter the "orientation" of the data ellipsoid can be shifted in a gross way by reordering the magnitudes of the characteristic roots. For example, if the λ_1 and λ_K are simply switched, the data ellipsoid changes its orientation so that $\mathbf{p}_K$ is now the major axis of the ellipsoid and $\mathbf{p}_1$ is the direction of least variation.

After desired changes in Λ and P are made, X is simply "reconstituted." The matrix U need not be altered. With respect to a constant term, note that even if the X matrix originally decomposed *had* a constant term the reconstituted X will not. If a constant term is desired for subsequent purposes, it should be added after the reconstitution of X.

IV. MULTICOLLINEARITY IN NONLINEAR STATISTICAL MODELS

In the linear statistical model there is a direct relationship between multicollinearity, as we usually think of it, near-exact linear dependencies among the columns of the X matrix, and negative consequences on the performance (i.e., precision) of the LS or maximum likelihood (ML) estimator of the regression parameters. Nonlinear statistical models, whether they be nonlinear regression models or general nonlinear models like multnominal logit that are usually estimated via ML methods, can also suffer from ill-conditioned or multicollinear data, although here the link between cause and effect can be obscure. To be specific, in the context of nonlinear models, studying the multicollinearity problem involves exploring the relationship between near-exact linear dependencies among a set of explanatory variables and the asymptotic covariance matrix of the estimator of the model's parameters. Studying this question is of course only a step toward trying to deterine the effects of multicollinearity in the sample data on the small sample performance (which may include precision and bias aspects) of a particular estimator. The latter question is difficult to attack analytically. Although exact (or approximate) finite-sampling distributions are known for some estimators in some contexts, the simplifying assumptions under which the results are derived do not leave much room to explore the effects of multicollinearity. Both questions can be explored via Monte Carlo methods, however, and some analytical results on the effects that multicollinearity can have on asymptotic covariance matrices are obtainable on a model-specific basis. In this section we will briefly explore these ideas.

A. The Nonlinear Least Squares Regression Model

Consider the standard nonlinear regression model

$$y_t = f(\mathbf{x}_t, \boldsymbol{\beta}_0) + e_t \qquad t = 1, \ldots, T,$$
$$= f_t + e_t, \tag{4.1}$$

where $\mathbf{x}_t$ is a vector of exogenous variables, and $\boldsymbol{\beta}_0$ is the $(K \times 1)$ vector of true parameter values. The error e_t is an i.i.d. random variable with mean 0 and variance σ_0^2. The nonlinear least squares (NLLS) estimator of $\boldsymbol{\beta}_0$ is the value of $\boldsymbol{\beta}$, say, $\hat{\boldsymbol{\beta}}$, that minimizes

$$S_T(\boldsymbol{\beta}) = \sum_{t=1}^{T} [y_t - f(\mathbf{x}_t, \boldsymbol{\beta})]^2. \tag{4.2}$$

Under the usual assumptions,

$$\sqrt{T}(\hat{\boldsymbol{\beta}} - \boldsymbol{\beta}_0) \xrightarrow{d} N(0, \sigma_0^2 C^{-1}),$$

where

$$C = \lim \frac{1}{T} \sum_{t=1}^{T} \left[\frac{\partial f_t}{\partial \boldsymbol{\beta}} \bigg|_{\boldsymbol{\beta}_0} \cdot \frac{\partial f_t}{\partial \boldsymbol{\beta}'} \bigg|_{\boldsymbol{\beta}_0} \right] = \lim \frac{1}{T} G_0' G_0$$

where G_0 is the $(T \times K)$ matrix $G = (\partial f / \partial \boldsymbol{\beta}')$ evaluated at $\boldsymbol{\beta}_0$.

In practice this asymptotic result would be approximated by using

$$\hat{\boldsymbol{\beta}} \sim N(\boldsymbol{\beta}_0, \sigma_0^2 (G_0' G_0)^{-1}),$$

and for the purposes of hypothesis testing or interval estimation we would estimate σ_0^2 using $\hat{\sigma}^2 = S_T(\hat{\boldsymbol{\beta}})/T$ and evaluating $G = \partial f / \partial \boldsymbol{\beta}'$ at $\hat{\boldsymbol{\beta}}$ (call it $\hat{G}$). Thus the effects of multicollinearity in the NLLS model are manifested in the matrix $(G_0' G_0)^{-1}$, which we estimate by $(\hat{G}' \hat{G})^{-1}$, henceforth used as a basis for evaluating the precision of our NLLS estimator in large samples.

Our intuition that the matrix $(G_0'G_0)^{-1}$ must be the object of investigation if we wish to analyze the "asymptotic" effects of multicollinearity is furthered by examining the Gauss–Newton iterative scheme for obtaining the NLLS estimator $\hat{\beta}$. The $(n + 1)$st round estimate is

$$\hat{\beta}_{n+1} = \hat{\beta}_n - [\hat{G}_n'\hat{G}_n]^{-1}\hat{G}_n'\hat{e}_n,$$

where $\hat{G}_n$ is $G|_{\hat{\beta}_n}$, and $\hat{e}_n = y - f(\hat{\beta}_n)$. The matrix $\hat{G}_n$ serves as a regressor matrix in this iterating scheme.

From these analogies it is clear that we can study the effects of multicollinearity on the NLLS estimator $\hat{\beta}$ by analyzing $\hat{G}'\hat{G}$ as we would $X'X$ in a linear regression model. The more difficult problem is in determining *how* linear associations among the columns of X affect this asymptotic multicollinearity. In order to attack that question it is clear that we must consider how linear associations among the columns of X are related to linear associations among the columns of G. This must be done on a case-by-case basis.

To illustrate the nature of the problem, let us consider the CES (constant elasticity of substitution) production function that is widely used to illustrate the NLLS model (see, for example, Judge et al., 1985, Chap. 6). This model has the form

$$\ln Q_t = \beta_0 + \beta_1 \ln[\beta_2 L_t^{\beta_3} + (1 - \beta_2)K_t^{\beta_3}] + e_t,$$

where Q_t, L_t, and K_t are output, labor input, and capital input, respectively. For this model the vector $\partial f_t/\partial\beta$ is as shown in Eq. (4.3):

$$\begin{bmatrix} \dfrac{\partial f_t}{\partial\beta_0} \\[2ex] \dfrac{\partial f_t}{\partial\beta_1} \\[2ex] \dfrac{\partial f_t}{\partial\beta_2} \\[2ex] \dfrac{\partial f_t}{\partial\beta_3} \end{bmatrix} = \begin{bmatrix} 1 \\[2ex] \ln[\beta_2 L_t^{\beta_3} + (1 - \beta_2)K_t^{\beta_3}] \\[2ex] \dfrac{\beta_1(L_t^{\beta_3} - K_t^{\beta_3})}{\beta_2 L_t^{\beta_3} + (1 - \beta_2)K_t^{\beta_3}} \\[2ex] \dfrac{\beta_1[\ln(L_t)\beta_2 L_t^{\beta_3} + \ln(K_t)(1 - \beta_2)K_t^{\beta_3}]}{\beta_2 L_t^{\beta_3} + (1 - \beta_2)K_t^{\beta_3}} \end{bmatrix}. \qquad (4.3)$$

The question to be tackled is how would a near-exact linear dependence between 1, L_t, and K_t affect the relationship among the columns of $\partial f_t / \partial \boldsymbol{\beta}'$. The answer will depend not only on the multicollinearity in the data but also on the values of the parameters and on the functional form f_t itself. Despite the potential difficulty in determining how linear dependencies in the data work through the model to the asymptotic covariance matrix, the methods described in Section III for generating collinear data are still applicable.

B.   Maximum Likelihood Estimation

The problems of assessing the effects of multicollinearity in the data on ML estimator performance are essentially similar in scope to those associated with NLLS estimation of a nonlinear regression function. If the log-likelihood function is denoted $L(\boldsymbol{\beta})$, where $\boldsymbol{\beta}$ is a vector of unknown parameters, then under the usual regularity conditions for the ML estimator of $\boldsymbol{\beta}$, say, $\hat{\boldsymbol{\beta}}$, we obtain

$$\sqrt{T}(\hat{\boldsymbol{\beta}} - \boldsymbol{\beta}) \xrightarrow{d} N(0, \lim[I(\boldsymbol{\beta})/T]^{-1}),$$

where $I(\boldsymbol{\beta}) = -E \, \partial^2 L/\partial\boldsymbol{\beta} \, \partial\boldsymbol{\beta}'$. In finite samples we would approximate this asymptotic result as

$$\hat{\boldsymbol{\beta}} \sim N(\boldsymbol{\beta}, [I(\boldsymbol{\beta})]^{-1})$$

and evaluate $I(\boldsymbol{\beta})$ at $\hat{\boldsymbol{\beta}}$. The effects of multicollinearity thus affect the ML estimator through $[I(\hat{\boldsymbol{\beta}})]^{-1}$ which we hope reflects the actual finite sample variability of our ML estimator. The actual evaluation of how multicollinearity affects ML estimation is further complicated by the fact that there are three popular nonlinear optimization procedures used to obtain ML estimates, each with its *own* natural estimator of $I(\boldsymbol{\beta})$. The iteration schemes can all be represented as

$$\hat{\boldsymbol{\beta}}_{n+1} = \hat{\boldsymbol{\beta}}_n + C_n^{-1} \frac{\partial L}{\partial \boldsymbol{\beta}} \bigg|_{\hat{\boldsymbol{\beta}}_n},$$

where

$$C_n = -\frac{\partial^2 L}{\partial \boldsymbol{\beta} \, \partial \boldsymbol{\beta}'} \bigg|_{\hat{\boldsymbol{\beta}}_n}$$

for the Newton–Raphson algorithm;

$$C_n = I(\hat{\boldsymbol{\beta}}_n)$$

for the method of scoring; and

$$C_n = \left(\sum_{t=1}^{T} \frac{\partial L_t}{\partial \boldsymbol{\beta}} \cdot \frac{\partial L_t}{\partial \boldsymbol{\beta}'} \right) \Big|_{\hat{\boldsymbol{\beta}}_n}$$

for the method of Berndt et al. (1974), in which $L_t = \ln f_t$ and f_t is the value of the relevant density or probability function for the tth observation (assuming that L is based on a random sample). Each algorithm has as a natural estimator of $I(\boldsymbol{\beta})$ the inverse of the matrix C_n, evaluated at the ML estimator $\hat{\boldsymbol{\beta}}$. Consequently we may perceive the asymptotic effects of multicollinearity differently depending on which estimaton algorithm we adopt.

As an example of studying multicollinearity in the context of ML estimation, consider the binary choice model where an observable random variable y_i takes the values 1 or 0, with probabilities P_i and $1 - P_i$, respectively. The probability P_i depends on a vector of explanatory variables and unknown parameters $\boldsymbol{\beta}$ as $P_i = F(\mathbf{x}_i'\boldsymbol{\beta})$ when $F(\cdot)$ is usually the CDF (cumulative distribution function) of a standard normal random variable (probit analysis) or the CDF of a logistic random variable (logit analysis). For both models the information matrix has the form

$$I(\boldsymbol{\beta}) = \sum_{i=1}^{T} \alpha_i \mathbf{x}_i \mathbf{x}_i',$$

where

$$\alpha_i = f(\mathbf{x}_i'\boldsymbol{\beta})$$

for the logit model in which $f(\cdot)$ is the logistic PDF (probability density function), and

$$\alpha_i = [f(\mathbf{x}_i'\boldsymbol{\beta})]^2 / F(\mathbf{x}_i'\boldsymbol{\beta})(1 - F(\mathbf{x}_i'\boldsymbol{\beta}))$$

for the probit model, in which f and F are the PDF and CDF of a standard normal random variable. In these models we can use the principal components transformation to help us study the effects of multicollinearity. Let P be the matrix of characteristic vectors of $X'X$ so

$$Z = XP \quad \text{and} \quad Z'Z = P'X'XP = \Lambda = \text{diag}(\lambda_1, \ldots, \lambda_K).$$

If there is a single near-exact linear dependency among the columns of X, then $\lambda_K \doteq 0$. Consequently $\mathbf{z}_K = X\mathbf{p}_K \doteq \mathbf{0}$, since $\lambda_K =$

$\mathbf{z}'_K\mathbf{z}_K \doteq 0$. This implies

$$\mathbf{x}'_i\mathbf{p}_K = \mathbf{p}'_K\mathbf{x}_i \doteq 0 \qquad \forall i,$$

or

$$\mathbf{z}_i = P'\mathbf{x}_i = \begin{bmatrix} \mathbf{p}'_1 \\ \mathbf{p}'_2 \\ \vdots \\ \mathbf{p}'_K \end{bmatrix}\mathbf{x}_i \doteq \begin{bmatrix} z_{i1} \\ z_{i2} \\ \vdots \\ z_{i,K-1} \\ 0 \end{bmatrix} \qquad \forall\, i. \tag{4.4}$$

Consequently, if we consider the transformed binary choice model, we can write Eqs. (4.5) and (4.6)

$$y_i = F(\mathbf{x}'_i\boldsymbol{\beta}) = F(\mathbf{x}'_iPP'\boldsymbol{\beta}) = F(\mathbf{z}'_i\boldsymbol{\theta}) \tag{4.5}$$

$$I(\boldsymbol{\theta}) = \sum_{i=1}^{T} \alpha_i\mathbf{z}_i\mathbf{z}'_i$$

$$= \sum_{i=1}^{T} \alpha_i \begin{bmatrix} z_{i1} \\ \vdots \\ z_{i,K-1} \\ 0 \end{bmatrix}[z_{i1} \quad \cdots \quad z_{i,K-1}, \quad 0]$$

$$= \sum_{i=1}^{T} \alpha_i \begin{bmatrix} z_{i1}^2 & z_{i1}z_{i2} & \cdots & 0 \\ z_{i2}z_{i1} & z_{i2}^2 & \cdots & 0 \\ \vdots & \vdots & & \vdots \\ 0 & 0 & \cdots & 0 \end{bmatrix} \tag{4.6}$$

$$= \begin{bmatrix} I_{11} & \mathbf{0} \\ \mathbf{0}' & 0 \end{bmatrix},$$

regardless of the values of α_i. Thus the asymptotic variances and covariances of $\tilde{\theta}_K$ may be large. As in the linear model, since $\tilde{\boldsymbol{\beta}} = P\tilde{\boldsymbol{\theta}}$, the magnitude of the elements of the jth row of P indicate how severely the jth element of $\boldsymbol{\beta}$ will be affected by the imprecision in $\tilde{\theta}_K$. Consequently we can generate multicollinear data for this model in the same way we did for the linear model and expect similar results.

V. MODELING EXTRAPOLATION IN THE LINEAR
STATISTICAL MODEL

One of the functions of the regression model is to provide a basis for prediction. In this section we explore how multicollinearity affects prediction. In particular, we focus upon the question of how multicollinearity affects out-of-sample prediction. This focus requires a measure of multivariate data extrapolation which will take into account not only changing levels of explanatory variables but also changing patterns of multicollinearity.

To motivate this problem let us recall the basic results for the simple linear regression model $y_t = \beta_1 + \beta_2 x_t + e_t$. The variance of the forecast error of the LS predictor of $E(y_0 | x_0)$ is

$$E[\hat{y}_0 - Ey_0]^2 = \sigma^2 \left[\frac{1}{T} + \frac{(x_0 - \bar{x})^2}{\sum (x_t - \bar{x})^2} \right], \tag{5.1}$$

where $\bar{x} = \sum x_t / T$. The further x_0 is (extrapolated) from $\bar{x}$, the larger the variance of the forecast error. In this model multicollinearity appears as a lack of variation in x_t about its mean $\bar{x}$; and clearly the less variation x_t exhibits, the greater the forecast variance. Thus the effects of multicollinearity and extrapolation are easy to see in the simple model.

In the multiple regression model

$$\mathbf{y} = X\boldsymbol{\beta} + \mathbf{e},$$

the variance of the LS predictor $\mathbf{x}_0'\mathbf{b}$ is

$$\text{var}(\mathbf{x}_0'\mathbf{b}) = \sigma^2 \mathbf{x}_0'(X'X)^{-1}\mathbf{x}_0 = \sigma^2 \mathbf{x}_0' P\Lambda^{-1}P'\mathbf{x}_0$$

$$= \sigma^2 \mathbf{x}_0' \sum_{i=1}^{K} \lambda_i^{-1} \mathbf{p}_i \mathbf{p}_i' \mathbf{x}_0$$

$$= \sigma^2 \sum_{i=1}^{K} \frac{(\mathbf{x}_0'\mathbf{p}_i)(\mathbf{p}_i'\mathbf{x}_0)}{\lambda_i}. \tag{5.2}$$

The conventional wisdom about the effects of multicollinearity on prediction are based on (5.2). If there is multicollinearity, then one or more of the values λ_i will be small. If, however, the values of the explanatory variables $\mathbf{x}_0$ obey the same pattern of multicollinearity as the sample data, then the variance of the LS predictor need not be inflated. To see this, recall that

$$X'X\mathbf{p}_i = \lambda_i \mathbf{p}_i$$

and

$$\mathbf{p}_i'X'X\mathbf{p}_i = \lambda_i \mathbf{p}_i'\mathbf{p}_i = \lambda_i.$$

If λ_i is small, then $\mathbf{z}_i = X\mathbf{p}_i$ must contain small elements too since

$$\mathbf{z}_i'\mathbf{z}_i = \sum_{j=1}^{T} z_{ji}^2 = \lambda_i.$$

That is, if $\lambda_i \doteq 0$, then $z_{ji} \doteq 0$ $\forall j$. Thus, if $\mathbf{x}_0$ is "like" the sample data in the sense that $\mathbf{x}_0'\mathbf{p}_i \doteq 0$, then in (5.2) small denominators may just be offset by small values of the numerator. Thus, certainly if we look at insample predictions, where $\mathbf{x}_0' = \mathbf{x}_t'$ and $\mathbf{x}_t'$ is one of the rows of X, we should not expect severe multicollinearity to adversely affect the performance of the LS predictor.

Much of the theoretical work in statistics on the properties of alternative estimators of $\boldsymbol{\beta}$ in the linear model is based on evaluation of their risk functions, specified as

$$\begin{aligned} R(\hat{\boldsymbol{\beta}}, \boldsymbol{\beta}, Q) &= EL(\hat{\boldsymbol{\beta}}, \boldsymbol{\beta}, Q) \\ &= E[(\hat{\boldsymbol{\beta}} - \boldsymbol{\beta})'Q(\hat{\boldsymbol{\beta}} - \boldsymbol{\beta})], \end{aligned} \tag{5.3}$$

where Q is a positive definite and symmetric matrix. If $Q = X'X$, then the risk function gives the average squared error when using $X\hat{\boldsymbol{\beta}}$ as an estimator (or predictor) of $X\boldsymbol{\beta}$. We transform the regression model as

$$\mathbf{y} = X\boldsymbol{\beta} + \mathbf{e} = XQ^{-1/2}Q^{1/2}\boldsymbol{\beta} + \mathbf{e} = Z\boldsymbol{\theta} + \mathbf{e}, \tag{5.4}$$

where $Z = XQ^{-1/2}$; $\boldsymbol{\theta} = Q^{1/2}\boldsymbol{\beta}$; and $Q = P\Lambda^{1/2}P'$. Then, if we premultiply (5.4) by Z', we have

$$Z'\mathbf{y} = Z'Z\boldsymbol{\theta} + Z'\mathbf{e}$$

or

$$\mathbf{w} = \boldsymbol{\theta} + \mathbf{v}. \tag{5.5}$$

Thus the linear model (5.5) for the mean of a multivariate normal random vector [since $\mathbf{v} \sim N(0, \sigma^2 I)$] is simply a reparameterization of the regression model. Furthermore, studying the properties of alternative estimator of $\boldsymbol{\theta}$ under loss

$$L(\hat{\boldsymbol{\theta}}, \boldsymbol{\theta}, I) = (\hat{\boldsymbol{\theta}} - \boldsymbol{\theta})'(\hat{\boldsymbol{\theta}} - \boldsymbol{\theta})$$

is equivalent to studying the corresponding estimator of β, namely, $\hat{\beta} = Q^{-1/2}\hat{\theta}$, under the risk function (5.3) with $Q = X'X$. The statistical model (5.5) has been widely studied, and consequently much is also known about the linear regression model under mean square error (MSE) of prediction loss. Specifically I am referring to the "improved" estimaton literature that has its genesis with James and Stein (1961).

Discussion has begun, however, about the sampling performance of improved estimators with respect to out-of-sample MSE of prediction (Freidman and Montgomery, 1985; Copas, 1986; Hill and Fomby, 1986). A logical risk function to consider is (5.3), but with $Q = X_0'X_0$, where X_0 is an $(m \times K)$ matrix of values $(m \geq K)$ of explanatory variables at which we wish to predict Ey_0, with

$$y_0 = X_0\beta + e_0 \qquad (5.6)$$

and $e_0 \sim N(0, \sigma^2 I_m)$ and independently of e.

The question of current interest is how multicollinearity in X and X_0 affects the out-of-sample MSE of prediction, and how Monte Carlo experiments can be designed to study the out-of-sample predictive ability of alternative estimators. As a starting point we consider the prediction risk of the LS predictor

$$\hat{y}_0 = X_0 b = X_0(X'X)^{-1}X'y. \qquad (5.7)$$

The risk of $\hat{y}_0$ is

$$R(b, \beta, X_0'X_0) = E[(X_0 b - X_0\beta)'(X_0 b - X_0\beta)]$$

$$= E[(\hat{y}_0 - Ey_0)'(\hat{y}_0 - Ey_0)]$$

$$= \sigma^2 \operatorname{tr} X_0(X'X)^{-1}X_0' = \sigma^2 \operatorname{tr} X_0'X_0(X'X)^{-1}. \qquad (5.8)$$

Thus the prediction risk of the LS predictor depends on the cross-product matrices for X_0 and X. What can be shown, though, is that we can decompose the risk (5.8) into separate components that are easily interpreted. To that end, we define

$$X = [i_T, X_1], \qquad X_0 = [i_m, X_2]$$

$$X_1^* = M_1 X_1 = (I_T - i_T i_T'/T)X_1$$

$$X_2^* = M_2 X_2 = (I_m - i_m i_m'/m)X_2 \qquad (5.9)$$

$$d = (\bar{x}_2 - \bar{x}_1) = X_2' i_m/m - X_1' i_T/T.$$

The vector $\mathbf{i}_j$ is a $(j \times 1)$ vector of ones; the matrices X_1 and X_2 are the nonconstant regressors of X and X_0; X_1^* and X_2^* are the data matrices in deviation from the mean form; and $\mathbf{d}$ is the difference in the mean values of the regressors in matrix X_2 and X_1. With this notation it is straightforward to show that

$$R(\mathbf{b}, \boldsymbol{\beta}, X'X)$$

$$= \frac{\sigma^2 m}{T} + \sigma^2 \, \mathrm{tr}[(X_2^* + \mathbf{i}_m\mathbf{d}')'(X_2^* + \mathbf{i}_m\mathbf{d}')(X_1^{*\prime}X_1^*)^{-1}]$$

$$= \frac{\sigma^2 m}{T} + \sigma^2 \, \mathrm{tr}[(X_2^{*\prime}X_2^* + \mathbf{d}\mathbf{i}_m'\mathbf{i}_m\mathbf{d}')(X_1^{*\prime}X_1^*)^{-1}] \qquad (5.10)$$

$$= \sigma^2\left[\frac{m}{T} + \mathrm{tr} \; V_1'V_2\Lambda_2 V_2'V_1\Lambda_1^{-1} + m \, \mathbf{d}'V_1\Lambda_1^{-1}V_1'\mathbf{d}\right],$$

where $X_1^{*\prime}X_1^* = V_1\Lambda_1 V_1'$ and $X_2^{*\prime}X_2^* = V_2\Lambda_2 V_2'$. Here V_1 and V_2 are matrices of characteristic vectors, and Λ_1 and Λ_2 are diagonal matrices of charcteristic vests of $X_1^{*\prime}X_1^*$ and $X_2^{*\prime}X_2^*$, respectively.

The expression (5.10) decomposes the prediction risk into its basic elements. The prediction risk of LS is directly related to σ^2 and m and inversely related to T. In (5.10) the matrices V_1 and V_2 determine the directions of the major and minor axes of the data ellipsoids for X and X_0 (centered at the regressor means) and Λ_1 and Λ_2 reflect the variability of the data in those directions. Thus these four matrices reflect the multicollinearity in-sample and out-of-sample from the point of view of predictive risk. The vector $\mathbf{d}$ of differences between means of course reflects the distance between the centers of the data ellipsoids. Given the in-sample and out-of-sample multicollinearity, the greater $\mathbf{d}$, the distance between the mean vectors, the greater the prediction risk.

Given (5.10) we see that not only does predictive risk depend on σ^2, m, T, and $\mathbf{d}$, but also on the differences between the rotation in the data ellipsoids (V_1 and V_2) and differences in the patterns of variation (Λ_1 and Λ_2). The data ellipsoids are *rotationally equivalent* if $V_1 = V_2$, so $V_1'V_2 = I$. The data ellipsoids are *variationally equivalent* if $\Lambda_1 = \Lambda_2$.

If we use $\mathbf{d} = 0$, $V_1 = V_2$, and $\Lambda_1 = \Lambda_2$ as a starting point, the effects of differences in the in-sample and out-of-sample data can be explored systematically.

For the purpose of exploring the effects of changes in $\mathbf{d}$, V_1, V_2, Λ_1, and Λ_2 via Monte Carlo procedures, we may proceed as follows: We let U_1 be a $T \times (K - 1)$ matrix of standardized variables such that $U_1'U_1 = I_{(K-1)}$ and the sample mean of each column of U_1 is zero, so $U_1'\mathbf{j}_T = \mathbf{0}$, where $\mathbf{j}_T$ is a $(T \times 1)$ vector of ones. We define $X_1 = U_1\Lambda_1^{1/2}V_1'$, so $X_1'X_1 = V_1\Lambda_1 V_1'$. By choosing $\Lambda_1 = \mathrm{diag}(\lambda_1, \ldots, \lambda_{K-1})$ and V_1 orthogonal, we define a matrix X_1 with specific variablity characteristics. Note that $X_1'\mathbf{j}_T = V_1\Lambda_1^{1/2}U_1'\mathbf{j}_T = \mathbf{0}$, so these design variables have zero mean. Since only the difference between the means enters risk, this normalization does not matter. We define $X = [\mathbf{j}_T X_1]$, so

$$X'X = \begin{bmatrix} T & \mathbf{0}' \\ \mathbf{0} & X_1'X_1 \end{bmatrix}.$$

Now we let $\Lambda_2 = \mathrm{diag}(\gamma_1, \ldots, \gamma_{K-1})$; V_2 be an orthogonal matrix; and $\mathbf{d}$ a $(K - 1) \times 1$ vector. We let U_2 be an $m \times (K - 1)$ matrix $(m > K - 1)$ such that $U_2'U_2 = I$ and $U_2'\mathbf{j}_m = \mathbf{0}$. We define

$$X_2 = U_2\Lambda_2^{1/2}V_2' + \mathbf{j}_m\mathbf{d}$$

and

$$X_0 = [\mathbf{j}_m X_2].$$

Note that $X_2'X_2 = V_2\Lambda_2 V_2' + m\mathbf{d}\mathbf{d}'$ since $U_2'\mathbf{j}_m = \mathbf{0}$, and $X_2'\mathbf{j}_m = m\mathbf{d}$ so

$$X_0'X_0 = \begin{bmatrix} m & m\mathbf{d}' \\ m\mathbf{d} & V_2\Lambda_2 V_2' + m\mathbf{d}\mathbf{d}' \end{bmatrix} = \begin{bmatrix} m & m\mathbf{d}' \\ m\mathbf{d} & X_2'X_2 \end{bmatrix}.$$

Given these specifications, the MSE of out-of-sample predictions for LS is (5.10) as desired.

Since there are many "dimensions" of multicollinearity to explore, it is useful to think about extreme situations. For example, if we assume that the data scatters are fixed and the length of $\mathbf{d}$ is fixed, prediction risk is minimized if $\mathbf{d}$ is in the direction of the major axis of the within-sample data scatter. The alignment of $\mathbf{d}$ along the minor axis of the within-sample data scatter maximizes risk. Also, if the within-sample data scatter is fixed, and $\mathbf{d}$ and Λ_2 are fixed, then the prediction risk is minimized when $V_1 = V_2$ so that the major and minor axes of the data ellipsoids are perfectly aligned. Prediction risk is maximized (for given V_1, Λ_1, $\mathbf{d}$, Λ_2) when the major and minor axes are exactly aligned but in the opposite order. For a geometric exposition of these and related propositions that can be useful in planning a Monte Carlo experiment to study predictive risk, see Fomby and Hill (1986).

VI. SUMMARY

This paper has explored the concept of multicollinearity in the usual linear regression model, in nonlinear statistic models, and in the content of prediction. The effects of multicollinearity in the linear statistical model are well known. By considering multicollinearity from three separate points of view we can visualize modeling multicollinearity in three separate ways. Thinking of multicollinearity as a general intercorrelation among explanatory is common in macroeconomic applications and thus viewing the regressor variables as outcomes of a particular univariate or multivariate process is reasonable. If multicollinearity is represented as near-exact linear relations among the explanatory variables, then the use of an auxiliary regression framework to generate regressor values is appropriate. Finally if multicollinearity is generally defined as a lack of equal variation in all directions of the observation space, then use of the singular value decomposition to specify the design matrix is very useful. Regarding mulicollinearity in this way also sheds some light on the centering–noncentering and scaling debate. In particular, to understand the two sides it is necessary to view the data scatter from different vantage points in the observation space.

In the context of nonlinear regression or general nonlinear statistical models, the question of multicollinearity's effects on the properties of estimators is more difficult. The reason is that the effects of multicollinearity in the data on the asymptotic covariance matrix of the usual estimators depends upon the values of the model's parameters and the form of the nonlinear relationship. Matters are further confounded, of course, by the fact that the asymptotic covariance matrix may not be a good guide to finite sample variability. In fact, Griffiths et al. (1987) note that the asymptotic properties in the probit model appear to be delayed by the presence of multicollinearity.

Finally, in prediction, we find that three aspects of the data scatter affect the MSE of prediction of the LS predictor, and of other predictors as well as one would suspect. Predictive risk is affected by (1) the distance between data scatters, (2) the orientation of the data ellipsoids relative to one another as well as the orientation of the in-sample data relative to the vector of differences between the sample means of the explanatory variables, and (3) the elongation of the ellipsoids.

The issue of how we design Monte Carlo experiments that explore properties of estimators in various contexts is an important one. It is not satisfactory to *only* study estimators in circumstances that are simple enough so that analytical results can be obtained. While this is certainly one way to make progress, it is not the only way. But bringing the power of the computer to the problem is not enough. Numerical experiments that are not well designed offer no feeling for the robustness of results, nor do they lead to conjectures (which otherwise would be a basis for asking interesting theoretical questions). The position of this paper is that the more thoroughly we understand the model under study the more intelligently Monte Carlo experiments can be designed and the more, as a consequence, we can learn from them.

ACKNOWLEDGMENTS

The author would like to acknowledge partial financial support for this research from the Real Estate Research Institute, Louisiana State University.

REFERENCES

Anderson, T. (1984) *An Introduction to Multivariate Statistical Analysis*, 2nd ed. New York: Wiley.

Berndt, E., B. Hall, R. Hall, and J. Hausman (1974) "Estimation and Inference in Nonlinear Structural Models." *Annals of Economic and Social Measurement* 3, 653–665.

Copas, J. P. (1986) "Regression, Prediction and Shrinkage." *Journal of the Royal Statistical Society, Series B* 45, 311–354.

Fomby, T. and R. C. Hill (1986) "The Geometry of Least Squares Prediction." Working paper, Economics Department, Southern Methodist University, Dallas.

Friedman, D. and D. Montgomery (1985) "Evaluation of the Predictive Performance of Biased Regression Estimators." *Journal of Forecasting* 4, 153–163.

Griffiths, W., R. C. Hill, and P. Pope (1987) "An Investigation into the Small Sample Properties of Covariance Matrix and Pre-Test Estimators for the Probit Model." *Journal of the American Statistical Association*, 82, in press.

Hill, R. C. and T. Fomby (1986) "The Effects of Extrapolation on Minimax Stein-Rule Prediction." Presented at the American Statistical Association Meetings, Chicago, August.

James, W. and C. Stein (1961) "Estimation with Quadratic Loss. Pp. 316–379 in *Proceedings of the Fourth Berkeley Symposium on Mathematical Statistics and Probability*. Berkeley: University of California Press.

Judge, G., W. Griffiths, R. C. Hill, H. Lütkepohl, and T. Lee (1985) *The Theory and Practice of Econometrics*, 2nd ed. New York: Wiley.

Vinod, H. D. and A. Ullah (1981) *Recent Advances in Regression Methods*. New York: Dekker.

NONPARAMETRIC MONTE CARLO DENSITY ESTIMATION OF RATIONAL EXPECTATIONS ESTIMATORS AND THEIR t RATIOS

Simon Power and Aman Ullah

ABSTRACT

This paper explores the integration of nonparametric density estimation and Monte Carlo methods in a study of two single-equation estimators in the context of a rational expectations simultaneous equations model. Nonparameteric density estimation is shown to significantly enhance the value of Monte Carlo experiments. The results suggest that the substitution method estimator (Sargent, 1973, 1976; Wallis, 1980) may dominate the errors-in-variables estimator (McCallum, 1976).

KEYWORDS   kernel estimator; hypothesis testing; simulation.

Advances in Econometrics, Volume 6, pages 157–186
Copyright © 1987 by JAI Press Inc.
All rights of reproduction in any form reserved.
ISBN: 0-89232-795-2

I. INTRODUCTION

Monte Carlo experiments are frequently used in econometrics and more generally in statistics to compare the small sample performance of different estimation techniques for particular applications (e.g., by Fomby and Guilkey, 1983; Mikhail, 1975). They are especially useful in situations where exact sampling distributions or approximations to them are unavailable or not easily interpretable.

The aim of this paper is to demonstrate a method by which the value of Monte Carlo experiments may be significantly enhanced, namely, nonparametric density estimation. This technique allows us to actually estimate the sampling distribution of an estimator in a particular situation rather than just being able to calculate parameteric or nonparametric summary statistics, which can frequently be difficult to assimilate. In addition, sampling distributions of asymptotic t statistics can be estimated, thus allowing the evaluation of inference procedures based on asymptotic results.

The application chosen to illustrate this technique, the comparison of two single-equation estimators in the context of a rational expectations simultaneous equations model, is particularly appropriate as it represents an important and topical case where, although exact sampling distribution or approximation results are currently unavailable, empirical use of these estimation techniques and inference procedures based thereupon has been widespread (e.g., see Barro, 1977; Blanchard, 1983).

Section II briefly summarizes the method of nonparametric density estimation and explains how it can be utilized in Monte Carlo studies; Section III introduces the model to be used; Section IV describes the two estimation methods to be compared; Section V outlines the details of the experiments; Section VI considers the generation of the data; and Section VII reports the results and draws some conclusions.

II. NONPARAMETRIC DENSITY ESTIMATION

A. Brief Review

Many different methods of nonparametric density estimation have appeared in the literature, including histograms, orthogonal series, penalty functions, splines, Fourier inversions, nearest neighbors, delta sequences, stochastic approximations, and kernels. The various advantages of the more complex methods over the simple histograms are discussed in Silverman (1986). For a recent survey, see Rao (1983). The most popular of these estimation methods has proved to be the method of kernels, and we concentrate on this method below.

The probability density function of a random variable X at a point x may be defined as

$$f = f(x) = \frac{d}{dx} F(x) = \lim_{h \to 0} \frac{F(x + h/2) - F(x - h/2)}{h}$$

$$= \lim_{h \to 0} h^{-1} P[x - (h/2) < X < x + (h/2)],$$

where $F(x) = P[X < x]$ is the cumulative probability density function.

Given a random sample, $x_1, x_2, \ldots, x_n$, of independently identically distributed observations on X, a natural candidate for a consistent estimator of $f(x)$ is given by

$$\hat{f}_n = \hat{f}_n(x) = \frac{F_n(x + h/2) - F_n(x - h/2)}{h}$$

$$= (nh)^{-1}[\text{number of } x_1, x_2, \ldots, x_n \text{ in} \\ (x - h/2, \quad x + h/2)]$$

$$= (nh)^{-1} \sum_{i=1}^{n} I\left(\frac{x_i - x}{h}\right),$$

where $F_n(x)$ is the empirical cumulative probability density function of $x_1, x_2, \ldots, x_n$; the window width $h = h_n$ is a positive function of the sample size such that $h_n \to 0$ as $n \to \infty$; and $I(w)$ is an indicator function such that $I(w)$ is equal to 1 if $-\frac{1}{2} < w < \frac{1}{2}$, and 0 otherwise. Note that $\int I(w) \, dw = 1$.

Rosenblatt (1956) showed that the consistency property of this estimator remains invariant if the indicator function $I(w)$ is replaced by any other nonnegative function $K(w)$ satisfying $\int K(w) \, dw = 1$, this yielding the "kernel" estimator

$$\hat{f}(x) = (nh)^{-1} \sum_{i=1}^{n} K\left(\frac{x_i - x}{h}\right), \tag{1}$$

which is also asymptotically unbiased.

Parzen (1962) generalized these results by showing that the kernel function need not be nonnegative. Indeed, any Borel measurable function $K(w)$ satisfying

$$\int K(w)\, dw = 1, \qquad \sup|K(w)| < \infty, \qquad \int |K(w)|\, dw < \infty,$$

and

$$\lim |wK(w)| = 0 \quad \text{as} \quad |w| \to \infty,$$

will result in a kernel estimator which is mean square consistent at every continuity point of f provided $h_n \to 0$ and $nh_n \to \infty$ as $n \to \infty$. Moreover, under these conditions on h_n, Parzen (1962) proved that the asymptotic distribution of $(\hat{f}(x) - E\hat{f}(x))/\sqrt{V(\hat{f}(x))}$ is standard normal. It is also known (see, e.g., Cacoullos, 1966; Singh and Ullah, 1985) that under an additional restriction on h

$$\frac{\hat{f}(x) - f(x)}{\sqrt{V(\hat{f}(x))}} \sim AN(0, 1),$$

this allowing the construction of asymptotic $100(1 - \beta)\%$ confidence intervals for $f(x)$ at each point x as

$$\hat{f}(x) \pm z_{\beta/2}(nh)^{-1/2}\left(\hat{f}(x) \int K^2 \right)^{1/2}, \tag{2}$$

where $z_{\beta/2}$ is such that if Z is a standard normal variate then

$$P[-z_{\beta/2} < Z < z_{\beta/2}] = 1 - \beta.$$

Given these results, an important practical question which arises concerns the choice of kernel and window width. For the case of a kernel, $K(w)$, in (1) such that

$$\int K(w)\, dw = 1, \qquad \int wK(w)\, dw = 0,$$

and

$$\int w^2 K(w)\, dw < \infty,$$

Rosenblatt (1956) has obtained the finite sample bias and mean squared error (MSE) of $\hat{f}$ (see also Silverman, 1986; Singh and Ullah, 1985). Further, these authors have shown that the optimal choice of h which minimizes the integrated MSE of $\hat{f}$ is $\propto n^{-1/5}$. Consequently, Singh and Ullah (1985) and Ullah and Singh (1985) have indicated that, since the variance of $\hat{f}$ gets inflated whenever the variance of x, σ^2, and hence of K gets inflated, a good choice of h is given by $\sigma n^{-1/5}$. In practice σ may be replaced by s, the sample standard deviation (SD) of x. As regards K, it follows from the work of Epanechnikov (1969) that any reasonable choice, e.g., the standard normal kernel, is optimal in the sense of minimizing the integrated MSE. For additional technical details on the determination of K and h, see Rao (1983, Chap. 2).

Extensions of the kernel estimator to multivariate density and regression function estimation are discussed in, e.g., Bierens (1985), Rao (1983), Silverman (1986), and Ullah and Singh (1985).

B. Application to Monte Carlo Studies

Here we consider the kernel method of nonparametric density estimation for the Monte Carlo evaluation of the small sample properties of two single-equation estimators in the context of a rational expectation simultaneous equations model. Essentially, we estimate the sampling distributions of the two estimators of the various coefficients and the asymptotic t statistics corresponding to the null hypotheses that the estimated coefficients are equal to their known (to the Monte Carlo researcher) true values by means of the kernel estimator. Thus, in formula (1) the x_i's become the Monte Carlo point estimates and Monte Carlo asymptotic t statistics [the Monte Carlo point estimates minus the value of the coefficient under the null hypothesis divided by the Monte Carlo asymptotic standard errors (SEs)], respectively, while the x becomes the point at which the density is being estimated.

In all cases a standard normal kernel

$$K(w) = (2\Pi)^{-1/2} \exp(-\tfrac{1}{2}w^2),$$

is used with the window width, h, set equal to $sn^{-1/5}$, where s is the sample SD of the Monte Carlo estimates (Monte Carlo asymptotic t statistics) and n is the number of such Monte Carlo estimates (Monte Carlo asymptotic t statistics) or equivalently the number of replications. These choices of kernel and window width have been discussed above.

We estimate the density at 50 equally spaced points in the range $\pm 4s$, and we compute asymptotic 95% confidence intervals for each of the estimated density points using the formula given in (2), which for the standard normal kernel becomes

$$\hat{f}(x) \pm 1.96(\hat{f}(x))^{1/2}(2nh\sqrt{\Pi})^{-1/2}.$$

III. THE MODEL

The model for which we wish to compare our two estimation techniques is a simple simultaneous equations model involving rational expectations variables. Many econometric models involve expectations variables reflecting the fact that many economic decisions involve expectations of future realisations of economic variables which are necessarily unknown at the time the decisions are made. Two basic methods of handling these expectations variables have been utilized in econometric modeling: the first employs survey data of one kind or another, while the second uses some kind of expectations model (Holden et al., 1985). The rational expectations model (Muth, 1961) represents one of these expectations models. It is particularly attractive from a theoretical perspective, because unlike some of the earlier expectations models it does not imply that economic decision makers will make systematic mistakes.

To make this more concrete, consider the model

$$BY_t + \Gamma X_t + A_{t-1}Y_t = U_t, \tag{3}$$

where Y_t is a $G \times 1$ vector of endogenous variables at time t; X_t is a $K \times 1$ vector of exogenous variables at time t; $_{t-1}Y_t$ is the rational expectation of Y_t formed at time $t - 1$; U_t is a $G \times 1$ vector of normally distributed white noise random disturbances at time t; and B, Γ, and A are matrices of unknown parameters of order $G \times G$, $G \times K$ and $G \times G$, respectively.

We assume for simplicity that the exogenous variables X_t are generated by the following process:

$$X_t = C(L)X_t + e_t, \tag{4}$$

where $C(L)$ is a pth-order matrix polynomial in the lag operator L, that is, $LX_t = X_{t-1}$, etc., and e_t is assumed to be a $K \times 1$ vector of white noise random disturbances independent of U_t. To solve model (3) for the rational expectations vector $_{t-1}Y_t$, we first take the mathematical expectation conditional on the information set

$$I_{t-1} = \{X_{t-1}, X_{t-2}, \ldots, Y_{t-1}, Y_{t-2}, \ldots,$$

$$U_{t-1}, U_{t-2}, \ldots, e_{t-1}, e_{t-2}, \ldots\} \text{ of both sides, yielding}$$

$$B_{t-1}Y_t + \Gamma_{t-1}X_t + A_{t-1}Y_t = 0, \tag{5}$$

and then rearrange giving

$$_{t-1}Y_t = -(B + A)^{-1}\Gamma_{t-1}X_t, \tag{6}$$

which by (4) may then be rewritten as

$$_{t-1}Y_t = -(B - A)^{-1}\Gamma \sum_{i=1}^{p} C_i X_{t-i}. \tag{7}$$

This last equation, as can readily be ascertained, is now free of expectations terms and is referred to as the rational expectations solution of the model. This solution may now be substituted into (3) and hence render the original model into the transformed model

$$BY_t + \Gamma X_t - A(B + A)^{-1}\Gamma \sum_{i=1}^{p} C_i X_{t-i} = U_t, \tag{8}$$

which is composed exclusively of observable variables. Subject to the necessary identification conditions (Pesaran, 1981; Wegge and Feldman, 1983), this model may theoretically be estimated efficiently by *full-information maximum likelihood* (FIML) (Wallis, 1980).

In practice, however, despite the fact that FIML estimation is theoretically efficient, the technique has a number of drawbacks (e.g., see Fair, 1984; Sargent 1978); consequently applied researchers in macroeconomics have had recourse to single-equation estimation techniques, and it is these which will form the subject of our discussion below.

IV. ESTIMATION METHODS

We now consider two single-equation estimation techniques: first, the substitution method estimator due to Sargent (1973, 1976) and Wallis (1980); secondly, the errors-in-variables estimator due to McCallum (1976).

Without loss of generality, consider a single equation from (3), where for simplicity of exposition we change notation and, moreover, assume that only one rational expectations variable appears in the equation:

$$y_t = [_{t-1}z_t \, Z_t]\delta + u_t, \tag{9}$$

where y_t is a scalar endogenous variable; $_{t-1}z_t$ is the rational expectation of an endogenous variable; Z_t is a row vector containing k endogenous variables and $h - k - 1$ exogenous variables; δ is an $h \times 1$ vector of unknown coefficients; and u_t is a normally distributed white noise random disturbance.

The substitution method proceeds by noting that the rational expectations solution (7) may alternatively be written in terms of the forecasting equation

$$Y_t = -(B + A)^{-1}\Gamma \sum_{i=1}^{p} C_i X_{t-i} + \mathcal{H}_t, \tag{10}$$

where $\mathcal{H}_t$ is the vector of forecast errors, $Y_t - _{t-1}Y_t$. By the rational expectations hypothesis, this vector is orthogonal to the information set at time $t - 1$, that is, $E[\mathcal{H}_t \,|\, I_{t-1}] = 0$.

This implies that one can obtain a consistent estimate of the rational expectation $_{t-1}z_t$ by regressing z_t on p lagged values of all the exogenous variables in the model (3) and taking the fitted value $\hat{z}_t$. The substitution method then replaces the rational expectation, $_{t-1}z_t$, in (9) with $\hat{z}_t$ and estimates the resulting equation by two-stage least squares (2SLS) or instrumental variables (IV) treating $\hat{z}_t$ as a predetermined variable. One disadvantage of this method is that the estimated asymptotic standard errors computed by a standard package may be underestimated owing to the fact that the additional uncertainty arising from the replacement of $_{t-1}z_t$ with $\hat{z}_t$ has not been taken into account (Hayashi, 1980). A similar problem involving surprise models and, more generally, the whole issue of generated regressors has now spawned a considerable literature (e.g., Mishkin, 1983; Murphy and Topel, 1985; Pagan, 1984, 1985). In the experiments to follow we calculate the regular, i.e., the incorrect, asymptotic SEs, it being considered interesting to see the extent of this underestimation in practice, together with two sets of corrected asymptotic SEs based on White (1984, pp. 159–160, Corollary 6.21), as adjusted in Phillips (1985) and Newey and West (1986), and an extension of the results in

Murphy and Topel (1985). For convenience, these SEs will be referred to in the sequel as *regular*, *White*, and *Murphy and Topel*, respectively.

The errors-in-variables approach to the estimation of (9) proceeds instead by replacing the rational expectations variable, $_{t-1}z_t$, by its realized value, z_t, and then adding a compensating term to the random disturbance. Denoting the forecast error $z_t - {}_{t-1}z_t$ by η_t, we then obtain

$$y_t = [z_t\, Z_t]\delta + u_t - \delta_1\eta_t = Q_t\delta + v_t, \tag{11}$$

where δ_1 is the first element of δ, and v_t is the composite disturbance $u_t - \delta_1\eta_t$. Using z_t as a proxy for $_{t-1}z_t$ results in the composite disturbance v_t being potentially correlated with all the elements of Q_t not included in I_{t-1} except those predetermined variables which are perfectly predictable at time $t - 1$, for example, time trends and constants. To consistently estimate this equation, therefore, we need instruments composed from lagged endogenous or exogenous variables or perfectly predictable exogenous variables. In this case the estimated asymptotic SEs will also be consistent, this following from the fact that the composite disturbance is serially uncorrelated, given one further assumption, namely, conditional homoscedasticity, that is, $E(v_t^2 \mid F_t) = \sigma_v^2$ for all t, where F_t denotes the instrument set (Hansen, 1982; Cumby et al., 1983).

V. EXPERIMENTS

The particular rational expectations model used in our Monte Carlo experiments is a special case of (3):

$$
\begin{bmatrix} 1 & 0 & -\beta_1 \\ -\beta_2 & 1 & 0 \\ -\beta_3 & -\beta_4 & 1 \end{bmatrix}
\begin{bmatrix} y_{1t} \\ y_{2t} \\ y_{3t} \end{bmatrix}
+
\begin{bmatrix} -\gamma_1 & 0 & 0 & -\gamma_2 & -\gamma_3 \\ 0 & -\gamma_4 & -\gamma_5 & 0 & -\gamma_6 \\ -\gamma_7 & 0 & -\gamma_8 & 0 & -\gamma_9 \end{bmatrix}
\begin{bmatrix} x_{1t} \\ x_{2t} \\ x_{3t} \\ x_{4t} \\ x_{5t} \end{bmatrix}
$$

$$
+
\begin{bmatrix} 0 & -\alpha_1 & 0 \\ 0 & 0 & 0 \\ 0 & 0 & 0 \end{bmatrix}
\begin{bmatrix} {}_{t-1}y_{1t} \\ {}_{t-1}y_{2t} \\ {}_{t-1}y_{3t} \end{bmatrix}
=
\begin{bmatrix} u_{1t} \\ u_{2t} \\ u_{3t} \end{bmatrix}.
$$

This model, involving only one rational expectations variable, was chosen as it is both relatively simple and reasonably realistic.

In addition, all the equations are overidentified by at least four in the hope that this will ensure the existence of fourth-order population moments and hence make the SEs on the sample variances and MSEs below meaningful—this hope being based on the similarity of the two estimation techniques to 2SLS, given the exact results in the literature on the relationship between the degree of overidentification and existence of moments in the regular simultaneous equations model (Mariano and Sawa, 1972; Sawa, 1972).

For the experiments we used two variants, both of which have identical structural parameters, given in Table 1, chosen at random from the interval $(-1, +1)$, subject only to restrictions necessary for solution and identification, namely, that the matrices B and $(B + A)$ be nonsingular (Pesaran, 1981; Wegge and Feldman, 1983). The only difference between the two variants is that the data for the first variant, referred to hereafter as the "tight fit" variant, are generated from a multivariate normal random disturbance vector U_t having a smaller variance covariance matrix, i.e., a smaller multiple of the basic variance–covariance matrix

$$\begin{bmatrix} 0.1 & 0.002 & 0.002 \\ 0.002 & 0.1 & 0.002 \\ 0.002 & 0.002 & 0.1 \end{bmatrix},$$

than the second, hereafter referred to as the "loose fit" variant, the multiples being 2 and 8.5, respectively. These particular multiples were chosen by the rather ad hoc procedure of running ordinary least squares (OLS) on the equation with the rational expectation, having replaced both the endogenous variable and the rational expectations variable with their expected values, and then adjusting the multiple of the basic variance–covariance matrix until we obtained an R^2 of approximately 0.9 for the first variant and approximately 0.7 for the second variant.

The exogenous variables x_{1t}, x_{2t}, x_{3t}, and x_{4t} were generated from independent univariate AR(1) processes with the autoregressive parameters set at 0.8 to mimic the empirical fact that macroeconomic time series are typically strongly autocorrelated, with the errors on these processes generated independently of the structural disturbances from a standard normal distribution. Here x_{5t} is a constant term. These exogenous variables were generated once and for all, and neither regenerated for each replication nor

Table 1. Values of the
Structural Parameters

Parameter	Value
β_1	0.21
β_2	0.95
β_3	−0.87
β_4	0.17
γ_1	0.55
γ_2	0.91
γ_3	−0.87
γ_4	0.61
γ_5	−0.71
γ_6	0.31
γ_7	−0.75
γ_8	−0.59
γ_9	−0.75
α_1	−0.27

for each variant. The covariance matrix of these exogenous variables is given in Table 2.

We estimated only the equation containing the rational expectations variable. A thousand replications and three sample sizes—20, 50, and 100—were used throughout, as was direct simulation, i.e., we did not use variance reduction techniques such as control variates or antithetic variates. We did, however, use common data sets, as recommended by Hendry (1984); i.e., not only did we use the same sets of data for each estimator, but also we reused the data from, say, the 20-sample size as part of the data for the 50-sample size—this reduces variability between sample size comparisions. In addition, the fixing of the exogenous variables across all replications and experiments helps to reduce variability across both sample size and estimator comparisons.

The pseudorandom number generator used was SUPERDUPER (Marsaglia, 1976), which is a combination of congruential and shift-register generators. This is a very-high-quality generator and has passed extensive tests for randomness (Marsaglia, 1976; McLeod, 1981). Standard normal variates were obtained by the Beasley and Springer (1977) procedure and then transformed to multivariate normal variates, where appropriate, by the method

Table 2.   Covariance Matrix of the
Exogenous Variables

Sample Size 20:

	x_1	x_2	x_3	x_4	x_5
x_1	0.99				
x_2	0.76	5.66			
x_3	−0.10	−1.10	1.24		
x_4	0.04	−1.90	1.08	2.20	
x_5	0.00	0.00	0.00	0.00	0.00

Sample Size 50:

	x_1	x_2	x_3	x_4	x_5
x_1	1.25				
x_2	0.01	3.45			
x_3	0.86	−1.48	4.16		
x_4	0.12	−0.92	0.20	2.11	
x_5	0.00	0.00	0.00	0.00	0.00

Sample Size 100:

	x_1	x_2	x_3	x_4	x_5
x_1	1.61				
x_2	0.61	2.82			
x_3	0.72	−0.71	3.25		
x_4	−0.33	−1.02	−0.20	2.83	
x_5	0.00	0.00	0.00	0.00	0.00

of Nagar (1969). All experiments were programmed in FORTRAN, using IMSL subroutines, and executed on the University of Western Ontario's Cyber 835.

Finally, the variables used to form the instruments in the error-invariables estimation procedure were all the exogenous and endogenous variables in the model lagged one and two periods.

VI.   DATA GENERATION

As the generation of the data for a rational expectations simultaneous equations model Monte Carlo experiment requires a few more steps than that for a regular simultaneous equations model Monte Carlo experiment (e.g., see Raj, 1980) and is relatively unfamiliar, we make this process explicit.

Consider Eq. (3), which we repeat for convenience

$$BY_t + \Gamma X_t + A_{t-1}Y_t = U_t.$$

The reduced form of this model is

$$Y_t = -B^{-1}A_{t-1}Y_t - B^{-1}\Gamma X_t + B^{-1}U_t, \tag{12}$$

and the rational expectations solution is

$$_{t-1}Y_t = -(B + A)^{-1}\Gamma_{t-1}X_t. \tag{13}$$

Step 1. Generation of the series on X_t: This series was generated from independent, univariate AR(1) processes beginning 45 periods before the sample was taken in order to eliminate start up effects.

Step 2. Generation of the series on $_{t-1}X_t$: This series was generated, given our assumptions above, from $0.8x_{it-1}$, $i = 1, \ldots, 4$. The rational expectation of the constant term x_{5t} is, of course, just itself.

Step 3. Generation of the series on $_{t-1}Y_t$: Given the series on $_{t-1}X_t$ from Step 2, $_{t-1}Y_t$ was generated from the rational expectations solution (13). Note that as we are fixing X_t across all experiments and replications, we only needed to generate $_{t-1}Y_t$ once. Moreover, as only $_{t-1}Y_{2t}$ appears in the model, we only needed to generate this one rational expectation.

Step 4. Generation of the series on Y_t: Given the series on X_t from Step 1 and $_{t-1}Y_t$ from Step 3, we generated the data on Y_t from the reduced form [Eq. (12)] using the generated reduced form errors.

VII. RESULTS AND CONCLUSIONS

We now consider the results of our various experiments. For all cases we generated a substantial array of summary statistics, both parametric and nonparametric, in addition to the various nonparametric density estimates. Due to the limitations of space and the expository nature of this paper, however, we only report a small subset of these results in any detail, namely, sample size 50 and coefficients 1, 3, and 5. Results for the other cases are very similar. More extensive results are available elsewhere (Power, 1985).

The nonparametric density estimates for these experiments are given in Figures 1 through 6, where for ease of interpretation we

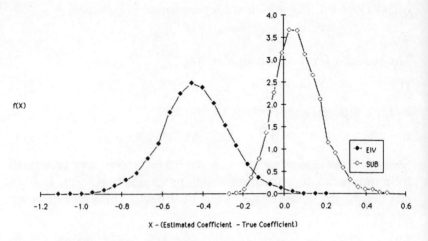

Figure 1. Coefficient 1: sample size 50; tight fit.

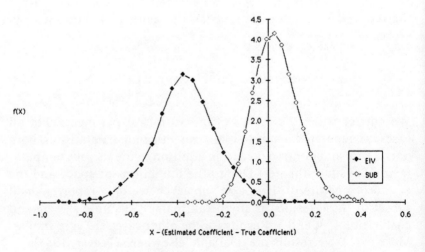

Figure 2. Coefficient 3: sample size 50; tight fit.

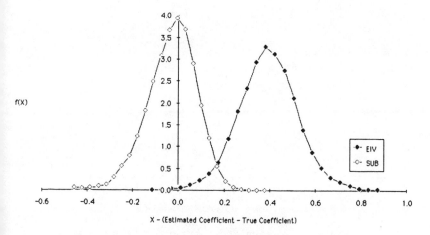

Figure 3. Coefficient 5: sample size 50; tight fit.

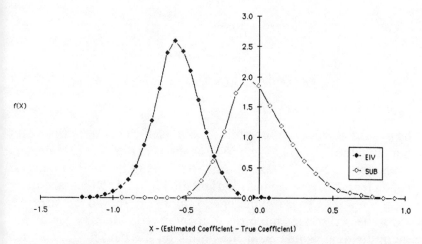

Figure 4. Coefficient 1: sample size 50; loose fit.

171

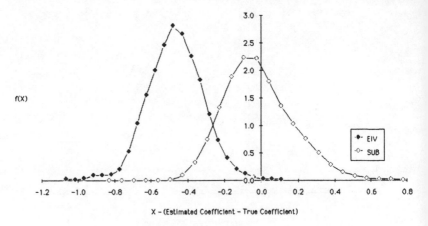

Figure 5.   Coefficient 3: sample size 50; loose fit.

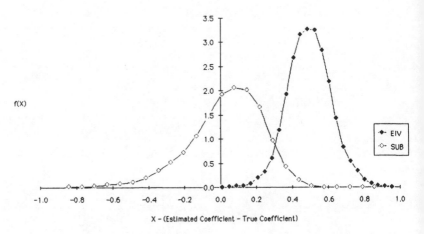

Figure 6.   Coefficient 5: sample size 50; loose fit.

have subtracted the true values of the coefficients from their estimated values. To give some idea of the accuracy of these density
estimates, we show asymptotic 95% confidence bounds for
coefficient 3 of the tight fit variant in Figure 7, which are quite
representative. These confidence bounds, it should be stressed,
show the loci of the endpoints of the 95% confidence intervals for
the individual estimates of the points on the density, rather than
95% confidence bounds for the overall density estimate.

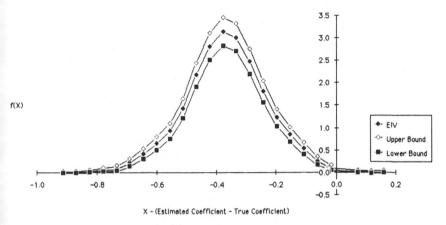

X - (Estimated Coefficient - True Coefficient)

Figure 7. Coefficient 3: sample size 50; tight fit; 95% confidence bounds.

A cursory examination of these density estimates reveals that, for these cases at least, the substitution method estimator (SUB) is considerably less biased than the errors-in-variables estimator (EIV), while with respect to dispersion SUB seems to do rather better than EIV in the tight fit variant and rather worse in the loose fit variant. Moreover, it is interesting to note that the bias of EIV is always opposite in sign to the true value of the coefficient (the true values from Table 1 are 0.21, 0.91, and −0.27 for coefficients 1, 3, and 5, repectively). In addition, whereas the EIV density estimates are pretty much symmetric in all cases, the SUB density estimates are always skewed in the opposite direction to the sign of the true coefficient values.

In short, it is clear that these nonparametric density estimates contain a great deal of information about the empirical sampling distributions; and although a number of the observations made above are readily apparent from traditional Monte Carlo summary statistics, some of which are reported in Table 3 [the statistics given are Percentage Bias (PBIAS), Percentage Variance (PVAR), and Percentage Mean Squared Error (PMSE), with SEs in parentheses (Raj, 1980)], the observation concerning skewness is not. This last point is not to say that Monte Carlo studies never present skewness statistics—clearly they do (e.g., see MacKinnon and White, 1985); rather, it is to underline the point that a density estimate will almost always reveal additional information to that available in summary statistics of whatever kind.

Table 3.   Monte Carlo Summary Statistics Sample Size 50

		1	3	5
Coefficient / Statistic / Estimator				
A. Tight fit variant:				
PBIAS	EIV	−208.29	−40.09	145.15
		(2.51)	(0.48)	(1.47)
	SUB	34.72	3.78	--10.95
		(1.71)	(0.34)	(1.25)
PVAR	EIV	63.07	2.27	21.70
		(3.36)	(0.12)	(1.12)
	SUB	29.05	1.14	15.50
		(1.94)	(0.08)	(0.90)
PMSE	EIV	496.92	18.35	232.37
		(10.86)	(0.40)	(4.40)
	SUB	41.11	1.28	16.70
		(2.63)	(0.09)	(1.03)
B. Loose fit variant:				
PBIAS	EIV	−226.7	−51.29	183.34
		(2.46)	(0.92)	(1.42)
	SUB	6.83	−1.01	9.71
		(3.59)	(0.71)	(2.55)
PVAR	EIV	60.31	2.70	20.05
		(3.61)	(0.16)	(1.16)
	SUB	128.70	5.09	64.77
		(13.80)	(0.66)	(5.68)
PMSE	EIV	771.97	29.01	356.20
		(13.18)	(0.56)	(5.29)
	SUB	129.17	5.10	65.71
		(14.07)	(0.65)	(5.42)

The overall dominance of SUB is expected from theory, given the fact that EIV cannot exploit current period exogenous variables as instruments in this situation. The increasing relative dispersion in the loose fit variant stems in all probability from the fact that SUB has to estimate the rational expectation in the first stage and that when the fit of the model is loose this estimation becomes subject to a relatively high variance, while still remaining relatively unbiased.

Turning now to the density estimates of the sampling distributions of the asymptotic *t* statistics presented in Figures 8 through 19, we can begin to draw some conclusions concerning inference based upon the asymptotic formulas. Again we give some idea of the accuracy of these density estimates by giving the asymptotic

(*Text continues on page 180*)

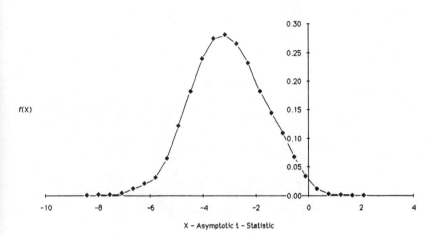

Figure 8. Coefficient 1: sample size 50; tight fit; EIV asymptotic *t* statistic.

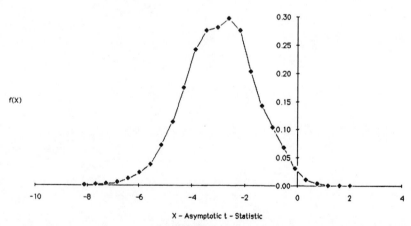

Figure 9. Coefficient 3: sample size 50; tight fit; EIV asymptotic *t* statistic.

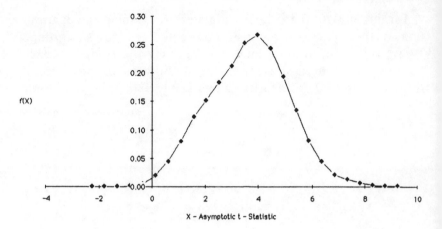

Figure 10. Coefficient 5: sample size 50; tight fit; EIV asymptotic *t* statistic.

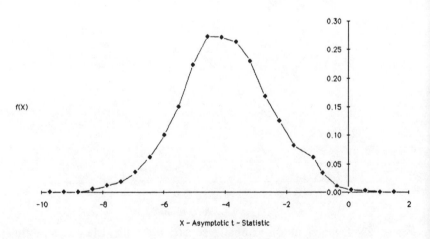

Figure 11. Coefficient 1: sample size 50; loose fit; EIV asymptotic *t* statistic.

176

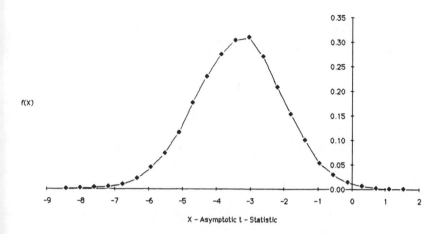

Figure 12. Coefficient 3: sample size 50; loose fit; EIV asymptotic *t* statistic.

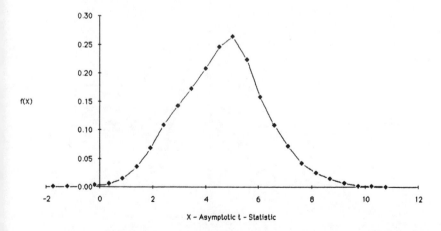

Figure 13. Coefficient 5: sample size 50; loose fit; EIV asymptotic *t* statistic.

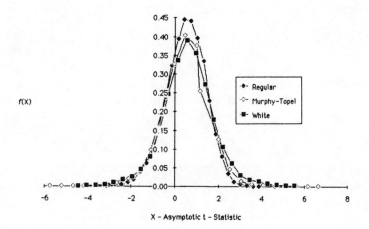

Figure 14. Coefficient 1: sample size 50; tight fit; SUB asymptotic *t* statistic.

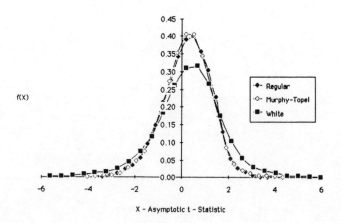

Figure 15. Coefficient 3: sample size 50; tight fit; SUB asymptotic *t* statistic.

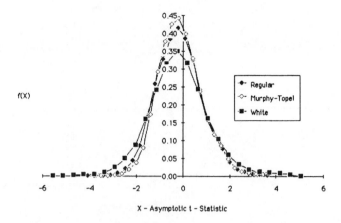

Figure 16. Coefficient 5: sample size 50; tight fit; SUB asymptotic
t statistic.

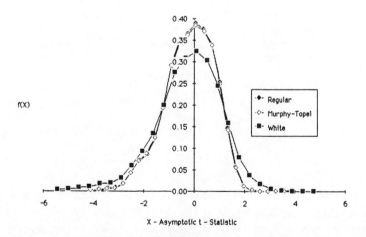

Figure 17. Coefficient 1: sample size 50; loose fit; SUB asymptotic
t statistic.

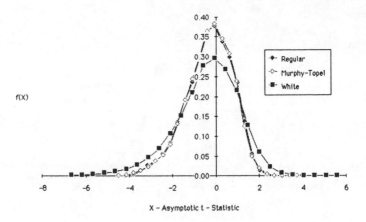

Figure 18. Coefficient 3: sample size 50; loose fit; SUB asymptotic
t statistic.

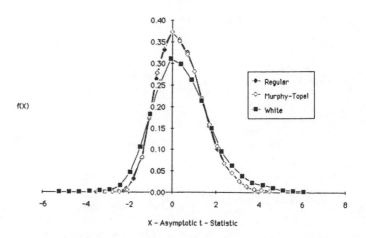

Figure 19. Coefficient 5: sample size 50; loose fit; SUB asymptotic
t statistic.

95% confidence bounds for coefficient 3 of the tight fit variant in
Figure 20. The striking feature of these results is that, whereas
SUB seems to result in reasonably accurate inferences using either
the regular, i.e., incorrect, or the Murphy and Topel asymptotic
standard errors and only slightly overrejects using the White
asymptotic standard errors (the critical *t* values for the appropriate
45 degrees of freedom for two-sided tests are ±1.301, ±1.681,

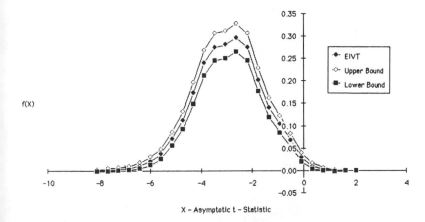

Figure 20. Coefficient 3: sample size 50; tight fit; EIV asymptotic
t statistic; 95% confidence bounds.

±2.016, and ±2.693 at the 20%, 10%, 5%, and 1% significance
levels, respectively), EIV does not and, in particular, overrejects
substantially. (Incidentally, the White variance–covariance matrix
was not positive definite in 42 and 29 replications for the loose
and tight fit variants, respectively. In these cases we substituted
the regular variance–covariance matrix.) To make this more concrete we numerically integrated under these estimated densities to
obtain estimates of the actual sizes of the tests. These we report
in Table 4, together with consistent estimates of their SEs from
the formula $(\hat{F}(x)(1 - \hat{F}(x))/n))^{1/2}$, where $\hat{F}(x)$ is the estimated
actual size of the test (Singh et al., 1983).

The fact that SUB seems to result in relatively accurate inferences
in this situation using either the regular, i.e., the incorrect, or the
Murphy and Topel asymptotic SEs and only slightly overrejects
using the White asymptotic SEs is reassuring, while the fact that
EIV results in such poor inference would indicate that the applied
researcher should exercise some caution in the interpretation of
hypothesis tests involving this estimation procedure.

Once again, the nonparametric density estimates give a very
transparent view of the situation and can clearly enhance the value
of traditional Monte Carlo results. A further advantage of nonparametric density estimation, not illustrated here, is that it is possible
to plot density estimates for a given estimator for several different
sample sizes on the same figure, thus yielding a clear graphic

Table 4. Estimated Actual Sizes of the Asymptotic t Tests

		1	3	5
Coefficient / Estimator / Nominal Size				
A. Tight fit variant:				
EIV	20	0.885	0.886	0.928
		(0.0101)	(0.0101)	(0.0082)
	10	0.827	0.825	0.884
		(0.0120)	(0.0120)	(0.0101)
	5	0.766	0.752	0.837
		(0.0134)	(0.0137)	(0.0117)
	1	0.607	0.561	0.721
		(0.0154)	(0.0157)	(0.0142)
SUB	20	0.225	0.217	0.201
(Regular)		(0.0132)	(0.0130)	(0.0127)
	10	0.107	0.103	0.096
		(0.0098)	(0.0096)	(0.0093)
	5	0.044	0.050	0.047
		(0.0065)	(0.0069)	(0.0067)
	1	0.006	0.009	0.011
		(0.0024)	(0.0030)	(0.0033)
SUB	20	0.268	0.214	0.168
(Murphy-Topel)		(0.0140)	(0.0130)	(0.0118)
	10	0.150	0.108	0.075
		(0.0113)	(0.0098)	(0.0083)
	5	0.082	0.056	0.035
		(0.0087)	(0.0072)	(0.0059)
	1	0.023	0.014	0.008
		(0.0048)	(0.0038)	(0.0028)
SUB	20	0.309	0.339	0.291
(White)		(0.0146)	(0.0150)	(0.0144)
	10	0.196	0.225	0.182
		(0.0126)	(0.0132)	(0.0122)
	5	0.127	0.154	0.118
		(0.0105)	(0.0114)	(0.0102)
	1	0.052	0.072	0.050
		(0.0070)	(0.0082)	(0.0069)

Table 4.   (Continued)

		1	3	5

Coefficient/ Estimator/ Nominal Size

B. Loose fit variant:

EIV	20	0.961	0.942	0.981
		(0.0061)	(0.0074)	(0.0043)
	10	0.934	0.898	0.965
		(0.0079)	(0.0096)	(0.0058)
	5	0.905	0.845	0.944
		(0.0093)	(0.0114)	(0.0073)
	1	0.813	0.688	0.875
		(0.0123)	(0.0147)	(0.0105)
SUB (Regular)	20	0.180	0.231	0.239
		(0.0121)	(0.0133)	(0.0135)
	10	0.096	0.125	0.138
		(0.0093)	(0.0104)	(0.0109)
	5	0.051	0.074	0.084
		(0.0070)	(0.0083)	(0.0088)
	1	0.012	0.027	0.030
		(0.0034)	(0.0051)	(0.0054)
SUB (Murphy-Topel)	20	0.184	0.222	0.238
		(0.0122)	(0.0132)	(0.0135)
	10	0.093	0.122	0.138
		(0.0092)	(0.0104)	(0.0109)
	5	0.053	0.072	0.085
		(0.0071)	(0.0082)	(0.0088)
	1	0.012	0.027	0.031
		(0.0035)	(0.0051)	(0.0055)
SUB (White)	20	0.287	0.345	0.332
		(0.0143)	(0.0150)	(0.0149)
	10	0.179	0.234	0.219
		(0.0121)	(0.0134)	(0.0131)
	5	0.116	0.164	0.149
		(0.0101)	(0.0117)	(0.0113)
	1	0.047	0.081	0.072
		(0.0067)	(0.0086)	(0.0082)

indication of how the sampling distribution changes with the sample size.

REFERENCES

Barro, R. J. (1977) "Unanticipated Money Growth and Unemployment in the United States." *American Economic Review* 67, 101–115.

Beasley, J. D. and S. J. Springer (1977) "Algorithm AS 111: The Percentage Points of the Normal Distribution". *Applied Statistics* 26, 118–121.

Bierens, H. (1985) "Kernel Estimators of Regression Functions". Research report No. 8518, Department of Economics, University of Amsterdam.

Blanchard, O. J. (1983) "The Production and Inventory Behavior of the American Automobile Industry". *Journal of Political Economy* 91, 365–400.

Cacoullos, T. (1966) "Estimation of a Multivariate Density". *Annals of the Institute of Statistical Mathematics* 18, 179–189.

Cumby, R. E., J. Huizinga and M. Obstfeld (1983) "Two-Step Two-Stage Least Squares Estimation in Models With Rational Expectations". *Journal of Econometrics* 21, 333–355.

Epanechnikov, V. A. (1969) "Nonparametric Estimation of a Multi-Dimensional Probability Density". *Theory of Probability and its Applications* 14, 153–158.

Fair, R. (1984) "Effects of Expected Future Government Deficits on Current Economic Activity". National Bureau of Economic Research (NBER) working paper No. 1293.

Fomby, T. B. and D. K. Guilkey (1983) "An Examination of Two-Step Estimators for Models with Lagged Dependent Variables and Autocorrelated Errors". *Journal of Econometrics* 22, 291–300.

Hansen, L. P. (1982) "Large Sample Properties of Generalised Method of Moments Estimators". *Econometrica* 50, 1029–1054.

Hayashi, F. (1980) "Estimation of Macroeconometric Models with Rational Expectations: A Survey". Discussion paper No. 444, Department of Economics, Northwestern University.

Hendry, D. F. (1984) "Monte Carlo Experimentation in Econometrics". Pp. 937–976 in Z. Griliches and M. D. Intriligator (eds.), *Handbook of Econometrics*, Vol. 2. Amsterdam and New York: North-Holland Publishing.

Holden, K., D. A. Peel, and J. L. Thompson (1985) *Expectations: Theory and Evidence.* London: Macmillan.

McCallum, B. T. (1976) "Rational Expectations and the Natural Rate Hypothesis: Some Consistent Estimates". *Econometrica* 44, 43–52.

MacKinnon, J. G. and H. White (1985) "Some Heteroskedasticity-Consistent Covariance Matrix Estimators with Improved Finite Sample Properties". *Journal of Econometrics* 29, 305–325.

McLeod, A. I. (1982) "Efficient FORTRAN Coding of a Random Number Generator". Technical report TR-82-08, Department of Statistics, The University of Western Ontario.

Mariano, R. S. and T. Sawa (1972) "The Exact Finite-Sample Distribution of the Limited Information Maximum Likelihood Estimator in the Case of Two Included Endogenous Variables". *Journal of the American Statistical Association* 67, 159-163.

Marsaglia, G. (1976) "Random Number Generation". In A. Ralston (ed.), *Encyclopedia of Computer Science*. New York: Petrocell & Charter.

Mikhail, W. M. (1975) "A Comparative Monte Carlo Study of the Properties of Econometric Estimators". *Journal of the American Statistical Association* 70, 94-104.

Mishkin, F. S. (1983) *A Rational Expectations Approach to Macroeconometrics*. Chicago: University of Chicago Press.

Murphy, K. M. and R. H. Topel (1985) "Estimation and Inference in Two-Step Econometric Models". *Journal of Business and Economic Statistics* 3, 370-379.

Muth, J. F. (1961) "Rational Expectations and the Theory of Price Movements". *Econometrica* 29, 315-335.

Nagar, A. L. (1969) "Stochastic Simulation of the Brookings Model". In J. S. Duesenberry (ed.), *The Brookings Model: Some Further Results*. Chicago: Rand McNally.

Newey, W. K. and K. D. West (1986) "A Simple, Positive Semi-Definite, Heteroskedasticity and Autocorrelation Consistent Covariance Matrix". National Bureau of Economic Research (NBER) technical working paper No. 55.

Pagan, A. (1984) "Econometric Issues in the Analysis of Regressions with Generated Regressors". *International Economic Review* 25, 221-247.

Pagan, A. (1985) "Two-Stage and Related Estimators and Their Applications". Discussion paper No. 741, Cowles Foundation, Yale University.

Pagan, A. and A. Ullah (1986) "The Econometric Analysis of Models with Risk Terms". The University of Western Ontario (mimeo).

Parzen, E. (1962) "On the Estimation of Probability Density and Model". *Annals of Mathematical Statistics* 33, 1065-1076.

Pesaran, M. H. (1981) "Identification of Rational Expectations Models". *Journal of Econometrics* 16, 387-388.

Phillips, P. C. B. (1985) "Time Series Regression with Unit Roots". Discussion paper No. 740, Cowles Foundation, Yale University.

Power, S. (1985) "Single-Equation Errors-in-Variables Estimation of Rational Expectations Models". Unpublished Ph.D. dissertation, Department of Economics, The University of Western Ontario.

Raj, B. (1980) "A Monte Carlo Study of Small Sample Properties of Simultaneous Equation Estimators with Normal and Nonnormal Disturbances". *Journal of the American Statistical Association* 75, 221-229.

Rao, B. L. S. P. (1983) *Nonparametric Functional Estimation*. Orlando, FL: Academic Press.

Rosenblatt, M. (1956) "Remarks on Some Nonparametric Estimates of a Density Function". *Annals of Mathematical Statistics* 27, 832-837.

Sargent, T. J. (1973) "Rational Expectations, the Real Rate of Interest, and the Natural Rate of Unemployment". *Brookings Papers on Economic Activity* 2, 429-472.

Sargent, T. J. (1976) "A Classical Macroeconomic Model of the United States". *Journal of Political Economy* 84, 207-238.

Sargent, T. J. (1978) "Estimation of Dynamic Labor Demand Schedules Under Rational Expectations". *Journal of Political Economy* 86, 1009-1044.

Sawa, T. (1972) "Finite Sample Properties of the k-Class Estimators". *Econometrica* 40, 653-680.

Silverman, B. W. (1986) *Density Estimation for Statistics and Data Analysis*. New York: Chapman & Hall.

Singh, R. S. and A. Ullah (1985) "Nonparametric Recursive Estimation of a Multivariate, Marginal, and Conditional DGP with an Application to Specification of Econometric Models". *Communications in Statistics: Theory and Methods* 15, 3489-3513.

Singh, R. S., T. Gasser, and B. Prasad (1983) "Nonparametric Estimates of Distribution Functions". *Communications in Statistics: Theory and Methods* 12, 2095-2108.

Ullah, A. and R. S. Singh (1985) "The Estimation of Probability Density Functions and its Applications in Econometrics". Technical report No. 6, The Centre for Decision Sciences and Econometrics, The University of Western Ontario.

Wallis, K. F. (1980) "Econometric Implications of the Rational Expectations Hypothesis". *Econometrica* 48, 49-73.

Wegge, L. L. and M. Feldman (1983) "Identifiability Criteria for Muth-Rational Expectations Models". *Journal of Econometrics* 21, 245-254.

White, H. (1984) *Asymptotic Theory for Econometricians*. Orlando, FL: Academic Press.

VALIDATING SIMULATION STUDIES

George F. Rhodes, Jr.

I. INTRODUCTION

A modest estimate indicates that several hundred years of research effort are devoted annually to simulation studies in economics and statistics. For example, Hauck and Anderson[1] surveyed 1198 papers published in five statistical journals for 1975, 1978, and 1981, finding that 216 papers (18%) reported simulation results. Even with a modest assumption like one-half year of effort per paper, that represents over 100 years of research effort. The research efforts reported in this volume alone must be measured in tens of years.

Uses for simulation studies range across the applied, theoretical, and policy studies of economists and statisticians. Simulation studies are playing increasing roles in rate and rule making before regulatory commissions, in econometric and statistical theory development, in selection of techniques for applied research, as

Advances in Econometrics, Volume 6, pages 187–213

well as in solutions for intricate empirical research projects. Simulation models are used in the classroom, the research institute, the consulting firm, public and quasi-public agencies, and the boardroom. One of the questions to be asked is whether the success at interpreting and documenting this outpouring of simulation studies has brought increases in knowledge proportional to the effort expended in doing them? If not, is the excess of cost over benefit due to inherent weaknesses in the technique or to lack of skill in using it, or have we simply failed to harvest all of the fruit from the studies? It is the aim of this paper to investigate some dimensions of these questions.

Interpreting and documenting the results from simulation studies has been a growing concern of statisticians. It has been recognized that rather rudimentary standards govern the reporting of simulation studies in statistics and economics, where there are standards at all.[2] I believe that this is because the framework for creating and interpreting simulation studies is itself too rudimentary. Documentation standards reflect the standards for designing and executing various simulation studies, including Monte Carlo and sampling experiments as well as simulation of decision models. Where there is clear knowledge of what can and what cannot be learned from the studies, appropriate documentation will follow almost automatically. Where there is only inadequate knowledge of what to expect from the studies and how to use them, documentation and interpretation are likely to remain rudimentary. Competent experimental design and execution will naturally produce matching documentation. With that belief in mind, the present essay will base suggested documentation and interpretation standards on the logic of simulation studies. This essay focuses on interpretation of simulation study results, with documentation as a derived concept. The essential objective is to interpret experimental results in a useful and useable manner, recognizing that documentation is a tool for interpretation rather than a direct objective in itself.

The basic question for interpreting and documenting simulation studies is this: "Does the process of the simulation study match the concept of the simulation study so that the results are informative within the research context" Interpretation and documentation standards for simulation studies are governed by knowing the kind of information that one can expect to derive from them. Knowing the capabilities as well as the limitations of simulation studies will motivate the effective documentation that is essential for productive interpretations.

II. WHAT IS A SIMULATION STUDY?

A simulation study is a statistical experiment. Before comparing different kinds of simulation studies, it will be worthwhile to outline the elements of statistical experiments.

A statistical experiment may be thought of as a series of set mappings. The beginning set is the population; the initial set function is the sample design, whose domain is the population and whose range is the sample space. The sample space is precisely determined by the population and the sample design. The second set function is the random variable, whose domain is the sample space and whose range is the set of real numbers. The set that is the range of the random variable function is itself often called "random variables." Additional mappings from the set of random variables are produced by functions called "estimators" and "test statistics." These mappings use the set of random variables as their domain, their range sets being called sample statistics. The set relations that characterize a statistical experiment are shown in Figure 1. The process of a statistical experiment is illustrated in Figure 1 by moving from left to right as the series of set mappings transform the domains at the left to the ranges at the right. Set functions are shown in italics.

Set	Fn.	Set	Fn.	Set	Fns.	Set
Population	*Sample Design*	Sample Space	*Random Variable*	Random Variables	*Estimators Test Statistics*	Sample Statistics

Figure 1

Statistical experiments may be divided into categories according to alternative features and purposes of the experimental design. Four categories of experiments have been chosen for discussion: natural experiments, Monte Carlo experiments, sampling experiments, and decision model simulations.

Natural experiments focus on the characteristics of existing natural populations, such as populations of consumers, workers, or firms. Population behavior as exhibited in sample distribution functions and statistics is studied and described. Natural experiments may measure unemployment rates or reveal consumer purchasing patterns. Recent research has introduced the concept of a *superpopulation*, which may also be the focus of study for natural experiments. Thus, one can study the behavior of the existing finite population or of the conceptually infinite superpopulation.[3]

Monte Carlo experiments are designed to generate random numbers in order to simulate a physical process. The process may be either random or deterministic. "In the case of a probabilistic problem the simplest Monte Carlo approach is to observe random numbers, chosen in such a way that they directly simulate the physical random processes of the original problem, and to infer the desired solution from the behavior of these random numbers."[4] The experiment may be used to approximate solutions to equations representing the process as well as to simulate samples from the population that would be generated by the process. Or Monte Carlo experiments may be designed to estimate parameters for both natural and artificial populations, as when in an early application they were used to estimate values of the physical constant pi (π).

Sampling experiments also focus on populations, but on populations of sample and test statistics rather than on natural populations. Thus, in a sampling experiment one creates a large batch of sample statistics computed as estimators and test statistics. These samples of estimates and test statistics are then used to analyze the behaviors and properties of their parent populations. In econometrics, sampling experiments have been used to compare properties of alternative estimators; to discern properties of estimators measured by moments, bias, and concentration; to measure the accuracy of asymptotic approximations to power functions; to "solve" nuisance parameter problems; and to study the finite sample distribution functions of estimators and test statistics. Comparing alternative simultaneous equation parameter estimates and assessing the accuracy of approximations to exact critical regions in simultaneous equations inference have been the most prevalent uses of sampling experiments in economics. However, they have not by any means settled these issues.

Decision model experiments are used to simulate and compare the outcomes of physical processes under alternative conditions. Policy simulations in economics are decision model experiments. They are designed to simulate reactions by sectors of the economy to different policies, exogeneous shocks, or regulation schemata. They may also simulate cost and production functions in firms and systems, especially in regulated sectors of the economy. Later in this paper a special section is devoted to documentation standards for policy simulations. Those standards may indeed provide a pattern for the entire problem of documentation standards. In physical processes, one may simulate reactions by varying temperature, pressure, or volume. Such experiments amount to comparing characteristics of populations generated by varying random processes. Simulations create samples from the varying populations.

Statistical experiments are carried out in three basic steps: the first step is design of the experiment; the second, execution of the experimental design; and the third, analysis and interpretation of the results.

The design of a statistical experiment involves either creating or choosing five basic elements: the population and the four set mappings, sample design, random variable, estimators, and test statistics[5] (refer to Figure 1). The design of a statistical experiment is complete when these elements are identified and specified.

In simulation studies it may be necessary to create a *sample generator*, which is a set function that will use a distribution function and a sample design as inputs to create samples drawn from the population under the sample design. A sample generator must be created when the experiment calls for sampling from an artificial population, as opposed to an existing natural population. To accommodate the obvious use of computers in simulation studies, a *cybernetic sample generator* may also need to be defined. A cybernetic sample generator is a model, perhaps embedded in a computer code, of a sample generator that is capable of generating the complete sample space without producing, undetected, any samples not in the sample space. (A cybernetic sample generator should always be a model of a sample generator but will never be equivalent to it.) Specifying the population, creating the sample design (along with the sample generator and cybernetic sample generator) will allow creation of the sample space. Additional steps required are definition of the random variable functions and of the estimator and test statistic functions.

The execution of the simulation study creates the physical realization of the experimental design. It means creating actual samples from the sample space, whether from a natural population or from a created population through a cybernetic sample generator. This is the second stage in a simulation study.

In the third stage the set of sample statistics is treated as a sample from the population of sample statistics, and the sample and results are *analyzed and interpreted* to complete the purposes of the study.

In the language of economics, demand for research results from simulation studies is a derived demand. The results will be used by other researchers as inputs to their own projects. Then, in order to be persuaded to use the results from simulation studies, downstream producers will need to know that the input is worth the price, that the value of the marginal product is at least equal to the marginal cost. Viewed in this way, documentation standards are recognized as tools for measuring the value of information.

In determining the value of information produced by another researcher, an economist faces three basic issues: (1) Is the study design capable of producing valuable information? (2) Did the execution of the study actually produce the information sought? (3) What are the valid interpretations of the results? For each of these issues, one may think of a checklist of threshold questions to be answered in measuring the value of the information produced by the study. Answering the third question will tell the potential user whether the results will be productive inputs in his/her own project.

1. Is the Study Design Capable of Producing Valuable Information?

To answer this question for a potential consumer of information a researcher would want to address the two implicit components of a thorough answer. The first issue is simply, "What is the information yielded by the study?" The most direct, competent response to this issue is to identify the information that the study will produce. Additional documentation will assist in appraising the value of the information. It will answer such questions as the following: Does the study address an important open issue? How do I know that the question has not been answered analytically? How do I know that it has not already been resolved by another simulation study?

The second issue is also direct: "Is the study design logically capable of producing the information sought" Or "Is there anything in the study design that would prevent it from achieving the purposes identified?" Of course, the basic evidence to be presented here is the study design itself. What guides the completeness of the presentation? It is knowing that the potential consumer must be able to judge whether the study is logically capable of producing the product. He/she must also be able to tell whether the study design is deductively flawed in any manner that would reduce or eliminate the value of the product. A potential consumer will want documentation that will allow answers to such questions as these: How do I know that the simulation study design will produce answers to the essential questions? How does this simulation study apply to my research?

Evidence as to the logical consistency of the study is found in the sample generator. Documenting the conceptual and logical validity of the study means specifying the basic components of the design: the populations, the sample design, and the sample generator.

2. Did the Execution of the Study Actually Produce the Information Sought?

The burden of proof resting on the researcher here is to show that that actual execution conformed to the design of the study. The primary focus is on the cybernetic sample generator. Did it actually generate the sample called for in the design? Here the consumer will be cognizant of the ways in which the execution may contradict the design of the study.

A cybernetic sample generator will ordinarily consist of two components: a random number generator producing samples from population U with distribution function $F(x)$ together with a set function ($f:x$ to z) transforming points from U into sample points from population V with distribution function $G(z)$. The consumer of simulation study information will want to know what has been done to ensure that indeed the sample generated from population V, with distribution function $G(z)$, is the sample required by the study design.

Essential questions to be answered by the documentation here include the following:

1. Is the sample drawn according to the sampling design? What is often addressed here is the issue: Does the random number generator really generate random numbers? Since most simulation studies are designed to use simple random samples, this is an essential issue. But it is not necessary to use simple random samples. To be documented here are two essential points: first, that the sampling design is fully specified in a manner consistent with the purposes of the study; and, second, that the sample is created as designed.

2. Is the sample drawn from the appropriate population? A sample drawn according to the sample design from the wrong population will not yield the sample of sampling statistcs sought. What is needed here is evidence that the population generated actually has the properties required by the sample design. Not only does it need parameters as designed, but the basic distribution function has to be the one specified. Tests of fit and other appropriate evidence showing compliance with the sample design should be completed and reported.

Ensuring that the simulation study produced the information sought requires that the experiment was completed in substantial compliance with the design. Compliance, or failure thereof, must be documented before the reliability of the results can be appraised.

3. What Are the Valid Interpretations of the Results?

Interpretation of results begins with a complete account of the experiment. In addition to the experimental design and the execution of the study, it will document the outcome of the experiment, including whether hypotheses were rejected or not and whether measurements are reliable. Documentation standards here are direct: Does the account show whether the objectives of the study were fulfilled? Which objectives were fulfilled? Which were not? This is the foundation documentation for interpreting the results. Previous documentation allowed the potential user to assess the quality and reliability of the study. This documentation conveys the outcome so that he/she can decide whether to use the information.

Interpretation will continue with comparisons between the subject study and related studies. This contrast and comparison is perhaps the most conspicuous element absent from extant reports of experiments. Yet, in many ways it is the most essential. Only by comparison and contrast can the value of the study be assessed. Further, only by coordination with other studies can the full range of results from available experiments be known and exploited. It is therefore essential to answer these questions: How do the results interface with results from other simulation studies? How do they interface with actual empirical research? Documenting answers to these questions will allow composition of a comprehensive view of what is known about the subject under study. What is sought is knowledge as to where the study results fit into the puzzle that will make a complete picture. This documentation is especially necessary in light of the inherent "problem of induction."

Not only should the documentation compare and contrast the results with other experiments, but it should also compare the results with what is known analytically by deductive proof. Documentation should answer such questions as the following: Are the results consistent with analytical results, both direct and intuitive? What do they tell us about prospects for success in further analytical research? What information do the results provide that will guide further analytical research?

There are some questions common to all types of issues and experiments that guide the interpretation of results. They include, for example, questions about the generality of the results. What is the applicable domain for the results? How general are the results? These questions come up in every experimental setting, but especially in sampling experiments in econometrics, where model form seems to play such a strong role in determining properties of populations of estimators and test statistics.

III.   POTENTIAL LIMITATIONS OF SIMULATION STUDIES

Potential users of simulation study results will want to know if they have inherent limitations that preclude certain interpretations or generalizations. Potential limitations are found in two sources: universal limitations based on the logic of simulation studies, and specific limitations based on the design and execution of individual experiments.

To discover universal limitations one answers the question, "What cannot be learned from simulation studies?" The primary universal limitation of simulation studies is the limitation inherent in any inferential reasoning. This is the foundation of an often-cited criticism, namely, that the results of any simulation cannot be generalized. It is "the problem of induction" so clearly discussed by David Hume and later applied so cogently by Popper.[6] Without an adequate solution to *the problem of induction*, this limitation remains an absolute limitation to what can be learned from simulation studies.

It may also be worthwhile to ask, "What are the essential differences between simulation studies and statistical experiments performed by sampling from natural populations?" Simulation studies ordinarily avoid the first issue that comes up in any statistical experiment, namely, "What is the distribution function for the population?" Because the simulation study creates the population distribution function, this source of uncertainty in the study is precluded, assuming the cybernetic sample generator is an accurate model of the sample generator. The sample space is known with certainty.[7]

To discover the limitations of a particular study one can ask, "What cannot be concluded from this simulation study?" While potential users of simulation studies must always ask this question, it is difficult to answer in a general way. It will perhaps be worthwhile to illustrate the types of analysis to follow with some examples, showing different types of weaknesses that may be manifest in simulation studies. These particular weaknesses may arise even for well-designed studies.

The first issue to be treated is that of specifying models for studying estimators and test statistics along with choosing parameter values for the models. Tintner provides a model of the meat market that is also simple enough to provide a pattern for simulation studies.[8] The pattern of the model is as follows:

demand equation $y_1 + b_{12}y_2 + c_{11}z_1 + c_{14}z_4 = u_1;$

supply equation $y_1 + b_{22}y_2 + c_{22}z_2 + c_{23}z_3 + c_{24}z_4 = u_2.$

We examine the concentrated likelihood functions for estimating b_{12} under two specifications: $c_{23} = 0$ and $c_{23} \neq 0$. These two cases are shown in Figures 2 and 3, respectively.[9] The vertical scales of Figures 2 and 3 are normalized by the likelihood function values at infinity; of course, the actual variance ratios never exceed unity. Dreze's discussion follows:

> These figures show clearly how much the concentrated likelihood function is modified by the inclusion of z_3 in the model. Figure [3] also reveals how flat that function becomes over a wide range including the maximum, when z_3 is included. Nearly constant values are obtained over the whole range from 3.5 to 8; the accuracy of the data and computations does not seem to permit a more precise location of the maximum, and point estimates are quite unreliable.

What can be learned from this example is this: Rather considerable uncertainty may be introduced into an otherwise well-designed experiment by the particular model form chosen. Any experimental evidence about the finite-sample behavior of estimators for b_{12} from this model would have to be received very dubiously indeed by the potential consumers. It seems almost impossible to say anything definite about estimates in the range from 3.5 to 8.

Not only can model form introduce considerable uncertainty into the simulation study results, but the selection of parameter values can also have powerful impact. This is seen clearly from experiments designed to assess the finite-sample performance of estimators and test statistics in simultaneous equations models. Estimators and test statistics for simultaneous equations models tend to behave predictably for large values of the concentration parameter. But they are far less predictable for small values of the concentration parameter. Nevertheless, many of the simulation studies designed to discover finite-sample behavior, as well as studies designed to evaluate asymptotic approximations of critical regions, are designed only with relatively large values for concentration parameters. Concentration parameters for 29 equations from small models are shown by Anderson et al.[10] These values tend to be small, so that asymptotic approximations are not known to be reliable. On the other hand, the experiments aimed at evaluating asymptotic approximations for finite samples have frequently been designed with large concentration parameters. The consequence is that such studies cannot reliably assess the finite sample performance of the statistics.

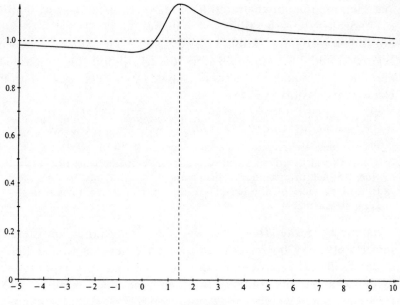

Figure 2

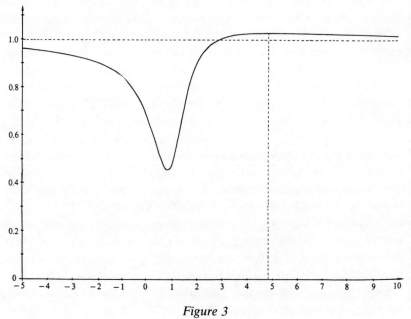

Figure 3

The choice of data, coupled with the estimator mappings studied and the cybernetic sample generator, may also render simulation studies unreliable. In the study published by Summers this problem was severe enough to preclude reliable rankings of alternative estimators, even though such rankings were the objective of the study.[11] In that study the computer coding was not accurate enough to effectively deal with the multicollinearity introduced by the choice of sample data. The result was a range of uncertainty for estimator mappings measured at 2-4 or more times population design parameters, thereby precluding any possibility of reliably ranking the alternative estimators.[12]

IV. MEASURING COMPLETENESS OF THE DOCUMENTATION

How do I know when the simulation study is documented thoroughly enough? Such a question is asked not only by researchers reporting their work but also by project sponsors, journal editors and referees, and those who read the reports. One suspects that the basic documentation in the researcher's own files cannot be too comprehensive. One also suspects from personal experience, as well as from discussions with colleagues, that it is never comprehensive enough. There are almost always pieces discovered to be missing when one is returning to the files after months or years have passed. But that is not the subject of this paper. Our concern is with the public interpretation and documentation of experiments as reported in research reports, journals, monographs, etc.

What is proposed here is a threshold standard of completeness based on some concepts of economic efficiency. The standard is introduced by a biographical account of Henry Eyring, noted chemist and educator: "Eyring's training was that of an experimentalist, but his contributions while at Princeton were almost exclusively in the realm of theoretical chemistry, wherein the published results of others became the bases of illuminating analyses which led to new concepts and increased understandings of a wide range of scientific phenomena." A visitor to Eyring's laboratory wrote: "After talking about his current researches, he showed me around his laboratory and introduced his students to me. I saw only slide rules and several calculators on tables, but could not find even a simple piece of experimental apparatus in his laboratory. It was my first experience to observe such a chemical laboratory."[13]

An additional example is provided by Johannes Kepler's reference to the astronomical observations supplied by Tycho Brahe: "To us Divine goodness has given a most diligent observer in Tycho Brahe, and it is therefore right that we should with a grateful mind make use of this gift to find the true celestial motion."[14]

The standard of completeness illustrated in these two accounts and proposed here is this: Would the published documentation allow other researchers to fully exploit the experimental results, thereby obtaining maximum benefits from the study? This is an essential matter of research economy. Efficient use of research resources demands taking advantage of economies of scope, scale, and density when interpreting and reporting simulation studies. Failure to document simulation studies to the extent that others can deduce and derive further results from them wastes resources. It is, in the language of economics, a failure to take advantage of great economies of scale, scope, and density. It fails to capitalize on potentially powerful externalities.

The standard is proposed especially for journal editors and referees as well as authors. Perhaps it will turn out to be a useful standard for deciding whether to publish papers. Is it possible that papers that do not have significant research economies in the form of externalities and economies of scale, scope, and density should be passed over in favor of papers that do? Will imposing such a standard alleviate the wasted space implied by recent surveys indicating the average number of readers of research articles beyond the editors to be 1?[15] This threshold standard of completeness is proposed here not as a maximum but as a *minimum*.

V. DECISION MODEL SIMULATIONS: A SPECIAL CASE

Mention of decision model simulations automatically brings to mind simulations of macroeconomic aggregates and models of them. The idea is that they are used for making fiscal, monetary, energy, welfare, tax, and other major socioeconomic policies in many Western nations. While they may be, the evidence that they are actually so used directly, or even indirectly, seems quite speculative. John Kenneth Galbraith, in *Economics and the Public Purpose*, argues persuasively against the belief that models are used in macroeconomic policy making and suggests some alternative hypotheses explaining the apparent state of affairs.[16]

But there are policymaking realms where the use of simulation models has a direct impact on policy decisions. Two of those realms are regulatory agencies and courts. Experts testifying before regulatory commissions will frequently include information from simulated models in their opinions. For example, many regulatory proceedings are based on measurements of fixed and variable costs, with measurement of costs based on simulation models. Recognition of the ubiquitous role of model simulations in regulatory proceedings and other policy decision institutions has led Congress to call for *model validation* methods to be developed and employed. The standards for introducing model simulations into judicial proceedings are based on legal rules of evidence. It turns out that the standards imposed by the rules of evidence match nicely with the concepts of scientific evidence, especially as applied for interpretation and documentation. With that in mind, standards for documenting and interpreting decision model simulations before a commission hearing or court are proposed not only for direct use in policymaking institutions but also for general use in communications among researchers.

A.   Introduction to Concepts of Evidence

Policy simulation models may be used by government as instruments for apportioning private rights and public interests. Within the structure of U.S. legal proceedings there are three tribunals where private rights and public interests are apportioned according to rules designed to ensure due process of law: commission hearings, judicial review of commission hearings, and civil litigation. Use of simulation models or information based on them in any of these settings would be associated with the legal term *finding of fact*. "Finding of fact" and related concepts constitute the legal principles and standards that are explored in this subsection as a foundation for documenting and interpreting decision model simulations. What is proposed is a subset of a comprehensive model validation methodology.

1.   *Finding of Fact*

The term *finding of fact* designates a decision taken by a commission or court. To say that a statement constitutes a finding of fact is to say that the hearing examiner has decided to use the statement in deciding issues before the commission and fixing remedies to them. (The decisions handed down by commissions are often called "remedies.") When presented before a hearing commission, a model, or components of a model, or forecasts based on a model would be called findings of fact, or briefly "findings," *if* the commission decides to use those information statements in its deliberations toward choosing remedies. Thus, when a simulated decision model or information based on that model becomes a finding of fact, that model has indeed become a policy model. It has been used in apportioning private rights and public interests.

When a commission issues a decision it is required to set forth, along with the decision, the findings of fact upon which the decision is based. Findings of fact are the conclusions reached to settle disputed issues. Both commission and court decisions are subject to judicial review: commission decisions are reviewed by federal courts, and lower court decisions by appellate courts. The review process includes determination as to whether rulings were based on substantial evidence. The appellate court may decide that the findings are not supported by substantial evidence or that the findings do not properly support the remedies. In fact, the third most common ground for judicial review of commission remedies is that the commission's order was not supported by findings, and the fourth most common ground is that the findings were not supported by substantial evidence.[17] Thus, a commission remedy or court decision may be overturned on the grounds that findings are not relevant or are not properly supported.

The process of finding a fact, then, has some specific require-ments and is an essential part of preserving due process of law. Findings of fact are decisions reached on disputed issues; they must be based on substantial evidence and they must be relevant to issues before the commission.

2. Decision Model Simulations as Findings of Fact

Since a model is never perfect and never perfectly or definitively confirmed it is reasonable to ask whether there is any principle of law or rule of evidence that precludes model information as findings of fact. The answer to this query is a conditional "No." There does not appear to be any a priori legal reason to exclude models as findings of fact as long as development and use of the model does not violate due process of law. With respect to econometric models, Steele has offered the following:

> It would be safe to assert ... that the [U.S.] Supreme Court would not rule against the use of an econometric model as a commission regulatory device. As a method or tool of analysis the basic econometric approach would undoubtedly be an acceptable commission technique so long as the model had been developed in a manner that did not violate procedural due process of law.[18]

The important condition here is that development and use of the model does not violate due process of law.

Preservation of the right of affected parties to due process of law in any remedies taken by commissions or courts is the major responsibility of judges and hearing examiners. In the specific case of using simulations of decision models as findings of fact the issues are whether (a) the model information is supported by substantial evidence and (b) whether the model information is relevant to issues and disputes before the commission. Successful advocacy of model information would require convincing the hearing examiner that model information is relevant and that it has substantial support. Without evidence that the model information satisfies the relevancy and substantial support critieria, the commission or court would be violating due process of law to use it as finding of fact. This condition naturally leads to questions regarding standards of evidence and objective determination of relevance and substantial support.

3. *Legal Evidence and Policy Models*

In this subsection we discuss some broad principles associated with the introduction of model information into a hearing or trial and the attempt to support that information as a finding of fact. We are here interested in the broad principles governing such attempted use of simulated models as they relate to standards for documentation, interpretation, or model validation.

a. Burden of proof. As a general rule, a party asserting a positive fact in a legal proceeding incurs the burden of proving the assertion. For example, in a hearing before the Interstate Commerce Commission (ICC) to determine needs for additional capacity in interstate natural gas pipelines one party may assert, "By 1990 the price of natural gas to retail customers will exceed $4.00 per thousand cubic feet." This assertion carries with it the burden of proving to the ICC that this statement is supported by substantial evidence and that the commission ought to rely on it in deliberations and rulings. This responsibility is called the *burden of proof.*

The burden of proof encompasses two separate but related burdens. First is the *burden of producing satisfactory evidence* of the fact in issue. In the example above the burden would require producing evidence that the price of natural gas will be more than $4.00 per thousand cubic feet by 1990. Second is the *burden of persuading the examiner* that the allegation is true. Thus, the party adducing a fact has the burdens of producing relevant evidence and of persuading the commission or court that the fact is true.

b. Adversary proceedings. Of course, positive assertions of fact are likely to be challenged by opposing parties in the hearing or litigation process. Preservation of due process mandates the opportunity to cross-examination, rebuttal testimony, and opposing evidence. Steele has argued that "when a complete econometric model is introduced in a hearing, it should be treated as though it were a hostile witness by those who did not have a hand in its development."[19] Thus, the burden of proof includes the burden of sustaining the adduced evidence and persuasive testimony in the face of direct and indirect counterattack by opposing parties.

As a matter of fact, the adversay method of proceeding is fundamental to the preservation of due process. Steele has asserted that *uncritical acceptance of a model by a commission hearing may be interpreted to constitute a capricious finding of fact.*[20] What this means is that part of the burden of proof consists of showing that supporting evidence withstands hostile cross-examination, rebuttal testimony, and contrary evidence.

Affected opposing parties are likely to carry the proceedings beyond cross-examination and rebuttal testimony. They are likely to directly support their own cases and attempt to have their own contentions found as facts. Such behavior is in keeping, of course, with due process of law. It also leads to an interesting apparent contradiction in the proceedings and a resolution based on an important legal principle.

c. Weight of evidence. There is no principle of law or rule of evidence preventing a hearing or court from entertaining contradictory findings of fact. For example, the ICC may find as facts the contradictory claims: (1) in 1990 the retail price of natural gas will exceed \$0.004/cubic foot; (2) in 1990 the retail price of natural gas will not exceed \$0.004/cubic foot. The commission may be persuaded that parties making these claims have satisfied their burdens of proof and entertain both claims. Mere introduction of the claims will not suffice to produce this condition. Each party will indeed be required to provide substantial support and persuasive testimony.

Where contradictory findings of fact are admitted their impact on policies and remedies is determined by the amount and quality of supporting evidence. The legal concept referred to here is known as "weight of evidence." It says that assertions of fact are to be used in deliberations and remedies in proportion to the amount and quality of supporting evidence. In the dispute regarding the price of natural gas in 1990, both price forecasts may have sufficient support to warrant findings as fact. However, one of them may be supported by considerably more evidence than the other. The finding with greater support, or "weight of evidence," will be accorded more weight in deliberations and rulings. The weight of evidence principle provides the legal method for reconciling contradictory findings of fact.

B. Legal Concepts and Model Evaluation

The legal concepts *finding of fact* and *weight of evidence* provide both a threshold standard and a measurement scale for documentation and interpretation. The threshold standard is based on whether a model has sufficient support to be found as fact. This is a yes/no decision. The weight of evidence criterion provides a measure for ranking alternative models and model information. It provides a standard based on an orderable measure of weight of evidence.

There is extensive literature on the concepts and rules of evidence that allows comprehensive and detailed application of legal concepts to documenting and interpreting simulation models. This paper does not purport to offer such a development. Rather, the purpose here is to apply the principles of finding of fact, burden of proof, weight of evidence, and adversary proceedings to the major problems of documenting and interpreting simulation studies, particularly decision model simulations. What is concluded is that the broad concepts of findings of fact, burden of proof, weight of evidence, and adversary proceedings offer foundation for developing coherent, surveyable, and practicable standards for reporting and documenting simulation studies.

C.   Goals of Modeling and Model Evaluation

1.   *Getting Models Accepted for Use in Policymaking*

One objective measure of success in policy modeling is getting a model into use by the policymakers for whose use it is developed. Of course, a policymaker's or policy adviser's failure to use a model is not by itself evidence that a model is not up to reasonable standards. But it does show that the model builder has not convinced the policymaker or his/her staff that the model can be used beneficially in policymaking. Among the many reasons that could lead to a policy analyst's rejection of a model is the analyst's suspicion that the model is "unrealistic"—that it does not represent the relevant aspects of reality as perceived by the policymaker.

There are myriad imaginable uses for policy models in a political and administrative structure as large, complex, and diverse as exists in the United States. The diversity and complexity of policymaking in this framework will not always allow clear evidence that a model was used for making policy. But there is one place where use of model information clearly indicates that the model was used as a policy tool—an instrument for apportioning private rights and public interests. That is the case where a model, or information based on the model, is cited as a finding of fact in recorded proceedings of a commission hearing. (Recall that a commission must set forth the findings upon which a ruling is based.) The rulings of regulatory and other commissions are certainly policies. Consequently, one objective standard for determining whether a model could be used for policymaking is found in the requirements for achieving finding of fact status in commission hearings.

It appears that hearing examiners and trusted policy advisers will require the same kinds of evidence and persuasion before accepting a model for use in policymaking. They need to be convinced that the model information is relevant and based on substantial evidence. The formal rules of evidence governing legal proceedings require the party asserting a fact to persuade the examiner or the court that model information intended to support the fact is (a) relevant and (b) based on substantial evidence. Furthermore, the evidence must be offered in a form intelligible to the hearing examiner or trusted policy adviser. Hearing examiners and policy advisers are unlikely to be persuaded to use a model as a policy instrument if it is not communicated to them clearly in a familiar language.

In summary, it appears that a model builder or model analyst can profitably use the standards for finding of fact in legal proceedings as objective criteria in deciding whether a model can meet the first major aim of policy-oriented models—actual use in the policy process. Further, the model builder can adopt the same documentation standards. Model documentation will need to demonstrate relevance and substantial support in language familiar to the trusted policy adviser and hearing examiner. These concepts have been discussed before (e.g., by Greenberger et al.,[21] esp. Chaps. 2 and 10). What is added here is the proposition that legal standards of evidence serve as foundation criteria for evaluating potential contributions to policymaking offered by specific models.

2. Achieving Sufficient Documentation

a. Expectations. Structuring model documentation and validation methods with a view toward introducing the model in a formal hearing can ensure that the four major objectives of the model documentation are met. Listed in natural order the four objectives are as follows:

1. To put the myriad pieces of modeling work together and keep them intact
2. To speed up detection of design and execution errors in models and their correction, thus speeding up the subsequent improvement of models
3. To facilitate modeling in anticipation of changes in policy-making needs and to speed up modeling responses to such changes
4. To achieve overall efficiency in modeling efforts.[22]

We recommend as a pattern for model documentation the preparation required to introduce a model before a commission hearing with the goal of having the model, including its forecasts and economic information, found as facts. Model documentation following this pattern should line up evidence for and against the model so as to meet the goals listed.

1. Presentation of a model and substantial support for it requires introduction of the model in systematic fashion. Each assertion must be built upon previously presented evidence. To convince the hearing examiner or policy adviser that model information ought to be a finding of fact requires a cohesive presentation showing the components of the model, how they fit together, and the evidentiary support for both the components and the system. Documenting the modeling work so that it satisfies rules of evidence will ensure that the myriad pieces are presented cohesively and in language familiar to examiners and policy advisers. The standard of presenting a modeling project according to rules of evidence will automatically lead to presentation suitable for policymakers not in a formal proceeding.

   There is substantial precedent for presentation of model information before regulatory commissions in written form.[23] What this suggests is a standard for written model presentation that would be suitable for use in commission proceedings. This establishes a uniform standard that at once is sufficiently rigorous to meet the first goal of the methodology and yet is reasonable in its resource demands.

2. Commission hearings are adversary proceedings where information is subject to legitimate challenge in order to preserve due process. Preparation of evidence to support information as findings will naturally include severe examination in order to discover weaknesses that may be used in cross-examination and rebuttal. The parallel activity in science is the requirement that each researcher is his/her own most severe critic. Following the tactic of detecting and correcting design, execution, or other errors in advance of documentation efforts is surely essential. Then the notion of sustaining substantial support for model information in an adversary proceeding provides a solid frame of reference for model evaluation. To maintain this frame of reference should ensure progress in detecting design and execution errors and thereby achieving the second purpose of documentation.

3. Commission hearings tend to make public policy as well as to provide specific remedies to affected and interested parties. McCormick has put it this way:

Agency hearings tend to produce evidence of general conditions as distinguished from facts relating solely to the respondent. Administrative agencies more consciously formulate policy by adjudicating—as well as rulemaking—than do courts. Consequently, administrative hearings require that the hearing officer considers the impact of his decision upon the public interest as well as upon the particular respondent.[24]

To have model information found as fact will require showing that the model is relevant to the issues before the commission. This in turn requires the party introducing the information to correctly perceive the policy issues at stake as well as alternative policy issues and proposed remedies that may arise during the hearing. What proponents of the model will want is (i) to show that the model information is relevant and (ii) to be prepared to show whether the model can successfully treat alternative issues and objections that may come up in the proceedings.

The need to anticipate changes in policymaking needs in order to provide timely responses to such changes is essential in both adversary proceedings and policy deliberations outside the formal setting. The framework of contingency planning for changes in policymaking needs in legal proceedings imposes a rigor and discipline that is beneficial in all areas of evaluating policy-oriented models. The need to anticipate changing needs of policymakers and their advisers is no less acute in the general arena than in specific commission hearings. The focus of attention and need to provide substantial support found in adversary proceedings leads to the necessary contingency planning; meeting this need supplies a necessary component in standards for documenting simulation models.

4. Interpretation and documentation standards based on the concept of a model as a finding of fact will increase overall efficiency in modeling efforts. To undertake a model building or model validation project using this frame of reference means that activities are directed toward introduction of information to policy analysts and policymakers with the goal of establishing findings of fact. The goals and objectives of the project are clearly understood. Relevant policymaking needs are specified. The burdens of proof are properly

allocated. Proper allocation of burdens of providing evidence and persuasion in advance of model building would require the model builders to compile relevant documentation as model building occurs. The end result should be a model supported by sufficient relevant documentation to be introduced in a formal hearing. The burden of proof, of course, rests upon the model builder. One task of the model analyst is to ensure that the builder has met the burden of proof requirements.

What is recommended is that a policy-modeling project is carried out with the aim in mind of convincing a hearing examiner that the model constitutes a legitimate finding of fact. The model evaluation methodology is therefore based on concepts and rules of evidence governing introduction and support of model information designed to achieve this objective. Simply put, a practicable standard for model validation and documentation is based on whether the specific model could realistically be introduced and sustained as a finding in a commission hearing. Documenting simulation models based on this standard is designed to provide an answer to that question. Application of this methodology will (a) put the pieces of modeling work together and keep them intact; (b) speed the detection and correction of errors; (c) lead to anticipation of changing needs of policymakers, providing timely responses; and (d) increase the efficiency of simulation modeling.

D.   Summary of Standards for Documenting Simulated Decision Models

It appears that the needs and goals of policymakers and policy advisers are the same whether policies are made in commission hearings or in other settings. Policymaking in commission hearings follows rules of evidence designed to uphold due process of law in apportioning private rights and public interests. The foundation stone of the rules—hence, of preserving due process—is the *proper allocation and enforcement of the burden of proof.* Surveyable, coherent, and practicable standards for model documentation can be developed using legal rules of evidence as the guidelines.

The parallel between scientific standards, legal rules of evidence, and needs of policy advisers is readily apparent. The formality of the legal rules of evidence coupled with their precedents and antecedents provide an enviable pattern for validation of simulation models in other arenas. Emulation of the pattern should ensure that documentation designed around the concept of supporting model information as findings of fact will provide workable and reliable standards and procedures for validation, interpretation, and documentation of simulation models in virtually any field of study.

Documenting for Different Audiences

It is hardly new advice to say, "Write with a definite audience in mind." Yet in reading economics and statistics journals in the last decade or two, I conclude that this advice is followed only rarely. Researchers reporting simulation studies will have a variety of potential consumers for their products. Among them will be the following:

Information users—those who want to know the state of knowledge but who are not working directly in the field. This group may include researchers whose applied work requires using estimators and test statistics studied in the simulation studies. They want to know your results, if they are reliable, if they are applicable to their own projects, and how far they can go in generalizing your results to their own particular problems. Most econometricians have a constant flow of such questions from colleagues and their graduate student research assistants who want to know if results reported in research articles can be applied to their current research projects. Is there a way to write so that the question is answered in the article itself?

Participants—those who are actively doing similar research. This is perhaps the easiest audience to inform, mainly because you are part of it. As a participant, you know what documentation you need to have reported as you review the reports of colleagues. Is the interpretation and documentation such that other experiments can easily be carried out to replicate the one reported? To interface with it? Can you easily tell where the reported experiment fits into a comprehensive view of the subject matter? From reading the report, can you easily tell what the next steps in the overall research effort ought to be? Could you recommend the report to an advanced graduate student so that he/she could design dissertation research?

Policy advisors—people who are particularly interested in decision simulations as inputs to their own debates and advising roles. What special obligations attend the documentation for simulation studies designed to inform policy advisers and their clients? These were discussed earlier in Section V.

Other professionals—who may have applied simulation techniques in their own fields of study but are looking for new techniques and applications to their own research. For example, there has been considerable activity recently in simulating fractal growth in various branches of science. Computer-simulated plant evolution, showing how the earliest plants may have evolved, has been carried out on desktop computers[25] One potential standard for documentation is this: Could a researcher familar with simulation techniques read my report and know what I had done? The documentation standards of *American Scientist, Scientific American,* and *Science* provide patterns for this type of report.

NOTES

1. Walter W. Hauck and Sharon Anderson, "A Survey Regarding the Reporting of Simulation Studies." *The American Statistician* 38 (1984), 214-216.

2. David C. Hoaglin and David F. Andrews, "The Reporting of Computation-Based Results in Statistics." *The American Statistician* 29 (1975), 122-126; and Hauck and Anderson, op. cit.

3. An account of the relation between studies of finite and superpopulations is given in C.-M. Cassell, C.-E. Sarndal, and J. H. Wretmen, *Foundations of Inference in Survey Sampling* (New York: Wiley, 1977). Review of that brief book will complete the examination of this topic.

4. J. M. Hammersley and D. C. Handscomb, *Monte Carlo Methods* (London: Methuen, 1964), p. 2. This book provides a brief introduction to and some examples of Monte Carlo experiments.

5. It is recognized, of course, that not all experiments will require creating each of the four set mappings. Some Monte Carlo experiments may stop with creating a sample from the population, for example.

6. See K. R. Popper, *The Logic of Scientific Discovery* (London: Hutchinson, 1972), esp. Sec. 1; also see *The Poverty of Historicism* (New York: Harper Torchbooks, 1961).

7. Of course, the sample space is always known with certainty in principle, even if it is not the one specified in the study design. The sample generator, or cybernetic sample generator, samples from a specific population, so that ipso facto there exists a population for the simulation study. The question of interest

to the potential user of information is whether the researcher knows and has accurately reported what population actually generated the sample.

8. G. Tintner, *Econometrics* (New York: Wiley, 1952), Chap. 7.

9. The kind permission of *Econometrica* to reproduce these figures from Jacques H. Dreze, "Bayesian Limited Information Analysis of the Simultaneous Equations model." *Econometrica* 44 (Sept. 1976), 1045-1075, is gratefully acknowledged.

10. T. W. Anderson, Kimio Morimune, and Takamitsu Sawa, "The Numerical Values of Some Key Parameters in Econometric Modelling." Technical report No. 270, IMSSS, Stanford University, Sept. 1978.

11. Robert Summers, "A Capital Intensive Approach to the Small Sample Properties of Simultaneous Equations Estimators." *Econometrica* 33 (Sept. 1965), 1-39.

12. For details, see George F. Rhodes, Jr., "Non-Theoretical Errors and Testing Economic Hypotheses." *Economic Inquiry* 13 (Sept. 1975), 437-444.

13. From "Henry Eyring, President-Elect," by Carl J. Christensen, published in *Science*, Feb. 21, 1964, when Eyring was named president-elect of the American Association for the Advancement of Science.

14. The quotation is found in David A. Freedman, "Statistics and the Scientific Method." In W. M. Mason and S. E. Feinberg (eds.), *Cohort Analysis in Social Research: Beyond the Identification Problem* (New York: Springer, 1985); it is taken from J. L. E. Dryer, *A History of Astronomy from Thales to Kepler* (new York: Dover, 1953), p. 385. Freedman's thought-provoking article provides excellent background for this essay.

15. Keith Stewart Thompson, "Marginalia: The Literature of Science." *American Scientist* 72 (Mar.-Apr. 1984), 185-187, and citations therein.

16. J. K. Galbraith, *Economics and the Public Purpose* (New York: Signet, 1973). See also R. L. Basmann and G. F. Rhodes, Jr., "Can Econometricians Influence Public Policy" (mimeo, 1975).

17. Joe L. Steele, *The Use of Econometric Models by Federal Regulatory Agencies* (Lexington, MA: Heath/Lexington Books, 1971), p. 79.

18. Ibid., p. 82.

19. Ibid., pp. 90-91.

20. Ibid., p. 81.

21. Martin Greenberger, Matthew A. Crenson, and Brian L. Crissey, *Models in the Policy Process: Public Decision Making in the Computer Era* (New York: Russell Sage Foundation, 1976).

22. Comprehensive discussion of these principles and their use in model validation activities is found in R. L. Basmann and G. F. Rhodes, Jr., "Perspectives and Foundation Concepts for Evaluating Policy Models" (mimeo, Jan. 1981).

23. Edward W. Clearly (gen. ed.), *McCormick's Handbook of the Law of Evidence* (Mineola, NY: West Publishing), pp. 856-858.

24. Ibid., pp. 836-837.

25. See Leonard M. Sander, "Fractal Growth." *Scientific American* 256 (Jan. 1987), 94-101; Karl J. Niklas, "Computer-Simulated Plant Evolution." Ibid. 254 (Mar. 1986), 78-87; and T. A. Witten and M. E. Cates, "Tenuous Structures from Disorderly Growth Processes." *Science* 232, No. 4758 (June 27, 1986), 1607-1612.

SOME ADVANCES IN BAYESIAN ESTIMATION METHODS USING MONTE CARLO INTEGRATION

Herman K. van Dijk

ABSTRACT

In this paper some Monte Carlo integration methods are discussed that can be used for the efficient computation of posterior moments and densities of parameters of econometric and, more generally, statistical models. The methods are based on the principle of importance sampling and are intended for the evaluation of multidimensional integrals where the integrand is unimodal and multivariate skew. That is, the integrand has different tail behavior in different directions. Illustrative results are presented on the dynamic behavior and the probability of explosion of a small-scale macroeconomic model. This application involves nine-dimensional numerical integration.

Advances in Econometrics, Volume 6, pages 215–261
Copyright © 1987 by JAI Press Inc.
All rights of reproduction in any form reserved.
ISBN: 0-89232-795-2

I. INTRODUCTION

Two related problems in the development of Bayesian statistical methods for econometric models are the specification of prior information and the efficient computation of the corresponding posterior moments and densities. A particularly difficult problem in this context is the conflict between two—apparently reasonable—requirements on prior information, i.e., *analytical tractability* and *richness*. An important advantage of the class of analytically tractable priors is that the integrals defined in the implied posterior moments can be evaluated analytically. In other words, the integrals are known in terms of elementary functions. As a consequence the computations involved are relatively simple. This is important in view of the problems that arise when numerical integration methods have to be applied for the computation of posterior moments in spaces with high dimensionality. An example of a class of analytically tractable prior densities is the natural conjugate family (see Raiffa and Schlaifer, 1961). However, Rothenberg (1963, 1973, Sect. 6.4) has pointed out that the natural conjugate family is not rich enough for an important class of econometric models, namely, the class of simultaneous equation models (SEM). Further, the structural parameters of the SEM are not identified in case a natural conjugate prior is used and all structural parameters are unrestricted.

In this paper we do not discuss the formal specification of prior information but assume that a posterior density is available. Our objective is to describe some methods that are *computationally efficient* and that are *flexible* enough to allow for a rich set of possible prior densities for the parameters of interest to economists. The price for increased flexibility of the prior densities is that in several cases the integrals defined in the posterior moments and densities of the parameters of econometric models have to be computed by numerical integration methods. Examples include models where the prior is uniform and the likelihood function is skew or where the prior density is informative and skew. This occurs, for instance, in the structural form of a SEM, in a linear regression model with serially correlated errors, in disequilibrium models, or—more generally—in nonlinear models where no linear approximation is available (see, e.g., Bauwens, 1984; Kloek and van Dijk, 1978; van Dijk and Kloek, 1980, 1983, 1985, 1986; Boender and van Dijk, 1987; Kooiman et al., 1985).

Well-known numerical integration methods are Cartesian product rules that are based on Gaussian or Newton–Cotes quadrature formulas (see, e.g., Abramowitz and Stegun, 1964). The application of such methods appears to be hampered by the amount of computational work involved in dimensions greater than five, say. Consider the example where use is made of a 10-point Gaussian quadrature formula. In K dimensions one has to evaluate 10^K points. When K is greater than 5 or 6 the computational workload is heavy. Due to the advances in modern computer technology the problem of the computational workload may become less important. However, there will still exist a relative advantage in efficient computation for the Monte Carlo methods discussed below. One may argue that a 2- or 3-point Gaussian quadrature formula can be used instead of a 10-point formula. In such cases one quite often makes use of the Cartesian product rules in an iterative way in order to check the numerical accuracy. That is, after the first round of numerical integration, one makes use of 2^K times the number of points in a second round, and so forth. So, Cartesian product rules suffer from what is sometimes referred to as "the curse of dimensionality."

In this paper we make use of Monte Carlo numerical integration methods in order to compute the integrals defined in the posterior moments and the marginal posterior densities mentioned above. The Monte Carlo approach is concerned with experiments on pseudorandom numbers where use is made of a computer[1] (see, e.g., Hammersley and Handscomb, 1964). Numerical integration is an important area of application of the Monte Carlo approach. Basically, the integrals to be computed are interpreted as expectations of certain random variables in the Monte Carlo approach, and the numerical integration problem is changed into a statistical estimation problem.

In econometrics, the Monte Carlo integration approach has been used traditionally for the investigation of properties of the finite sample distributions of classical estimators in the context of a given model and a *given* point in the parameter space. As a consequence, the results of such Monte Carlo experiments are specific for one parameter point. A recent survey of this application of the Monte Carlo approach, which contains several suggestions for further research, has been given by Hendry (1984).

We make use of Monte Carlo integration in a different way than the approach mentioned above. First, there is a conceptual difference. Monte Carlo applied in classical estimation implies integration over the data space (drawing repeatedly samples of artificial economic data). Monte Carlo applied in Bayesian estimation implies integration over the parameter space. Second, in our case the values of the parameters of interest of an econometric model are *not* known. Third, the present analysis is empirical in the sense that we do not generate artificial economic data.

Our way of using Monte Carlo may be succinctly stated as follows: The starting point is the specification of a so-called *importance* function. This is a density function defined on the space of the structural parameters (or on the space of a subset of these parameters in case part of the integration is carried out analytically). Two requirements are imposed on this importance function. It should have convenient Monte Carlo properties in the sense that it is relatively easy to generate pseudorandom drawings from a probability distribution with a density function that is equal (or proportional) to the importance function. In addition, the importance function should be a good approximation of the posterior density. One can describe the basic steps of Monte Carlo integration as follows: A sample of random drawings of parameters of interest θ is drawn from the distribution mentioned above.[2] Each random drawing and each function of the random drawing wherein one is interested are multiplied by the ratio of the posterior density and the importance function. This ratio serves as a weight function. Then one computes posterior moments and densities by means of simple formulas that are based on standard sampling theory. (For more details, refer to Section III.)

The important advantage of Monte Carlo is that a large number of posterior moments can be estimated at a reasonable computational effort. For instance, in a single Monte Carlo integration procedure one is able to compute the posterior first-order moments, second-order moments, univariate marginal densities, and bivariate marginal densities of a vector of parameters of interest and of a vector (or matrix) of nonlinear functions of the parameters of interest. For some illustrative results using a nine-dimensional vector, refer to Section IV. There are several indications that Monte

Carlo is computationally efficient in problems with many dimensions, say, more than five or six. The basic reason is that Monte Carlo is a sampling method and hence the error goes to zero as $N^{-1/2}$, where N is the number of sample points. This rather informal statement is explained in Section II.

This paper is organized as follows: In the next section we discuss the basic computational steps that are part of most Monte Carlo integration procedures by means of two simple examples. In Section III we summarize some basic concepts of importance sampling. Illustrative results using this method are presented in Section IV for Klein's Model I, which involves a nine-dimensional numerical integration problem. Section V contains a description of an algorithm that is based on a combination of one-dimensional Gaussian quadrature and importance sampling that we have named *mixed integration*. Some suggestions for further work are given in Section VI.

II. DIRECT SIMULATION AND SIMPLE REJECTION

In this section we discuss two elementary Monte Carlo (MC) integration methods. Our purpose is to illustrate the sequence of computational steps of most MC integration methods through simple examples. Further, we give a listing of a computer program that is intended as an introduction to the more complex computer programs for importance sampling and mixed integration.

The multivariate integrals that we shall consider may be described briefly as follows. Let θ be an ℓ-vector of parameters of interest, and let $g(\theta)$ be an integrable function of θ. The posterior mean of $g(\theta)$ is defined as

$$Eg(\theta) = \frac{\displaystyle\int g(\theta)p(\theta)\,d\theta}{\displaystyle\int p(\theta)\,d\theta}, \qquad (2.1)$$

where $p(\theta)$ is a kernel of a posterior density function. That is, $p(\theta)$ is proportional and not equal to a density function, and the denominator of (2.1) plays the role of integrating constant, similar to the role of $\sqrt{2\pi}$ in the case of the normal distribution. Simple examples of $g(\theta)$ are $g(\theta) = \theta$ and $g(\theta) = \theta\theta'$. Note that g may be a vector or a matrix. We emphasize that $g(\theta)$ may also be a complicated nonlinear function of θ such as the implied multipliers of the structural parameters of an SEM (see, e.g., van Dijk and Kloek, 1980; also Section IV, below). There exist several other examples of nontrivial nonlinear functions of θ. For an example in the statistical literature we refer to Kass (1985), and for some examples in the econometric literature we refer to van Dijk (1985), Zellner (1985), and Geweke (1986).

Consider the problem of the computation of the integrals in Eq. (2.1) for the case where a computer procedure is available that enables one to generate a sample of pseudorandom drawings from a distribution function $F(\theta)$ with a density function equal (or proportional) to $p(\theta)$. Let $\theta^{(1)}, \ldots, \theta^{(N)}$ denote the generated random sample. Given that $g(\theta)$ has a certain regularity property (that is, g is measurable), it follows that $g(\theta^{(1)}), \ldots, g(\theta^{(N)})$ is also a random sample. Then we may approximate the posterior mean (2.1) by the sample mean, which is defined as

$$\bar{g} = \frac{1}{N} \sum_{i=1}^{N} g(\theta^{(i)}). \tag{2.2}$$

The computation of $Eg(\theta)$ by means of this procedure is referred to in the literature as *direct simulation,* since one is able to generate a random sample *directly* from the distribution studied by making use of a computer procedure that *simulates* a sequence of random numbers (otherwise stated, the computer procedure generates a sequence of *pseudo*random numbers). For more examples on direct simulation and for references on computer procedures that generate sequences of pseudorandom numbers for many families of distributions, see Hammersley and Handscomb (1964, Chap. 3), Newman and Odell (1971), Atkinson and Pearce (1976), Kinderman and Ramage (1976), Kinderman and Monahan (1980), Rubinstein (1981, Chap. 3), Marsaglia (1984), Ripley (1983), Bauwens (1984), and the references cited therein.

A flow diagram for direct simulation is given in Figure 1. Note that we make use of an arrow sign instead of an equality sign in Figure 1. For instance, one interprets $S^{(0)} \leftarrow 0$ as "the value zero is assigned to the variable $S^{(0)}$." Apart from the computer procedure that generates $\theta^{(i)}$, the basic computational steps are given

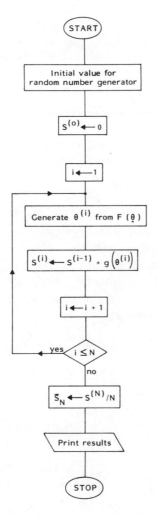

Figure 1. Flow diagram for direct simulation.

as

$$S^{(0)} \leftarrow 0 \tag{2.3}$$

$$S^{(i)} \leftarrow S^{(i-1)} + g(\theta^{(i)}) \qquad (i = 1, \ldots, N) \tag{2.4}$$

$$\bar{S}_N \leftarrow \frac{S^{(N)}}{N}. \tag{2.5}$$

The symbol $S^{(0)}$ stands for the initial zero value of the sum of the sequence of random variables $g(\theta^{(1)}), \ldots, g(\theta^{(N)})$; $S^{(i)}$ denotes the *i*th partial sum of this sequence, given as $S^{(i)} \leftarrow g(\theta^{(1)}) + g(\theta^{(2)}) + \cdots + g(\theta^{(i)})$. Equation (2.4) and Figure 1 illustrate that one does not have to store the large set of (pseudo) random numbers $g(\theta^{(1)}), g(\theta^{(2)}), \ldots, g(\theta^{(i)})$ in a computer, as is suggested by the formula for the *i*th partial sum, but one can make repeated use of a computer procedure that generates a pseudorandom number.

The accuracy of the approximation (2.2) may be studied by increasing the size of the sample from N to $2N$, to $3N, \ldots, MN$. The results can be printed at each value of jN, with $j = 1, \ldots, M$. Given certain regularity conditions, the Monte Carlo estimator $\bar{g}$ converges with probability 1 to $Eg(\theta)$. Some examples of this convergence process are presented below.

Another measure of numerical accuracy can also be derived from large sample theory. Under certain regularity conditions it follows from central limit theory that the estimator $\bar{g}$, Eq. (2.2), is approximately normally distributed with mean $Eg(\theta)$ and variance σ_g^2 / N, where σ_g^2 is given as

$$\sigma_g^2 = Eg^2(\theta) - [Eg(\theta)]^2. \qquad (2.6)$$

Under the assumption that the integrals in (2.6) exist, one may estimate σ_g^2 by the sample variance

$$\bar{\sigma}_g^2 = \frac{1}{N} \sum_{i=1}^{N} g^2(\theta^{(i)}) - \bar{g}^2. \qquad (2.7)$$

Given an estimator $\bar{\sigma}_g^2$ for σ_g^2, one can define a 95% confidence interval for $Eg(\theta)$ in the usual way as $[\bar{g} - 1.96\bar{\sigma}_g/\sqrt{N}, \bar{g} + 1.96\bar{\sigma}_g/\sqrt{N}]$. For an introduction to the sampling theory results that we use, see Mood et al. (1974, Chaps. 2 and 6); for a more advanced treatment, see Cramér (1946. Chap. 25 and 27). An example of a sequence of confidence intervals is presented below.

In order to illustrate the computational steps of an MC integration method, we consider the computation of a truncated five-dimensional standard normal integral by means of MC.[3] So, in this case we have $\ell = 5$; $p(\theta)$ is equal to a multivariate standard normal density function; and

$$\begin{aligned} g(\theta) &= 1 \qquad \text{if } \theta < a \\ &= 0 \qquad \text{otherwise,} \end{aligned} \qquad (2.8)$$

where a is a five-dimensional vector of known constants. Direct simulation is not a suitable integration method for this problem. Another Monte Carlo integration method for this problem may be formulated as follows: "Generate a vector of unrestricted normal random variables and test whether such a vector satisfies the restrictions of (2.8). Suppose that N_1 random drawings (out of a total of N drawings) satisfy the restrictions. Then we estimate the value of the integral P by means bo $\hat{P} = N_1/N$."

This method of computing a multivariate integral is an example of a Monte Carlo integration method known as *simple rejection*. [A standard example of simple rejection is given in, e.g., Rubinstein (1981, pp. 115–116).] The rejection step can be inserted in a simple way in the flow diagram of Figure 1 after the step where a random vector θ is generated from $F(\theta)$. A computer program, written in FORTRAN-77 is listed in Figure 2, and the results of some experiments are presented in Figures 3 and 4. The computer program illustrates the basic computational steps of most Monte Carlo integration procedures. That is, it starts with some statements that refer to initial values—in particular, the initial value of a random number generator and initial zero values. [We make use of the normal random number generator from Brent (1974), given as NAG-subroutine G05DDF.] The central part of the program refers to two so-called do loops. The inner loop, with the index i, refers to the computational steps given in Figure 1 and equation (2.4). (Note that in our program an estimate of the probability P in each round is denoted by the term *value* and the number of successes is denoted by the term *nacc*.) The outer loop refers to the number of times that intermediate results are printed. Let the index j refer to the number of times that a sample of size N is generated, for $j = 1, \ldots, M$ (j is labeled as "*jround*" in the program in order to avoid possible confusion between the integers i and j). Let $\hat{P}_j$ denote the estimated value of the integral P after j samples of size N. The values $\hat{P}_j$, for $j = 1, \ldots, M$, are related in a recursive way; i.e., we can write

$$\hat{P}_0 = 0 \tag{2.9}$$

and

$$j\hat{P}_j = (j-1)\hat{P}_{j-1} + \bar{S}_{N,j} \qquad (j = 1, \ldots, M), \tag{2.10}$$

```fortran
c       -------------------------------------------------------------------
c       -------------------------------------------------------------------
c
c       A Fortran-77 program for the evaluation of a truncated
c       multivariate normal integral.
c
c       ndim      : the dimension of the multivariate normal integral,
c       mround    : the number of times that an intermediate result is
c                   printed,
c       n         : the number of random drawings of the multivariate normal
c                   distribution for each round,
c       nacc      : the number of accepted random drawings of the
c                   multivariate normal distribution for each round,
c       ncum      : cumulative number of random drawings,
c       nacum     : cumulative number of accepted random drawings.
c       value     : computed value of integral in each round
c       cumvalue  : computed value of integral after jrounds
c
c
c       THETA(ndim) : a random drawing of the multivariate normal
c                     distribution,
c       BOUND(ndim) : a vector with upper bounds for the elements of
c                     THETA.
c
c       GENERATE(THETA,ndim) : a procedure that returns in THETA a random
c                     drawing taken from a ndim-dimensional
c                     multivariate normal distibution,
c       TEST(THETA,BOUND,ndim,tacc): a procedure that assigns the value
c                     .true. to tacc if the values of vector THETA are
c                     smaller then the upperbounds in vector BOUND,
c                     else tacc becomes .false.
c
c       -------------------------------------------------------------------
c
        integer ndim,mround,n
        parameter (ndim=5, mround=100, n=10000)
c
        logical tacc
        integer nacc,jround,i,ncum,nacum
        real*8 THETA(ndim),BOUND(ndim),value,cumval,p,q,ub,lb
c
        data BOUND/1.0d0,0.0d0,2.0d0,-1.0d0,-2.0d0/
c
        p = 0.0014838428435809d0
        q = 1.0d0 - p
c
 1001   format('0','The evaluated integral for round',i3,' is: ',f8.6,
      &         ' the cumulative value of the integral is: ',f8.6,', (',
      &         f8.6,',',f8.6,')')
        open(unit=6,file='[e.ect.hkvdijk]example1.res',status='new')
c
c       initial value of the pseudo-random number generator
c
        call G05CBF(100000*ndim)
c
c       initial zero value of number of accepted random drawings at round zero
c
```

Figure 2

224

```
      nacum = 0
c
      do jround = 1,mround
c
c     initial zero value of number of accepted random drawings for each round
c
          nacc = 0
c
          do i = 1,n
              call GENERATE(THETA,ndim)
              call TEST(THETA,BOUND,ndim,tacc)
              if (tacc) nacc = nacc + 1
          end do
          value = dfloat(nacc) / dfloat(n)
c
          nacum = nacum + nacc
          ncum = jround * n
          cumval = dfloat(nacum) / dfloat(ncum)
c
          lb = p - 1.9599639177322388d0 * dsqrt(p * q / dfloat(ncum))
          ub = p + 1.9599639177322388d0 * dsqrt(p * q / dfloat(ncum))
          write(6,1001) jround,value,cumval,lb,ub
      end do
c
      stop
      end
c     ---------------------------------------------------------------------
c     ---------------------------------------------------------------------
      subroutine GENERATE(THETA,ndim)
      integer ndim,i
      real*8  THETA(ndim)
      do i = 1,ndim
          THETA(i) = G05DDF(0.0d0,1.0d0)
      end do
c
      return
      end
c     ---------------------------------------------------------------------
c     ---------------------------------------------------------------------
      subroutine TEST(THETA,BOUND,ndim,tacc)
      logical tacc
      integer ndim,i
      real*8  THETA(ndim),BOUND(ndim)
      tacc = .true.
      do i = 1,ndim
          if (THETA(i) .gt. BOUND(i)) then
              tacc = .false.
              return
          end if
      end do
c
      return
      end
```

Figure 2. (*Continued*)

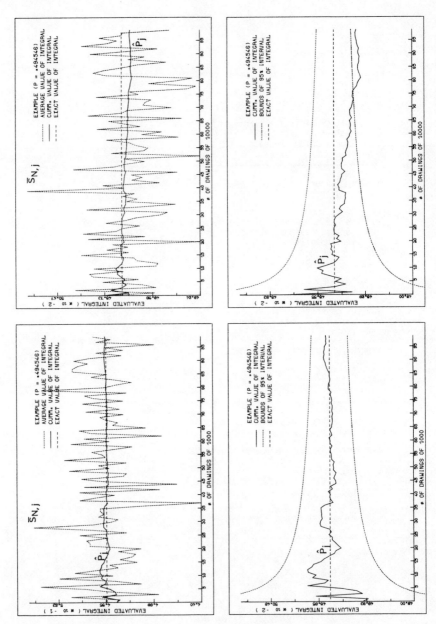

Figure 2. Sequences of estimates of the truncated multivariate normal integral $P = .494546$

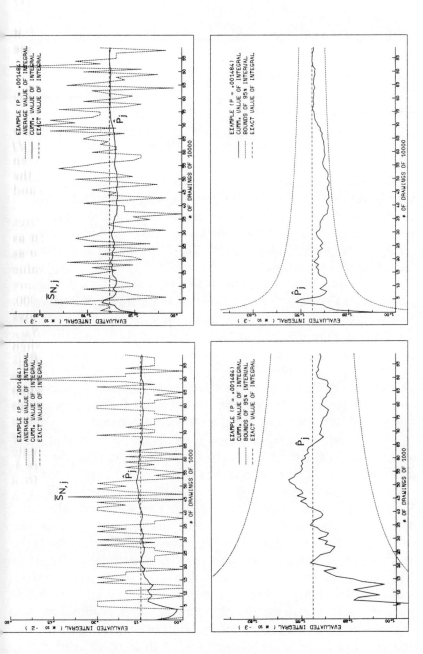

Figure 4. Sequences of estimates of the truncated multivariate normal integral $P = .001484$.

227

where

$$\bar{S}_{N,j} = \frac{S^{(jN)} - S^{(j-1)N}}{N} \qquad (2.11)$$

and $S^{(jN)}$ is defined in Eqs. (2.3)-(2.4). Note that for $j = 1$ it follows that (2.11) is equal to (2.5). Using (2.9) and (2.10), we see that $\hat{P}_j$ can be computed in a recursive way as

$$\hat{P}_j = \left(\frac{j-1}{j}\right)\hat{P}_{j-1} + \frac{\bar{S}_{N,j}}{j} \qquad (j = 1, \ldots, M). \qquad (2.12)$$

Equation (2.12) shows that convergence of $\hat{P}_j$ is guaranteed when j tends to infinity since $((j-1)/j) < 1$. Note, however, that $\bar{S}_{N,j}/j$ is not a constant but the realized value of a random variable. Even at a large value of j the additional term $\bar{S}_{N,j}/j$ may throw the sequence temporarily off-track, but this event should have less and less effect as j increases.

Some examples of sequences $\hat{P}_j$ and $\bar{S}_{N,j}$ are shown in Figures 3 and 4. In Figure 3 the true value of the integral P is given as $P = .494546$, which stems from taking the vector of constants a as $a = 1.12$; in Figure 4 the true value of P is .001484, and the value of the vector a is given in the computer program, listed in Figure 2. The sample size N is taken as $N = 1000$ and as $N = 10,000$. The results in Figure 3 indicate that the sequence $\hat{P}_j$ fluctuates around P due to to the random character of the sequence $\bar{S}_{N,j}$. Further, $\hat{P}_j$ stays well within the 95% confidence interval when $N = 1000$. When N is increased to 10,000, it is seen that $\hat{P}_j$ is outside the 95% confidence interval for a number of consecutive times when $j \geq 75$. This reflects the slow convergence process when j is large. We note that the scales on the vertical axes in Figures 3 and 4 have been determined in each figure by the difference between the largest and smallest numbers in order to show the variation in the sequences. The sequences $\hat{P}_j$ in Figure 4 fluctuate much less around their true value than the sequences of Figure 3. This is due to the fact that adding a very small number to a sequence of numbers has only a minor effect, in particular, when j is large. One may argue that the sequence $\hat{P}_j$ in Figure 4 mimics to a certain extent, in some intervals on the horizontal axis, the behavior of a linear difference equation with constant coefficients.

As an exercise one can determine the required size of the sample for a preassigned level of numerical accuracy. Suppose one is satisfied with two-digit accuracy at a 95% confidence level. That is, the required confidence interval bounds are given as .001484 − .00005 and .001484 + .00005 and we impose

$$1.96[P(1 - P)/N]^{1/2} \leq .00005$$

[compare the comment after Eq. (2.6)]. This implies that, roughly stated, N must be greater or equal to 20,000.

We end this section with a qualifying remark. Monte Carlo is not the most efficient method for the evaluation of a truncated multivariate normal integral (see, e.g., Quandt, 1983, Sec. 8.3, and the references cited therein). We repeat that our main purpose in this section is to indicate the basic computational steps of Monte Carlo integration and to illustrate the structure of a computer program using Monte Carlo.

III. BASICS OF IMPORTANCE SAMPLING

The posterior kernels of the parameters of interest of several econometric models have, to the best of our knowledge, no known Monte Carlo properties. That is, it is not known how one can generate random drawings from a distribution function with a density function equal (or proportional) to the kernels mentioned above. A well-known example of such an econometric model is the linear simultaneous equation model where some of the structural parameters are known exactly and where the prior information on the unrestricted parameters is taken from a noninformative approach. Further examples are dynamic regression models with serially correlated errors and disequilibrium models (see the references cited in Section I). As a consequence, direct simulation is not a suitable numerical integration method.

In such a case one can make use of the following simple solution. Interpret the integral given in the numerator of (2.1) as the expectation of the function $g(\theta)p(\theta)$ with respect to the uniform distribution $U(\theta)$, defined on the region of integration S. So, the numerator of (2.1) can be rewritten as $E_U[g(\theta)p(\theta)]$. Similarly, the integral in the denominator of (2.1) can be rewritten as $E_U[p(\theta)]$. Next, a sample of uniform random drawings of the vector θ is generated on the region of integration S. Let $\theta^{(1)}, \ldots, \theta^{(N)}$ denote the sequence of generated random drawings. Then, one can approximate (2.1) by

$$\bar{\bar{g}} = \frac{\dfrac{1}{N} \sum\limits_{i=1}^{N} g(\theta^{(i)}) p(\theta^{(i)})}{\dfrac{1}{N} \sum\limits_{i=1}^{N} p(\theta^{(i)})}, \qquad (3.1)$$

which can be written as

$$\bar{\bar{g}} = \sum_{i=1}^{N} g(\theta^{(i)}) p^*(\theta^{(i)}), \qquad (3.2)$$

where

$$p^*(\theta^{(i)}) = \frac{p(\theta^{(i)})}{\sum\limits_{i=1}^{N} p(\theta^{(i)})}. \qquad (3.3)$$

Note that $p^*(\theta^{(i)})$ is an estimator of the value of the normalized density function in the point $\theta^{(i)}$. The estimator (3.1) is a ratio of random variables. Given certain regularity conditions, it follows that (3.1) [and (3.2)] converges with probability 1 to (2.1) and that it is approximately normally distributed. The accuracy of the approximation (3.1) depends on the size N of the sample and on the variances of $g(\theta)p(\theta)$ and $p(\theta)$. These variances were very large in the cases that we studied, due to the large variation of $p(\theta)$. As a consequence, one needs a very large sample of random drawings in order to achieve an acceptable level of numerical accuracy (cf. Section II).

In order to improve on the approximation (3.1) [and (3.2)] we can proceed as follows. Let us define

$$w(\theta) = \frac{p(\theta)}{i(\theta)}, \qquad (3.4)$$

where $i(\theta)$, labeled *importance* function, is a density function on the region of integration S. [So, $p(\theta) = w(\theta)i(\theta)$, with $i(\theta) > 0$ on S.] Then we can replace $p(\theta)$ in (2.1) by $w(\theta)i(\theta)$. There are two requirements on $i(\theta)$: first, it should be a good approximation to $p(\theta)$; and, second, one should be able to generate a sample of random drawings from a distribution with density equal or proportional to $i(\theta)$. Let $\theta^{(1)}, \ldots, \theta^{(N)}$ be the generated sample. Then we can approximate (2.1) by

$$\hat{g} = \frac{\dfrac{1}{N} \sum\limits_{i=1}^{N} g(\theta^{(i)}) w(\theta^{(i)})}{\dfrac{1}{N} \sum\limits_{i=1}^{N} w(\theta^{(i)})}, \qquad (3.5)$$

which can be rewritten as

$$\hat{g} = \sum_{i=1}^{N} g(\theta^{(i)}) w^*(\theta^{(i)}), \qquad (3.6)$$

where

$$w^*(\theta^{(i)}) = \frac{w(\theta^{(i)})}{\sum\limits_{i=1}^{N} w(\theta^{(i)})}. \qquad (3.7)$$

Here, $w^*(\theta^{(i)})$ is the relative weight given to each random drawing $g(\theta^{(i)})$. Obviously, if $w^*(\theta^{(i)})$ is approximately equal to $1/N$ everywhere on the region S, it follows that one is (almost) back in the situation of direct simulation [compare the estimators (2.2) and (3.6)]. More practically stated, if the variance of $w(\theta)$ is much smaller than the variance of $p(\theta)$, one has achieved a large increase in numerical accuracy at a given sample size [compare (3.2) and (3.6)]. Details on the exact formulas that are needed to compute posterior first- and second-order moments, univariate and bivariate marginal posterior densities, and numerical error estimates are given in van Dijk et al. (1986).

Next, we discuss briefly some proposals for the importance function $i(\theta)$:

1. *The (truncated) multivariate Student t density.* If the surface of the posterior kernel is reasonably well behaved but there are some heavy tails, one can make use of the multivariate Student t density with the multivariate normal as a limiting case if the sample is large (see, e.g., Zellner, 1971, Appendix B2). As location and scale parameters of the multivariate Student t density, one can take the posterior mode and minus the inverse of the Hessian of the log posterior density, evaluated at the posterior mode. The mode can be determined by numerical optimization methods and the Hessian by means of numerical differentiation (see, e.g.,

van Dijk, 1984). For details on computer procedures that can be used to generate Student t random drawings, see Bauwens (1984), Kinderman and Monahan (1980), van Dijk et al. (1986), and the references cited therein. In case the posterior mode is on the boundary of the region of integration S, one has to make use of constrained numerical optimization methods. Some proposals for this are discussed in van Dijk and Kloek (1980).

2. *Poly-t density functions.* In case the posterior density is not well behaved, e.g., bimodal, one can make use of the poly-t class of density functions—in particular, when the posterior density is also a member of this class (see Bauwens, 1984). More research is needed in order to determine the usefulness of this family of density functions.

3. *Mixtures of normals or Student t densities.* Mixtures are very flexible and therefore suitable as importance function for irregularly shaped posterior densities. A difficult problem is, however, the specification of the values of the parameters of mixtures. A simple solution is given in van Dijk and Kloek (1985). More research is needed on this topic.

IV. PRIOR AND POSTERIOR ANALYSIS OF KLEIN'S MODEL I[4]

A. Model and Prior Information

In this section we apply the Monte Carlo approach to Klein's Model I, which is a small SEM based on annual data for the U.S. economy for the period 1921–1941 (see Klein, 1950). Given our prior information, this model has nine structural parameters of interest to economists, which implies that we compute nine-dimensional integrals numerically.

The statistical model can be summarized as follows. Our starting point is the well-known linear SEM

$$YB + Z\Gamma = U^*, \tag{4.1}$$

where Y is an $T \times (G + G')$ matrix of observations on $G + G'$ current endogenous variables, and Z is an $T \times K$ matrix of observations on the K predetermined variables. The rows of $U^* = (U \quad 0)$ are assumed to be independently normally distributed with mean zero and covariance matrix

$$\begin{bmatrix} \Sigma & 0 \\ 0 & 0 \end{bmatrix}, \tag{4.2}$$

where Σ (a nonsingular $G \times G$ matrix) corresponds to the stochastic equations. Further, current values of the disturbances are assumed to be independently distributed from current and lagged values of the predetermined variables, and the data matrix (Y, Z) has rank $G + K$.

The prior information on B, Γ, and Σ is specified as follows. The elements of the parameter matrices B, Γ, and Σ are divided into three groups: (i) *nuisance* parameters (constant terms, denoted by the vector α, and the covariance matrix Σ); (ii) *exactly known* elements of B and Γ; (iii) *unrestricted* elements of B and Γ, denoted by the vector θ. So, we have

$$B = B(\theta), \qquad \Gamma = \Gamma(\alpha, \theta). \tag{4.3}$$

The prior specification with respect to the nuisance parameters is taken from a noninformative approach. The prior density of the constant terms α is locally uniform and the prior density of Σ is proportional to $|\Sigma|^{-(1/2)h}$, where $h = -\frac{1}{2}(G + 1)$ and G is the number of stochastic equations. We have opted for this relatively low value of h so that the information contained in the likelihood function determines the posterior. As a consequence, analytical integration with respect to α and Σ is possible (see, e.g., van Dijk, 1984, Chap. 2).

With respect to the prior specification of the exactly known parameters, we proceed as follows: Identification is treated in the traditional way (for an alternative approach, see Kiefer, 1981). As a result we have a number of exactly known parameters (not only identifying zeros, but also normalizing unities) which are substituted in the likelihood function. The exactly known parameter values of B and Γ are implied by the specification of Klein's Model I. The structural equations of that model read as follows:

$$C = \theta_1 P + \theta_2 P_{-1} + \theta_3 W + \alpha_1 + u_1 \tag{4.4}$$

$$I = \theta_4 P + \theta_5 P_{-1} - \theta_6 K_{-1} + \alpha_2 + u_2 \tag{4.5}$$

$$W_1 = \theta_7 X + \theta_8 X_{-1} + \theta_9 t + \alpha_3 + u_3 \qquad (4.6)$$

$$X = C + I + G \qquad (4.7)$$

$$P = X - W_1 - T \qquad (4.8)$$

$$K = K_{-1} + I \qquad (4.9)$$

$$W = W_1 + W_2. \qquad (4.10)$$

Consumption expenditure (C) is structurally dependent on profits (P), profits lagged one year (P_{-1}), and total wages (W). Net investment expenditure (I) depends on profits, profits lagged, and the capital stock at the beginning of the year (K_{-1}); note the minus sign before θ_6 in the investment equation, (4.5). Finally, private wage income (W_1) depends on net private product at market prices (X), the same variable lagged (X_{-1}), and a trend term (t). The model is closed by four identities which provide links with three exogenous variables: the government wage bill (W_2); government nonwage expenditure, (G), including the net foreign balance; and business taxes (T). The model counts seven jointly dependent variables (C, I, W_1, X, P, K, W) and eight predetermined variables $(1, P_{-1}, X_{-1}, K_{-1}, G, T, W_2, t)$. All variables (except 1 and t) are measured in constant dollars.

For a more detailed exposition of the model, the reader is referrred to Klein (1950). Note, however, that the use of the symbols Y for net national income and G for government nonwage expenditure is not uniform in the literature on Klein's Model I. We shall use Y $(=X - T + W_2)$ for net national income. Klein (1950) uses G for government expenditure including wages $(=G + W_2$ in our notation). Other authors (e.g., Rothenberg, 1973), use Y instead of X for net private product. This notational point is relevant for the interpretation of a number of reduced and final form multipliers.

Finally, we shall discuss in this subsection the prior information on the parameters of interest θ. We shall specify a number of prior densities of θ and demonstrate how Monte Carlo may be used to investigate the implied prior information with respect to the reduced form parameters, the stability characteristics of the model, and the final form parameters (if these exist).

Our first and simplest prior for the vector θ is uniform on the nine-dimensional unit region[5] minus the region where $\| B \| < .01$. The latter region has been subtracted in order to guarantee that the implied prior moments of the multipliers exist. The likelihood determines the posterior in the truncated uniform region. It goes without saying that such a prior need not reflect in all detail the betting odds one might be willing to accept.

Next we investigate the implications of our prior information for the multipliers and dynamic characteristics of the model. We obtained the implied prior means and standard deviations of these functions of θ by drawing θ vectors from the nine-dimensional standard uniform distribution. Each θ vector was checked with respect to the condition $\| B \| > .01$. In case this condition was not satisfied, the vector was rejected and replaced by a new vector. Each experiment was stopped when 20,000 θ vectors satisfying the constraint were obtained.[6] For each θ vector we computed the implied reduced form parameters or short-run multipliers (SRM) and some other characteristics, to be discussed below. These are used for computation of the implied prior means and second-order moments and the implied univariate prior densities.

The reduced form equations form a system of linear difference equations. The three roots of the characteristic polynomial of this system summarize the dynamic properties of the system. If all roots are real, the system is monotone. If there is one real root and a pair of conjugate complex roots, the system is oscillatory. Further, if all roots are less than 1 in absolute value, the system is damped. If there is at least one root greater than or equal to 1, the system is explosive. (For more details, see Theil and Boot, 1962.) There exist four possible states of the system: damped oscillatory, damped monotone, explosive oscillatory, and explosive monotone. For each of these four states we computed the prior probabilities implied by the specified structural prior density. In case the system is oscillating, one may compute the period of oscillation; and in case the system is damped, one may compute the final form parameters or long-run multipliers (LRM).

As a next step we modified our first prior in several ways by adding sets of extra constraints. The set of constraints of prior 1 was maintained in all stages. The sets of extra constraints, which were introduced partly one at a time and partly in various combinations, will now be described:

1. The system is assumed to be stable. For that reason we only accepted vectors θ satisfying $|\mathrm{DRT}| < 1$, where DRT is the dominant root of the characteristic polynomial. In the present example this is of the third degree. The value of the dominant root of this third-degree polynomial may be computed by making use of analytical formulas (see, e.g., Abramowitz and Stegun, 1964, p. 17) or by making use of numerical methods. We made use of a numerical method given by the NAG-Library routine F02AFF.

2. The long-run effects in the structural equations $\theta_1 + \theta_2$, $\theta_4 + \theta_5$, $\theta_7 + \theta_8$ are all assumed to be in the unit interval.

3. The SRMs are assumed to be less than 5 in absolute value and to have the correct sign (positive for effects of W_2 and G; negative for effects of T).

4. The same set of constraints as mentioned in point 3, above, was applied to the LRMs (with an exception for the final form equation of K, where an upper bound of 10 was adopted).

5. The period of oscillation is assumed to be between 3 and 10 years. This is in accordance with the observed length of business cycles in the period 1890–1920 (see *Historical Statistics of the United States* 1975). Eight different priors were obtained by combining the sets of extra constraints, 1 to 5, in several ways. They are given as prior 1 (no sets of extra constraints); prior 2 (1); prior 3 (2); prior 4 (1, 2); prior 5 (2, 3), prior 6 (1, 2, 3); prior 7 (1, 2, 3, 4); prior 8 (1, 2, 3, 4, 5). [The numbers between parentheses ( ) refer to the sets of extra constraints.] We note that, due to space limitations, we present only results based in priors 2 and 8. More details are given in van Dijk (1984).

The posterior density of (θ, α, Σ) is obtained by combining the likelihood function of the SEM and the prior density by means of Bayes' rule. The marginal posterior density of the parameters of interest θ reads, in this case,

$$p(\theta \mid Y, Z) \propto p(\theta) \| B \|^T |S|^{-(1/2)(T-1)}, \qquad (4.11)$$

where S is defined as $S = U'NU$, with U given below Eq. (4.1) and $N = I - (1/T)zz'$ (z = zoya, i.e., a vector where all elements are unity). For details on the derivation of (4.11), see van Dijk (1984) or van Dijk and Kloek (1977).

B.   Prior and Posterior Results

In this subsection we present the prior and posterior means and standard deviations of the nine structural parameters θ (Table 1), the multipliers in the reduced and final form equations for national income (Table 2), the period of oscillation and the dominant root (Table 3), and we also present the prior and posterior probabilities

Table 1.   Means and Standard Deviations of Structural Parameters

	θ_1	θ_2	θ_3	θ_4	θ_5	θ_6	θ_7	θ_8	θ_9
FIML	−.23	.39	.80	−.80	1.05	.15	.23	.28	.23
(no prior)	(.58)	(.30)	(.04)	(.84)	(.42)	(.05)	(.09)	(.06)	(.06)
Prior 2	.40	.42	.37	.41	.36	.50	.65	.33	.50
	(.28)	(.28)	(.26)	(.28)	(.27)	(.29)	(.26)	(.24)	(.29)
Posterior 2′	.12	.19	.79	.06	.64	.15	.34	.23	.19
	(.08)	(.08)	(.04)	(.06)	(.10)	(.03)	(.05)	(.05)	(.04)
Prior 8	.25	.33	.39	.27	.30	.55	.43	.27	.50
	(.20)	(.23)	(.25)	(.20)	(.22)	(.26)	(.24)	(.20)	(.29)
Posterior 8′	.24	.06	.72	.14	.56	.20	.37	.24	.19
	(.08)	(.04)	(.05)	(.09)	(.12)	(.05)	(.04)	(.04)	(.05)

Table 2.   Means and Standard Deviations of Multipliers in the Reduced and Final Form Equations for National Income

	Short-Run Effects on Y (SRMs)			Long-Run Effects on Y (LRMs)		
	G	T	W_2	G	T	W_2
FIML	0.62	−0.36	1.50	1.96	−1.30	2.57
(no prior)						
Prior 2	2.20	−2.83	1.99	3.12	−2.55	3.06
	(1.57)	(1.94)	(1.45)	(151.0)	(58.0)	(134.0)
Posterior 2′	1.65	−1.32	2.30	2.38	−1.73	2.87
	(0.19)	(0.20)	(0.16)	(0.14)	(0.23)	(0.16)
Prior 8	2.00	−2.14	1.85	2.01	−2.20	1.93
	(0.71)	(0.83)	(0.73)	(0.78)	(0.74)	(0.86)
Posterior 8′	2.06	−1.81	2.49	2.25	−1.67	2.63
	(0.30)	(0.34)	(0.26)	(0.13)	(0.20)	(0.16)

Table 3. Means and Standard Deviations of Period of Oscillation and Dominant Root: Probabilities of States[a]

	Period of Oscillation (years)	|DRT|	Damped		Explosive	
			Oscillatory	Monotone	Oscillatory	Monotone
FIML (no prior)	34.83	.76	NA	NA	NA	NA
Prior 2	5.22 (4.74)	.78 (.17)	.96	.04	0	0
Posterior 2'	15.06 (2.90)	.84 (.08)	.9999	.0001	0	0
Prior 8	5.42 (1.57)	.72 (.18)	.98	.02	0	0
Posterior 8'	9.61 (0.37)	.77 (.08)	.9927	.0073	0	0

[a] NA = not available.

238

of the four states of the system (Table 3). Further, the marginal prior and posterior densities of the structural parameters are shown in Figure 5, univariate and bivariate marginal prior and posterior densities of the multipliers mentioned above are shown in Figures 6 and 7, and the prior and posterior densities of the period of oscillation and the dominant root are shown in Figure 8. We make use of a prime to denote a posterior density, e.g., 2' denotes the marginal posterior density based on prior 2. In all tables we give the full-information maximum likelihood (FIML) results (with asymptotic standard errors in Table 1) for comparison. In all cases we confine ourselves to presenting the results based on priors 2 and 8 (except for the bivariate densities, where we confine ourselves to prior 2 due to space limitations). The reason is that the difference between the results for priors 1 through 7 for the structural parameters and SRMs and for priors 2, 4, 6, and 7 for the LRMs were very small. We shall discuss this point in more detail below. All results presented are based on $N = 20,000$. In contrast, application of a 10-point Gaussian product rule of numerical integration requires 10^9 function evaluations. As the importance function we

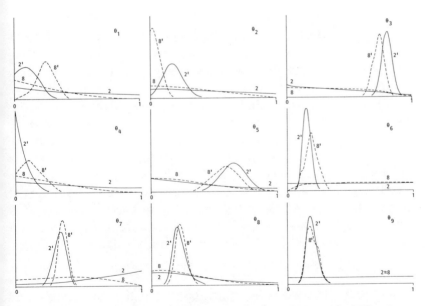

Figure 5. Marginal prior and posterior densities of structural parameters.

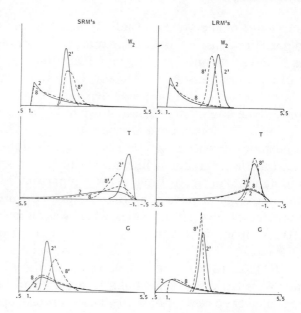

Figure 6. Prior and posterior densities in reduced and final form equations of national income.

make use of a truncated multivariate Student t density. For details, see van Dijk (1984, Chaps. 3 and 4) and van Dijk and Kloek (1980).

We start by observing that the FIML estimates of θ_1 and θ_4 have wrong signs. When analyzing this phenomenon it is found that three factors play a role. First, the data reveal collinearity of P and P_{-1}, which implies that the fit of the investment equation, for example, does not deteriorate much if θ_4 decreases while θ_5 increases. Second, there is a positive correlation between the residuals of the consumption and investment functions. If the covariance matrix Σ is postulated to be a diagonal matrix, the wrong signs are not observed. FIML results based on a diagonal matrix Σ are presented by Klein (1950). The hypothesis of a diagonal covariance matrix Σ is, however, strongly rejected in a likelihood ratio test $[\chi^2(3) = 28.46]$. Third, the Jacobian

$$\| B \| = \left|1 - (\theta_1 + \theta_4)(1 - \theta_7) - \theta_3\theta_7\right| \qquad (4.12)$$

is less than or equal to unity in the unit region but equals 1.60 in the FIML point. Recall that a factor $\| B \|^T$ occurs in the likelihood function and in the marginal posterior density $p(\theta \,|\, Y, Z)$,

(*Text continues on page 247*)

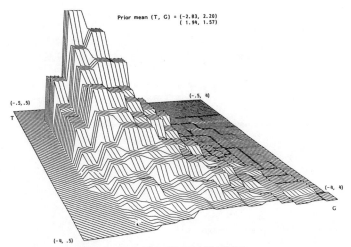

Prior mean (T, G) = (-2.83, 2.20)
(1.94, 1.57)

Prior density of short-run government-expenditures (G) and tax (T) multipliers

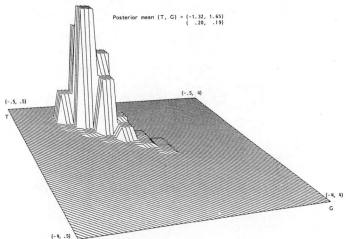

Posterior mean (T, G) = (-1.32, 1.65)
(.20, .19)

Posterior density of short-run government-expenditures (G) and tax (T) multipliers

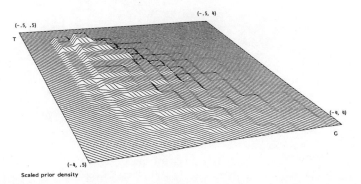

Scaled prior density

Figure 7

241

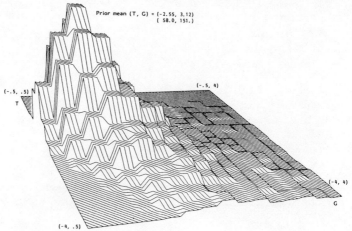

Prior mean (T, G) = (-2.55, 3.12)
(58.0, 151.)

(-.5, .5)
T

(-.5, 4)

(-4, 4)
G

(-4, .5)

Prior density of long-run government-expenditures (G) and tax (T) -multipliers

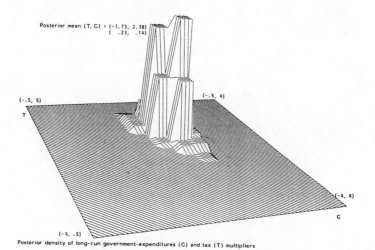

Posterior mean (T, G) = (-1.73, 2.38)
(.23, .14)

(-.5, 5)
T

(-.5, 4)

(-4, 4)
G

(-4, .5)

Posterior density of long-run government-expenditures (G) and tax (T) multipliers

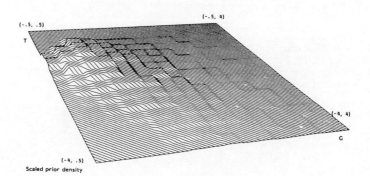

(-.5, .5)
T

(-.5, 4)

(-4, 4)
G

(-4, .5)

Scaled prior density

Figure 7. (*Continued*)

242

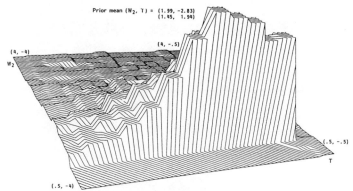

Prior density of short-run tax (T) and government-wages (W_2) multipliers

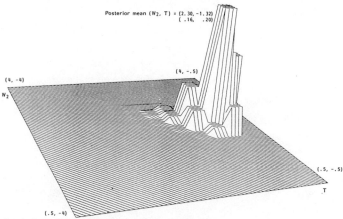

Posterior density of short-run tax (T) and government-wages (W_2) multipliers

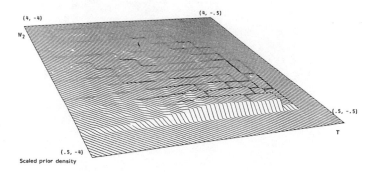

Scaled prior density

Figure 7. (*Continued*)

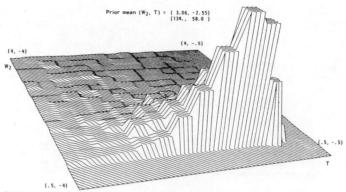

Prior mean (W_2, T) = (3.06, -2.55)
(134., 58.0)

Prior density of long-run tax (T) and government-wages (W_2) multipliers

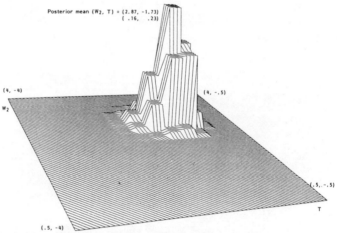

Posterior mean (W_2, T) = (2.87, -1.73)
(.16,   .23)

Posterior density of long-run tax (T) and government-wages (W_2) multipliers

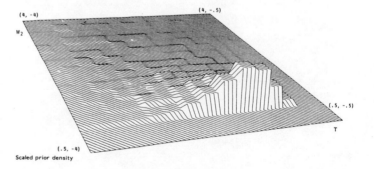

Scaled prior density

Figure 7. (*Continued*)

244

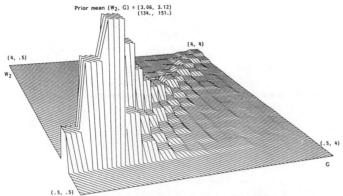

Prior mean $(W_2, G) = (3.06, 3.12)$
$(134., 151.)$

$(4, .5)$

W_2

$(4, 4)$

$(.5, 4)$

G

$(.5, .5)$

Prior density of long-run government-expenditures (G) and government-wages (W_2) multipliers

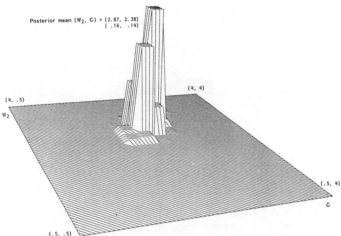

Posterior mean $(W_2, G) = (2.87, 2.38)$
$(.16, .14)$

$(4, .5)$

W_2

$(4, 4)$

$(.5, 4)$

G

$(.5, .5)$

Posterior density of long-run government-expenditures (G) and government-wages (W_2) multipliers

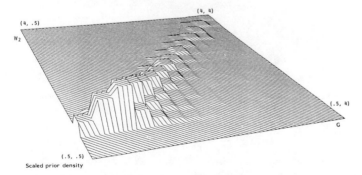

$(4, .5)$

W_2

$(4, 4)$

$(.5, 4)$

G

$(.5, .5)$

Scaled prior density

Figure 7. (*Continued*)

245

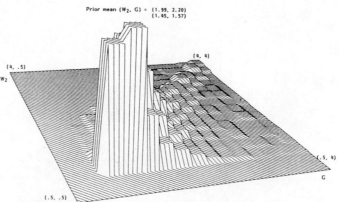

Prior mean (W_2, G) = $(1.99, 2.20)$
$(1.45, 1.57)$

Prior density of short-run government-expenditures (G) and government-wages (W_2) multipliers

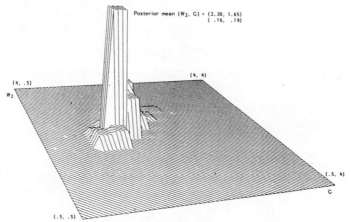

Posterior mean (W_2, G) = $(2.30, 1.65)$
$(.16, .19)$

Posterior density of short-run government-expenditures (G) and government-wages (W_2) multipliers

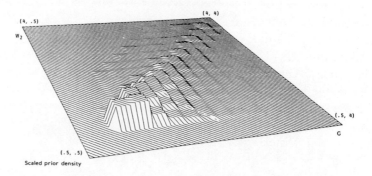

Scaled prior density

Figure 7. (Continued)

246

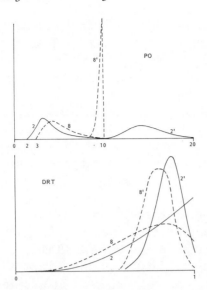

Figure 8. Prior and posterior densities of period of oscillation and dominant root.

Eq. (4.11). We note that in three-stage least squares (3SLS), where the Jacobian factor is absent in the function to be minimized but the nondiagonal elements of Σ are present, θ_4 has a wrong sign but only marginally so $(\hat{\theta}_4 = -.013)$ (Theil, 1971, p 517). If θ_4 is restricted to be zero, θ_1 gets the correct sign and this hypothesis is not rejected in a likelihood ratio test $[\chi^2(1) = 3.20]$. According to this diagnostic result there is no conflict between the sample information and our prior information, which states that θ_1 and θ_4 should be nonnegative. If we compare the FIML asymptotic standard errors and the posterior standard deviations of the structural parameters (Table 1), we see that this prior information plays a large role. This conclusion is confirmed in Figure 5.

Once we have accepted the prior information that all elements of θ are in the unit region, the extra sets of constraints 1, 2, 3, and 4, introduced in Section IV.A, turn out not to be restrictive. Given prior 1, the posterior probability that the system is explosive is .021. Given prior 2, the long-run posterior effects $\theta_1 + \theta_2$, $\theta_4 + \theta_5$, and $\theta_7 + \theta_8$ in the structural equations are all in the unit interval (Table 1). In this respect we note that the relevant covariances (not shown here in order to save space) are all negative. All SRMs and LRMs (Table 2) amply satisfy the upper-bound constraints.

They also satisfy the sign constraints, though some are close to zero. In these cases the prior and posterior densities (Figures 6 and 7) turn out to be skew, so the probability of wrong signs is extremely small. This explains why the differences between the posteriors 2 to 7 are very small.

The only set of extra constraints which adds substantial information to the sample is set 5, which says that the period of oscillation should be between 3 and 10 years. It is seen in Tables 1 through 3 and in Figures 5, 6, and 8 that this set, introduced in prior 8, influences almost every parameter. In particular, if θ_2 and θ_5 are relatively large (which corresponds to negative or small positive values of θ_1 and θ_4), the lags become large, and this in turn implies long periods of oscillation (compare Tables 1 and 3) and relatively small absolute values of most of the SRMs (Table 2).

So we have observed that the prior constraints on the period of oscillation have rather large effects. The question arises whether this information is acceptable. The posterior mean and standard deviation of the period of oscillation under prior 2 (Table 3) suggest that the hypothesis of a 10-year period is acceptable. Inspection of the prior and posterior densities of the period of oscillation in Figure 8 reveals that for the case of prior 2 the information from the likelihood function has modified the prior information substantially. The posterior probability that the period of oscillation is less than or equal to 10 years is less than .02. Further, the effect of constraint 5 is clearly reflected in the posterior density 8′. These results suggest rejection of the constraint 5.

We summarize the posterior results as follows: The prior restrictions that θ_1 and θ_4 should be nonnegative have a large effect on the posterior results. Given these prior restrictions, we have shown that only constraint 5 has a substantial, but undesired, effect on the posterior results, which suggests rejection of this prior constraint.

When considering these results we were tempted to look for specification errors. So far, Bayesian statistics lacks a well-developed standard battery of diagnostic checks, as has been developed for instance in the context of time-series analysis. A first set of diagnostic results is based on an analysis of the expected values of the posterior residuals that are defined as

$$EU = Y_s EB_s(\theta) + Z_s E\Gamma_s(\alpha, \theta),$$

where the index s refers to the set of variables and parameters that occur in the stochastic equations of Klein's Model I. Estimates of the posterior expected values of u_1, u_2, and u_3 [Eqs. (4.4)–(4.6)] are presented in Table 4, together with the residuals based on the FIML estimates of the vector θ. Further, the posterior densities of two functions of the posterior residuals are shown in Figure 9. That is, the serial correlation coefficients

$$\rho_j = \sum_{t=2}^{T} u_{jt}u_{jt-1} \bigg/ \sum_{t=2}^{T} u_{jt-1} \qquad (j = 1, 2, 3) \qquad (4.13)$$

and the well-known statistic of Durbin and Watson have been chosen as two diagnostic tools for the detection of correlation in the posterior residuals. The results indicate that there are errors in the dynamic specification of the consumption function. This finding is in accordance with results presented by Kiefer (1981). So, instead of reducing the parameter space by making use of the

Table 4. FIML Residuals and Mean Values of Posterior 2′ Residuals

	u_1		u_2		u_3	
	FIML	*Post. 2′*	*FIML*	*Post. 2′*	*FIML*	*Post. 2′*
1921	−1.07	−0.37	−3.85	−1.50	−1.57	−1.04
1922	−1.02	−0.91	2.13	0.49	0.77	0.88
1923	−1.07	−1.54	2.19	1.11	2.44	2.04
1924	−0.02	−0.54	−0.00	−1.33	0.05	0.05
1925	0.47	−0.08	2.06	0.54	0.45	0.06
1926	0.90	0.69	2.19	1.38	0.44	−0.05
1927	1.60	1.23	2.31	1.13	−0.23	−0.56
1928	1.80	1.03	2.57	0.36	0.71	0.42
1929	0.01	−0.69	4.24	2.04	1.98	1.46
1930	−1.86	−0.34	−4.61	−1.32	−1.02	−0.73
1931	−2.31	−0.57	−5.81	−1.41	−1.23	−0.34
1932	−2.99	−0.59	−8.23	−1.77	−2.68	−1.14
1933	0.76	0.80	−0.08	0.97	−1.05	−0.01
1934	−0.43	0.10	−2.28	−0.45	−0.46	0.15
1935	−0.03	0.15	−0.82	−0.01	−0.46	−0.09
1936	2.62	1.92	3.48	1.89	−0.32	−0.59
1937	−0.65	−0.49	−0.33	−0.18	0.80	0.73
1938	−0.76	0.03	−5.21	−3.47	−1.93	−1.39
1939	2.17	1.30	2.76	0.51	0.41	−0.16
1940	1.73	0.90	2.75	0.21	−0.25	−1.04
1941	−0.87	−2.04	4.56	0.81	3.16	1.33

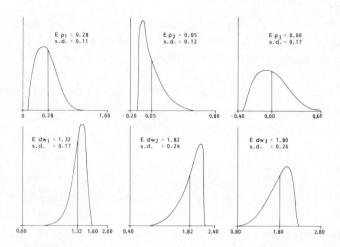

Figure 9. Marginal posterior densities of serial correlation coefficients (ρ) and Durbin–Watson coefficients (*dw*).

sets of prior constraints 1–5, we have to enlarge the parameter space by including, e.g., lagged consumption in Eq. (4.4). Preliminary results obtained with an enlarged version of Klein's Model I confirm this. This will be reported on in future work. We emphasize that one has to interpret these diagnostic results with care. They indicate, however, that there exists a need for diagnostic analysis on the correct specification of the information contained in the prior density and in the likelihood function.

V. MIXED INTEGRATION

Mixed integration, henceforth referred to as MIN, is a numerical integration method for the evaluation of multivariate integrals where the integrand is multivariate skew, that is, the integrand has different tail behavior in different directions. Such integrands contrast with integrands that have symmetric tail behavior, e.g., the multivariate normal density function and the multivariate Student *t* density function. Some examples of contours of multivariate skew functions are presented in Figure 10. The distinctive feature of MIN is that it employs a mixture of one-dimensional classical numerical quadrature and importance sampling. The method consists of two main steps. First, one generates a point $\theta^{(i)}$ from a

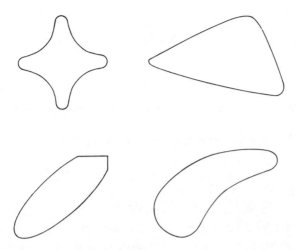

Figure 10. Examples of contours of multivariate skew functions.

multivariate normal distribution that has the posterior mode θ^0 as its center and minus the inverse of the Hessian of the logposterior, evaluated at the posterior mode, as its covariance matrix V. (We assume that θ^0 has been estimated by a preliminary optimization procedure.) A generated point $\theta^{(i)}$ defines a line through $\theta^{(i)}$ and θ^0. As a second step of the MIN method one performs one-dimensional numerical integration along the aforementioned line, where the integrand is the posterior kernel multiplied by a particular factor that is specified below. One may argue that the MIN technique conditions on skewness. That is, generating lines, or—more precisely stated—generating directions, by means of a multivariate normal sampling procedure occurs in a symmetric way. Conditional upon a generated direction, one perfoms a one-dimensional numerical integration step, which takes account of the possible skewness in the integrand.

We summarize the main idea of mixed integration as follows: MIN is based on a transformation of the random vector θ. That is, partition $\theta - \theta^0$ and V^{-1} as

$$\theta - \theta^0 = \begin{pmatrix} u \\ v \end{pmatrix}, \qquad V^{-1} = \begin{pmatrix} P & q \\ q' & r \end{pmatrix}, \tag{5.1}$$

where v and r are scalars. Define

$$d := (\theta - \theta^0)'V^{-1}(\theta - \theta^0)^{1/2} \tag{5.2}$$

and

$$\bar{v} := -u'q/r. \tag{5.3}$$

Then θ is transformed into (η, ρ), where

$$\eta := u/d, \qquad \rho := d \qquad \text{if } v \geq \bar{v}$$

and

$$\eta := -u/d, \qquad \rho := -d \qquad \text{if } < \bar{v}. \tag{5.4}$$

It is seen from (5.4) that the ℓ-vector of parameters of interest θ is changed into a pair (η, ρ), where the $(\ell - 1)$-vector η describes the direction of the vector $\theta - \theta^0$, and the scalar ρ describes the distance between θ and the posterior mode θ^0 in a metric that makes use of a covariance matrix V. That is, the scalar ρ satisfies $\rho^2 = (\theta - \theta^0)' V^{-1}(\theta - \theta^0)$, and a sign convention for ρ is added in order to guarantee that the transformation of θ into (η, ρ) is one-to-one. Let T denote the transformation formulae (5.4) that carry θ into (η, ρ). Then we can write $\theta = T^{-1}(\eta, \rho)$. The actual transformation employed involves a Jacobian determinant:

$$|J| = |\rho^{\ell-1}| |J(\eta)|, \tag{5.5}$$

where $|J(\eta)|$ is a determinant that depends only on η (cf. van Dijk, 1984; van Dijk et al., 1985). If we apply this transformation of variables to the case of the zeroth-order moment of θ, we obtain the following result:

$$\int p(\theta) \, d\theta = \phi_{01} + \phi_{02}, \tag{5.6}$$

where

$$\phi_{01} = \int_{\Omega} \left[\int_{R^+} p(T^{-1}(\eta, \rho)) |\rho^{\ell-1}| \, d\rho \right] |J(\eta)| \, d\eta$$

and

$$\phi_{02} = \int_{\Omega} \left[\int_{R^-} p(T^{-1}(\eta, \rho)) |\rho^{\ell-1}| \, d\rho \right] |J(\eta)| \, d\eta \tag{5.7}$$

The set Ω is the region of integration of η, and R^+ and R^- are, respectively, the positive and negative real lines, which are the regions of integration of ρ.

As a next step we make use of another feature of MIN. That is, we can apply the transformation of the random vector θ into the pair (η, ρ) also to the case where θ is normally distributed with mean θ^0 and covariance matrix V. The transformed density is proportional to $f(\rho)|J(\eta)|$, where $|J(\eta)|$ is the same determinant as given in (5.5). [For details on the specific forms of $f(\rho)$ and $J(\eta)$, see van Dijk et al. (1985).] It follows that random drawings $\eta^{(i)}$ can be generated from a distribution with a density function proportional to $|J(\eta)|$ by simply *generating random drawings* $\theta^{(i)}$ *from a multivariate normal distribution* with means θ^0 and covariance matrix V and then applying the transformation involved. So, given a sample of random drawings $(\theta^{(1)}, \ldots, \theta^{(N)})$, we obtain two subsamples, say, $(\eta_1^{(1)}, \ldots, \eta_1^{(N_1)})$ and $(\eta_2^{(1)}, \ldots, \eta_2^{(N_2)})$ with $N_1 + N_2 = N$. [Whether a random drawing of η belongs to the first or second set depends on the inequality conditions (5.4).]

In the actual computations we make use of the property that the generation of directions occurs in a symmetric way. That is, if $\theta^{(i)} - \theta^0$ is a generated point, we can take $\theta^0 - (\theta^{(i)} - \theta^0)$ as a next generated point since these two points are symmetric around θ^0 and they define opposite directions. The effects of such a sampling scheme, which is called *antithetic* sampling, is that each generated direction is used *twice* and that the one-dimensional integrals in ϕ_{01} and ϕ_{02} are computed on the *entire* real line. Therefore, we need not distinguish in the actual computations between ϕ_{01} and ϕ_{02}, except for the estimation of the numerical errors (see van Dijk and Hop, 1987). So, given a random sample $\theta^{(1)}, \ldots, \theta^{(N)}$, we have *one* set of generated directions $\eta^{(1)}, \ldots, \eta^{(N)}$, and the left-hand side of (5.6) is estimated by

$$\hat{\phi}_0 \propto \frac{1}{2N} \sum_{i=1}^{N} w_0(\eta^{(i)}), \tag{5.8}$$

where

$$w_0(\eta^{(i)}) = \int_{-\infty}^{+\infty} p(T^{-1}(\eta^{(i)}, \rho)|\rho^{\ell-1}| \, d\rho. \tag{5.9}$$

We divide in (5.8) by $2N$ since each generated direction $\eta^{(i)}$ is used twice. Note that we make use of a proportionality constant since the random sample $\eta^{(1)}, \ldots, \eta^{(N)}$ stems from a distribution with a density *proportional* (and not equal) to $|J(\eta)|$ and we have not written the proportionality constant in an explicit way. Since we deal always with ratios of integrals, these proportionality constants cancel.

Next, we discuss the computation of the posterior first-order moments by means of MIN, which illustrates the statement that

MIN conditions on skewness. We start with rewriting θ in the following way: Let y be an auxiliary random variable, defined as

$$y := \frac{\theta - \theta^0}{\rho} \tag{5.10}$$

so that

$$\theta = \theta^0 + \rho y. \tag{5.11}$$

Since θ^0 may be interpreted as a vector of known constants, it follows from (5.11) that

$$E\theta = \theta^0 + E\rho y. \tag{5.12}$$

Equation (5.12) illustrates that the term $E\rho y$ represents *skewness*. In the case of symmetry, when $E\theta = \theta^0$, one has the property $E\rho y = 0$. The computation of the posterior mean in case of skewness proceeds as follows: We write

$$E\theta = \theta^0 + \frac{\displaystyle\int \rho y p(\theta) \, d\theta}{\displaystyle\int p(\theta) \, d\theta}. \tag{5.13}$$

A mixed integration estimator for the integral in the numerator of Eq. (5.13) can be derived by going through the same transformation of variables as for the case of the denominator. By making use of results that are similar to the ones given in Eqs. (5.6)–(5.9) and (5.11), it follows that the vector of integrals in the numerator of (5.13) can be approximated by

$$\hat{\phi}_j \propto \frac{1}{2N} \sum_{i=1}^{N} y_j^{(i)} w_1(\eta^{(i)}) \qquad (j = 1, \ldots, \ell), \tag{5.14}$$

where

$$w_1(\eta^{(i)}) = \int_{-\infty}^{+\infty} \rho p(\theta^0 + \rho y^{(i)}) |\rho^{\ell-1}| \, d\rho. \tag{5.15}$$

Note that the integrand in (5.15) is equal to the integrand of (5.9) premultiplied by a factor ρ. A MIN estimator for $E\theta_j$ ($j = 1, \ldots, \ell$), can now be written as

$$\hat{\theta}_j = \theta_j^0 + \frac{\hat{\phi}_j}{\hat{\phi}_0} \qquad (j = 1, \ldots, \ell) \tag{5.16}$$

[compare Eqs. (5.6)–(5.9) and (5.13)–(5.15)]. Note that we made use of a proportionality sign in (5.8) and (5.14) but that we have used an equality sign in (5.16). Since the numerator and denominator in (5.16) have been estimated using the same random sample, it follows that the numerical constants, which were omitted in (5.8) and (5.14), cancel and so we can make use of an equality sign in (5.16). Second-order moments can be computed in a similar way as first-order moments. However, for the case of second-order moments one makes use of an integral $w_2(\eta^{(i)})$ [compare (5.15)] that has as integrand the function given in (5.9) premultiplied by a factor ρ^2.

The structure of the computer program for mixed integration is shown in the flow diagram in Figure 11. It may be seen that random drawings $\theta^{(i)}$ are generated from a normal distribution function. After the transformation of variables, which carries θ into (η, ρ), three one-dimensional integrals are computed. Particular examples of the function $h(\eta^{(i)})$ are given in (5.9) and (5.15).

We emphasize that in our applications the region of integration is bounded. As a consequence, the line integrals with respect to ρ are computed on a bounded interval. The upper and lower bound of this interval may be determined as follows: Given that $a_j < \theta_j < b_j$, for $j = 1, \ldots, \ell$, we can make use of (5.11) and write

$$a_j - \theta_j^0 < \rho y_j < b_j - \theta_j^0 \qquad (j = 1, \ldots, \ell). \qquad (5.17)$$

For each of the ℓ-dimensions, we can compute two values of ρ such that the inequalities are binding constraints. That is, if $y_j > 0$, then we define

$$\rho_j^* = \frac{a_j - \theta_j^0}{y_j}, \qquad \rho_j^{**} = \frac{b_j - \theta_j^0}{y_j} \qquad (j = 1, \ldots, \ell). \qquad (5.18)$$

If $y_j < 0$, then ρ_j^* and ρ_j^{**} are interchanged in (5.18). As a next step one determines the minimum value of $(\rho_1^{**}, \ldots, \rho_\ell^{**})$ and the maximum value of $(\rho_1^*, \ldots, \rho_\ell^*)$. These extreme values are the limits of integration for the line integrals.

Finally, we mention that mixed integration can also be used for the computation of moments of nonlinear functions of θ, such as implied multipliers of SEM. The restriction of mixed integration is that for each nonlinear function one has to compute a one-dimensional integral with respect to ρ, given a generated direction $\eta^{(i)}$. For an application of mixed integration which involves a

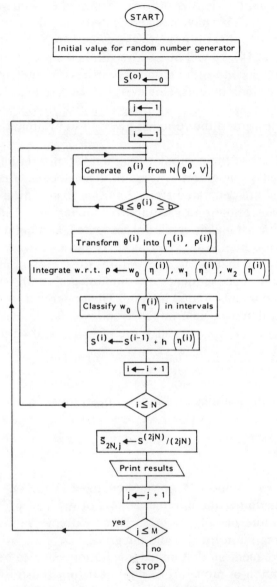

Figure 11. Flow diagram for mixed integration.

30-dimensional numerical integration problem, see van Dijk and Kloek (1986).

VI. CONCLUDING REMARKS

In this paper we have discussed some algorithms that can be used for the computation of posterior moments and marginal posterior densities of a vector of parameters θ for the case where the posterior kernel of θ is not a member of known family of density functions. If the surface of the posterior kernel is reasonably well behaved one may make use of the method of importance sampling with the (truncated) multivariate Student *t* density as an importance function. If the posterior surface is not well behaved (but uni-modal) one may use the method of mixed integration. In our experience, this method is flexible, robust, and parsimonious: that is, it is flexible since one follows the posterior kernel exactly with the computed line integrals; it is robust in the sense that it has handled several cases where the multivariate Student *t* density failed as an importance function; and it is parsimonious in the sense that mixed integration uses the same number of parameters as a normal importance function (i.e., location and scale param-eters). Mixed integration may not always be efficient in terms of CPU (central processing unit) time. A topic of further research is the search for flexible functional forms that can serve as an import-ance function. Finite mixtures appear to be very flexible, but they have also a large number of parameters that have to be specified a priori. A simple proposal in this area will be reported in a forthcoming paper. In order to experiment with the algorithms mentioned in this paper, we have prepared a set of standard programs (van Dijk and Hop, 1987). The development of Bayesian software is an active area of research.[7]

Another part of this paper was the application of Bayesian estimation methods to a particular econometric model. The results cast some doubt on the specification of the prior densities and on the specification of the likelihood function. So, apart from the development of Bayesian estimation procedures there is a need for procedures that evaluate the information in the prior and the likelihood function.

ACKNOWLEDGMENTS

This paper was produced as part of my work at the Econometric Institute, Erasmus University, Rotterdam, and Center for Operations Research and Econometrics (CORE), Université Catholique de Louvain. I am indebted to A. S. Louter of the Institute of Social Studies in The Hague and to J. P. Hop, J. Martens, and J. van Dijk of Erasmus University for their assistance in preparing the necessary computer programs and the list of figures.

NOTES

1. We note that there exist also physical devices that generate pseudorandom numbers. However, modern use of Monte Carlo integration methods involves usually a computer procedure for the generation of pseudorandom numbers.
2. We shall in most cases use the term *random drawing* instead of the more accurate but tedious expression *pseudorandom drawing*.
3. We note that in this case the value of the integral can be determined by making use of the table of the standard normal integral. More comments are given at the end of this section.
4. This section is an extension of van Dijk and Kloek (1980).
5. We use the term *unit interval* for the interval $(0, 1)$ and the term *unit region* for a Cartesian product of unit intervals.
6. We emphasize that this number is large so that the prior densities are reasonably accurate. The Monte Carlo estimates for the posterior moments are already reasonably accurate at 2000 random drawings.
7. Recently, Tierney and Kadane (1986) proposed a method for the computation of posterior moments and densities that avoids numerical integration.

REFERENCES

Abramowitz, M. and I. A. Stegun (1964) *Handbook of Mathematical Functions.* Washington, DC: National Bureau of Standards.
Atkinson, A. C. and M. C. Pearce (1976) "The Computer Generation of Beta, Gamma and Normal Random Variables." *Journal of the Royal Statistical Society, Series A* 139, 431–448.
Bauwens, L. (1984) *Bayesian Full Information Analysis of Simultaneous Equation Models Using Integration by Monte Carlo.* New York: Springer-Verlag.
Boender, C. G. and H. K. van Dijk (1987) "Bayesian Analysis of a Multi-criteria Decision Model." Report of the Econometric Institute, Erasmus University, Rotterdam, forthcoming.
Brent, R. P. (1974) "Algorithm 488, A Gaussian pseudo-random number generator [G5]." *Communications of the ACM* 17, 704–706.

Cramér, H. (1946) *Mathematical Methods of Statistics*. Princeton, NJ: Princeton University Press.

Geweke, J. (1986) "Exact Inference in the Inequality Constrained Normal Linear Regression Model." *Journal of Applied Econometrics* 1, 127-141.

Hammersley, J. M. and D. C. Handscomb (1964) *Monte Carlo Methods*. London: Methuen.

Hendry, D. F. (1984) "Monte Carlo Experimentation in Economics." In Z. Griliches and M. D. Intriligator (eds.), *Handbook of Econometrics*, Vol. 2. Amsterdam and New York: North-Holland Publishing.

Historical Statistics of the United States: Colonial Times to 1970, Bicentennial Edition (1975) Washington, DC: U.S. Bureau of the Census.

Kass, R. E. (1985) "Inferences About Principal Components and Related Quantities Using a Numerical Delta Method and Posteriors Calculated by Simulation." Technical report No. 346, Department of Statistics, Carnegie-Mellon University.

Kiefer, N. M. (1981) "Limited Information Analysis of a Small Underidentified Macroeconomic Model." *International Economic Review* 22, 429-442.

Kinderman, A. J. and J. F. Monahan (1980) "New Methods for Generating Students' *t* and Gamma Variables." *Computing* 25, 369-377.

Kinderman, A. J. and J. G. Ramage (1976) "Computer Generation of Normal Random Variables." *Journal of the American Statistical Association* 71, 893-896.

Klein, L. R. (1950) *Economic Fluctuations in the United States, 1921-1941*. New York: Wiley.

Kloek, T. and H. K. van Dijk (1978) "Bayesian Estimates of Equation System Parameters: An Application of Integration by Monte Carlo." *Econometrica* 46, 1-19; reprinted in A. Zellner (ed.), *Bayesian Analysis in Econometrics and Statistics*. Amsterdam and New York: North-Holland Publishing, 1980.

Kooiman, P., H. K. van Dijk, and A. R. Thurik (1985) "Likelihood Diagnostics and Bayesian Analysis of a Micro-economic Disequilibrium Model for Retail Services." *Journal of Econometrics* 29, 121-148.

Marsaglia, G. (1984) "The Exact-Approximation Method for Generating Random Variables in a Computer." *Journal of the American Statistical Association* 79, 218-221.

Mood, A. M., F. A. Graybill, and D. C. Boes (1974) *Introduction to the Theory of Statistics*, 3rd ed. New York: McGraw-Hill.

Newman, T. G. and P. L. Odell (1971) *The Generation of Random Varariates*. London: Griffin.

Numerical Algorithms Group (NAG) *Mark 10* (1983) Oxford, England: Oxford University Computing Laboratory.

Quandt, R. (1983) "Computational Problems and Methods." Chap. 12 in Z. Griliches and M. Intriligator (eds.), *Handbook of Econometrics*, Vol. 1. Amsterdam and New York: North-Holland Publishing.

Raiffa, H. and R. Schlaifer (1961) *Applied Statistical Decision Theory*. Boston: Graduate School of Business Administration, Harvard University.

Ripley, B. D. (1983) "Computer Generation of Random Variables: A Tutorial." *International Statistical Review* 51, 301-319.

Rothenberg, T. J. (1963) "A Bayesian Analysis of Simultaneous Equation Systems." Report No. 6315, Econometric Institute, Rotterdam.

Rothenberg, T. J. (1973) *Efficient Estimation with a priori Information.* New Haven, CT: Yale University Press.

Rubinstein, R. Y. (1981) *Simulation and the Monte Carlo Method.* New York: Wiley.

Tierney, L., and J. B. Kadane (1986) "Accurate Approximations for Posterior Moments and Densities." *Journal of the American Statistical Association* 81, 82-86.

Theil, H. (1971) *Principles of Econometrics.* New York: Wiley.

Theil, H. and J. C. G Boot (1962) "The Final Form of Econometric Equation Systems." *Review of the International Statistical Institute* 30, 136-152; reprinted in A. Zellner (ed.), *Readings in Economic Statistics and Econometrics.* Boston: Little, Brown, 1968.

van Dijk H. K. (1984) "Posterior Analysis of Econometric Models Using Monte Carlo Integration." Doctoral dissertation, Erasmus University, Rotterdam.

van Dijk, H. K. (1985) "A Note on Simple Algebraic Relations Between Structural and Reduced Form Parameters." Report No. 8549, Econometric Institute, Erasmus University, Rotterdam.

van Dijk, H. K. and J. P. Hop (1987) "PMMC: A Set of Computer Programs for the Computation of Posterior Moments and Densities Using Monte Carlo Integration." Report of the Econometric Institute, Erasmus University, Rotterdam, forthcoming.

van Dijk, H. K., J. P. Hop, and A. S. Louter (1986) "An Algorithm for the Computation of Posterior Moments and Densities Using Simple Importance Sampling." Report No. 8625/A, Econometric Institute, Erasmus University, Rotterdam; to appear in abridged form in *The Statistician.*

van Dijk, H. K. and T. Kloek (1977) "Predictive Moments of Simultaneous Econometric Models: A Bayesian Approach." In A. Aykaç and C. Brumat (eds.), *New Developments in the Application of Bayesian Methods.* Amsterdam and New York: North-Holland Publishing.

van Dijk, H. K. and T. Kloek (1980) "Further Experience in Bayesian Analysis Using Monte Carlo Integration." *Journal of Econometrics* 14, 307-328.

van Dijk, H. K. and T. Kloek (1983) "Monte Carlo Analysis of Skew Posterior Distributions: An Illustrative Econometric Example." *The Statistician* 32, 216-223.

van Dijk, H. K. and T. Kloek (1985) "Experiments with Some Alternatives for Simple Importance Sampling in Monte Carlo Integration (with Discussion)." Pp. 511-530 in J. M. Bernardo, M. H. DeGroot, D. V. Lindley, and A. F. M. Smith (eds.), *Bayesian Statistics,* Vol. 2. Amsterdam and New York: North-Holland Publishing.

van Dijk, H. K. and T. Kloek (1986) "Posterior Moments of the Klein-Goldberger Model." Pp. 95-108 in P. K. Goel and A. Zellner (eds.), *Bayesian Inference and Decision Techniques with Applications.* Amsterdam and New York: North-Holland Publishing.

van Dijk, H. K., T. Kloek, and C. G. E. Boender (1985) "Posterior Moments Computed by Mixed Integration." *Journal of Econometrics* 29, 3-18.

Zellner, A. (1971) *An Introduction to Bayesian Inference in Econometrics.* New York: Wiley.

Zellner, A. (1986) "Further Results on Bayesian Minimum Expected Loss (MELO) Estimates and Posterior Distributions for Structural Coefficients." in Daniel J. Slottje and George F. Rhodes, Jr. *Advances in Econometrics* 5, 171–182.

Research Annuals and Monographs in Series in
ECONOMICS

Research Annuals

Advances in Accounting
Edited by Bill N. Schwartz, *School of Business Administration, Temple University*

Advances in Accounting Information Systems
Edited by Gary Grudnitski, *Graduate School of Business, The University of Texas at Austin*

Advances in Applied Micro-Economics
Edited by V. Kerry Smith, *Department of Economics, Vanderbilt University*

Advances in Business Marketing
Edited by Arch G. Woodside, *A.B. Freeman School, Tulane University*

Advances in Distribution Channel Research
Edited by Gary L. Frazier, *University of Southern California*

Advances in Econometrics
Edited by George F. Rhodes, Jr., *Department of Economics, Colorado State University* and Thomas Fomby, *Department of Economics, Southern Methodist University*

Advances in Financial Planning and Forecasting
Edited by Cheng F. Lee, *Department of Finance, University of Illinois*

Advances in Futures and Options Research
Edited by Frank J. Fabozzi, Visiting Professor, *Sloan School of Management, Massachusetts Institute of Technology*

Advances in Health Economics and Health Services Research
Edited by Richard M. Scheffler, *School of Public Health, University of California*, Berkeley and Louis F. Rossiter, *Department of Health Administration, Medical College of Virginia, Virginia Commonwealth University*

Advances in Industrial and Labor Relations
Edited by David B. Lipsky, *New York State School of Industrial and Labor Relations, Cornell University*

Advances in International Accounting
Edited by Kenneth S. Most, *College of Business Administration, Florida International University*

Advances in International Marketing
Edited by S. Tamer Cavusgill, *Center for Business and Economic Research, Bradley University*

Advances in Marketing and Public Policy
Edited by Paul N. Bloom, *Department of Marketing, University of North Carolina*

Advances in Mathematical Programming and Financial Planning
Edited by Kenneth D. Lawrence, *Department of Industrial and Systems Engineering, Rutgers University*, John B. Guerard, Jr. *Department of Finance, Lehigh University* and Gary R. Reeves, *Department of Management Science, University of South Carolina*

Advances in Nonprofit Marketing
Edited by Russell W. Belk, *Department of Marketing, University of Utah*

Advances in Public Interest Accounting
Edited by Marilyn Neimark, *Baruch College, The City University of New York*

Advances in Statistical Analysis and Statistical Computing
Edited by Roberto S. Mariano, *Department of Economics, University of Pennsylvania*

Advances in Taxation
Edited by Sally M. Jones, *Department of Accounting, The University of Texas at Austin*

Advances in the Economic Analysis of Participatory and Labor Managed Firms
Edited by Derek C. Jones, *Department of Economics, Hamilton College* and Jan Svejnar, *Department of Economics, University of Pittsburgh*

Advances in the Economics of Energy and Resources
Edited by John R. Moroney, *Department of Economics, Texas A&M University*

Advances in the Study of Entrepreneurship, Innovation and Economic Growth
Edited by Gary Libecap, Director, *Karl Eller Center, University of Arizona*

Advances in Working Capital Management
Edited by Yong H. Kim, *Department of Finance, University of Cincinatti* and V. Srinivasan, *College of Business Administration, Northeastern University*

Perspectives on Local Public Finance and Public Policy
Edited by John M. Quigley, *Department of Economics and Graduate School of Public Policy, University of California, Berkeley*

Research in Accounting Regulation
Edited by Gary John Previts, *Department of Accounting, The Weatherhead School of Management, Case Western Reserve University*

Research in Consumer Behavior
Edited by Elizabeth C. Hirschman, *Department of Marketing, New York University* and Jagdish N. Sheth, *School of Business, University of Southern California*

Research in Domestic and International Agribusiness Management
Edited by Ray A. Goldberg, *Graduate School of Business Administration, Harvard University*

Research in Economic History
Edited by Paul Uselding, *Department of Economics, University of Illinois*

Research in Experimental Economics
Edited by Vernon L. Smith, *College of Business and Public Administration, University of Arizona*

Research in Finance
Edited by Andrew H. Chen, *Edwin L. Cox School of Business, Southern Methodist University*

Research in Governmental and Nonprofit Accounting
Edited by James L. Chan, *Office for Governmental Accounting Research and Education, University of Illinois at Chicago*

Research in Human Capital and Development
Edited by Ismail Sirgeldin, *Department of Population Dynamics and Political Economy, The Johns Hopkins University*

Research in International Business and Finance
Edited by H. Peter Gray, *Department of Economics, Rutgers University*

Research in International Business and International Relations
Edited by Anant R. Negandhi, *Department of Business Administration, University of Illinois*

Research in Labor Economics
Edited by Ronald G. Ehrenberg, *New York State of Industrial and Labor Relations, Cornell University*

Research in Law and Economics
Edited by Richard O. Zerbe, Jr., *Graduate School of Public Affairs, University of Washington*

Research in Marketing
Edited by Jagdish N. Sheth, *School of Business, University of Southern California*

Research in Political Economy
Edited by Paul Zarembka, *Department of Economics, State University of New York at Buffalo*

Research in Population Economics
Edited by T. Paul Schultz, *Department of Economics, Yale University*

Research in Public Sector Economics
Edited by P.M. Jackson, *Department of Economics, Leicester University*

Research in Real Estate
Edited by C.F. Sirmans, *Department of Finance, Louisiana State University*

Research in the History of Economic Thought and Methodology
Edited by Warren J. Samuels, *Department of Economics, Michigan State University*

Research in Transportation Economics
Edited by Andrew F. Daughty, *Department of Economics, The University of Iowa* and Clifford Winston, *The Brookings Institute*

Research in Urban Economics
Edited by Robert Ebel, Director, *Economics and Finance, Corporate Competitive Strategies, Northwestern Bell, Minneapolis*

Research on Technological Innovation, Management and Policy
Edited by Richard S. Rosenbloom, *Graduate School of Business Administration, Harvard University*

Monographs in Series and Treatises

Contemporary Studies in Applied Behavioral Science
Edited by Louis A. Zurcher, *School of Social Work, The University of Texas at Austin*

Contemporary Studies in Economic and Financial Analysis
Edited by Edward I. Altman and Ingo Walter, *Graduate School of Business Administration, New York University*

Contemporary Studies in Energy Analysis and Policy
Edited by Noel D. Uri, *Division of Antitrust, Bureau of Economics Federal Trade Commission*

Decision Research: A Series of Monographs
Edited by Howard Thomas, *Department of Business Administration, University of Illinois*

Handbook of Behavioral Economics
Edited by Benjamin Gilad and Stanley Kaish, *Department of Management Studies, Rutgers University, Newark*

Industrial Development and the Social Fabric
Edited by John P. McKay, *Department of History, University of Illinois*

Political Economy and Public Policy
Edited by William Breit, *Department of Economics, Trinity University* and Kenneth G. Elzinga, *Department of Economics, University of Virginia*

Please inquire for detailed subject catalog

JAI PRESS INC., 55 Old Post Road No. 2, P.O. Box 1678
Greenwich, Connecticut 06836
Telephone: 203-661-7602   Cable Address: JAIPUBL